THE PATTERN OF
NEW ZEALAND CULTURE

THE PATTERN OF
NEW ZEALAND
CULTURE

EDITED BY
A. L. McLEOD

CORNELL UNIVERSITY PRESS
ITHACA, NEW YORK

Library of Congress Catalog Card Number: 68-9751

PRINTED IN THE UNITED STATES OF AMERICA
BY VAIL-BALLOU PRESS, INC.

PREFACE

DURING the nineteenth century books about distant and presumably exotic lands and their peoples enjoyed an especially long vogue: readers, it seems, were insatiable in their desire to learn about the settlements that their kin had established in the obscure corners of the world. Most of these books were the products of travelers or short-term residents who were intellectually and in literary ability ill-suited to their self-appointed tasks. They described the natural wonders of flora and fauna, the handicaps to be overcome by European settlers relocated in the Antipodes or in the tropics, and recounted stories of adventure and excitement that would have enlivened popular Victorian romances.

Of this genre perhaps only Samuel Butler's *A First Year in the Canterbury Settlement* (1863), which records his impressions of life in New Zealand, has retained its interest and value. In contrast to the superficial observations and impressionistic judgments of other writers, Butler's work is characterized by perspicacity and penetra-

tion and is expressed in language of some elegance. He provided
what seems to have been an extraordinarily truthful account of the
state of mind and spirit of the New Zealand settlers of his period.
"New Zealand," Butler wrote,

seems far better adapted to develop and maintain in health the physical
than the intellectual nature. The fact is, people here are busy making
money: that is the inducement which led them to come in the first instance, and they show their sense by devoting their energies to the work.
. . . A mountain here is only beautiful if it has good grass on it. . . . If
it is good for sheep, it is beautiful, magnificent, and all the rest of it; if
not, it is not worth looking at.

In the intervening century the situation has changed. There is still
a major dependence on primary produce, on wool and wheat, cheese
and beef, to maintain a viable national economy, but intellectual
and cultural matters have long since been accorded the attention
appropriate to them in a modern society. As a result, there is an
identifiable New Zealand culture, one that resembles perhaps the
Australian more clearly than any other, yet is unique. Unfortunately, too many of us are not sufficiently familiar with it, and it is
the purpose of this book to describe and critically examine the
culture of contemporary New Zealand in the light of its historical
development for the benefit of the general reader.

The Pattern of New Zealand Culture is the fourth in a series
published by Cornell University Press. The first two books, *The
Culture of France in Our Time* (1954) and *The Culture of Contemporary Canada* (1957), were edited by Professor Julian Park of
the State University of New York at Buffalo; *The Pattern of Australian Culture* (1963) was edited by A. L. McLeod. The present
volume follows the same general editorial plan as the other volumes,
providing a general historical account of the several topics, a critical
assessment of the contemporary scene, and a tentative prognosis.
Since there is as yet no equivalent for New Zealand of Dr. George
Nadel's study, *Australia's Colonial Culture*, the historical-critical
method seems necessary. Each of the books in the series differs
somewhat in content from the others: the book on French culture,
for example, contains essays on law and religion, subjects that are not
treated in *The Culture of Contemporary Canada;* on the other hand,

PREFACE

the Canadian volume contains studies of French-Canadian culture and literary scholarship. *The Pattern of Australian Culture* has chapters on historiography, philosophy, and language, which are not to be found in the earlier volumes; since these areas of New Zealand culture are not so noticeably developed or as culturally significant, they have not been considered in separate essays, but rather treated wherever appropriate in the book. However, religion, politics, and mass communications being as important as they are in New Zealand, each has been considered separately. The purpose of the selection of topics has always been to provide a proper understanding of the cultural milieu of each of the countries, and the appended bibliographies are intended to provide interested readers with sources of additional information rather than to record the authors' source materials.

Mr. G. A. H. Kidd of the Department of Geography of the University of Otago drew the maps that illustrate the chapter on mass communications. Mrs. Eleanor Wyland and Mrs. Mildred Scarpati typed the manuscript: to both the editor acknowledges his gratitude. The selections from the poetry of R. A. K. Mason and Denis Glover are included by kind permission of the authors and The Caxton Press.

A. L. McL.

Rider University
April 1968

CONTENTS

ILLUSTRATIONS

Following page 176

MAPS

TABLES

THE PATTERN OF
NEW ZEALAND CULTURE

INTRODUCTION

A. L. MCLEOD

IN just a century and a quarter New Zealand has developed a characteristic national culture: it naturally is derivative, especially from that of Great Britain, but modifications, adaptations, extensions, and truncations have fashioned something new and distinctive.

Rudolf Rocker, in his stimulating *Nationalism and Culture*, argued that "culture as such is never national, because it always extends beyond the political frame of the State structure and is confined by no national frontier." But Rocker was writing within an essentially European frame of reference, certainly within a Continental one. In island nations such as Australia and New Zealand, where a European civilization has been transplanted in a Melanesian or Polynesian environment, the same situation does not necessarily exist. The influence of the culture that has developed within New Zealand has been limited to its few small island dependencies, and with the passage of time that culture has been less influenced by other cultures. In fact, the exceptional geographic isolation of New

1

Zealand from the mainstreams of Western cultural forces has permitted the development of a local cuture that is as national as can be envisioned.

Though Australia is just twelve hundred miles from New Zealand, the Tasman Sea has effectively isolated the two countries culturally as well as politically, so that neither is a dependency of the other. The early notion of colonial politicians and settlers who thought that it would be feasible to develop Australia and New Zealand as a single, homogeneous "Australasian" civilization has long since been abandoned. Naturally, it was thought that if settlers in South Australia, physically separated in the west by a thousand miles of land from the local wellspring of political and cultural forces in Sydney, could share a common experience, then settlers of identical ethnic backgrounds separated in the east at a similar distance by ocean would be able to do likewise, for commerce and communication between Sydney and the other two colonies was comparable in all essential particulars.

But Australian culture has been contained within the political boundaries of the Commonwealth, and New Zealand has developed its own cultural institutions and values and made its own contributions to the arts and sciences. And its culture has neither been noticeably influential beyond its territorial limits nor influenced by the French, Melanesian, Australian, and Polynesian that surround it.

It may well be that political independence demands cultural independence, and that the degree of one determines the extent of the other. During the First World War the Australian and New Zealand Army Corps served with distinction and brought fame to the acronym Anzac, but after each country was recognized as an independent power at Versailles and later in the League of Nations, the Anzac comity started to disappear; the New Zealanders wanted to be known as Kiwis, while the Australians preferred to be identified as Aussies. Both countries soon established their own legations and embassies abroad, their own minuscule navies and air forces, and sought their separate destinies. Each is justly proud of its achievements. Each has its own ethos, its own national identity, its own culture.

To many people outside New Zealand, the country is still thought

2

of as a somewhat idyllic and utopian antipodean microcosm of British civilization: democratic, picturesque, bucolic. They might have some difficulty in locating it on the world map, but they know that it exists, and they feel that they ought to know more about it.

To others, New Zealand is thought of in terms of its past achievements: almost exemplary integration of Caucasian and Maori races; pioneering social-welfare legislation; and technological advances such as the introduction of refrigerated shipping. When they think longer, they are inclined to think of it as a novel, uncrowded—albeit out of the way—tourist stop and bring to mind its geysers and glaciers, kiwis and tikis.

To still another group, New Zealand is a country that, although small in terms of population and land mass, extreme in its variations of climate and geography, and young in terms of both Maori and European settlement, has had a noteworthy influence on world affairs. They bring to mind certain individuals who have made significant contributions to world culture: in art, Frances Hodgkins; in music, Warwick Braithwaite (and the "Maoris' Farewell," known overseas as "Now Is the Hour"); in education, Professor A. H. Macdonald, the Cambridge classicist, and Professor Desmond Pacey, the historian of Canadian literature; in literature, Ngaio Marsh, the popular detective-story author and Katherine Mansfield, the short-story stylist; in science, Lord Ernest Rutherford, Nobel Laureate (1908) and discoverer of the nuclear structure of the atom, later professor of physics and director of the Cavendish Laboratory at Cambridge University; in sports, Peter Snell and Murray Halberg, who have set Olympic and world track records, and Sir Edmund Hillary, who first conquered Mount Everest.

But New Zealand as a national cultural entity is, like all others, the sum total of its organized community experience: its social and political values and institutions; its attitudes, goals, beliefs, and motivations; its priorities, products, and possessions; its recreations and pastimes no less than its achievements in the arts and sciences of "high" culture. And this total cultural milieu is the product of the many rather than the few, since the intellectual and artistic elite of New Zealand has always tended to migrate to what seemed to be more congenial places: to Australia and England at first, and to

Canada and the United States more recently. Some 63 per cent of New Zealand's Rhodes scholars—the largest percentage of any country's—have never returned to their homeland; but they have gained for it immense good will and reputation abroad. Because of the constant and statistically considerable emigration of the very best of New Zealand's artists and scholars, writers and scientists, the national culture owes more, perhaps, to amateurs and young people than most other cultures, and it is similarly indebted to the national emphasis on increased leisure. Josef Pieper argued in *Leisure: The Basis of Culture* (1952) that Western civilization had its foundations in the provision of leisure time, and this is certainly true of New Zealand culture.

The small intellectual community, vigorously hostile to its bland, smug environment, continually depleted and replenished, is largely alienated from the wider community whose tastes it ineffectually strives to elevate. Its endeavors are fundamentally quixotic, for its adversaries are the hegemony of the middlebrows and their penchant for Western, and more particularly American, popular culture.

The attitude of the New Zealand intellectual community is reminiscent of Roy Campbell's attitude to South Africa in the 1920's and is stated eloquently, if sardonically, by Denis Glover in "Soliloquies":

> When God made this place
> He made mountains and fissures
> Hostile, vicious, and
> Turned away His face.

But to appreciate the development of New Zealand culture we must consider its context, for as Alexis de Tocqueville pointed out in *Democracy in America*, the growth of nations reveals marks of their origins and "the circumstances that accompanied their birth and contributed to their development affect the whole term of their being."

According to Maori legend, New Zealand was discovered about A.D. 750, circumnavigated about 950, and revisited in 1150 by flotillas of Tahitians and other Pacific islanders before it was permanently

4

settled in the middle of the fourteenth century by a numerous contingent of Polynesians who, by surviving the perils of great distances of open sea in primitive canoes, exhibited navigational skills comparable only to those of the Vikings or Vice-Admiral William Bligh. Once settled in their new environment, they seem to have engaged in hunting the giant flightless bird, the moa, in coastal fishing, in primitive agriculture, and in the arts of weaving grass fibers, tattooing, carving, and domestic building. So satisfied were they, apparently, that they made no excursions westward to Australia or Tasmania.

European knowledge of New Zealand began with the discovery by Abel Tasman, captain of the Netherlands East Indies Company's vessel *Heemskerck*, of the west coast of South Island on 13 December, 1642. In an attempt to befriend the Maori, four of Tasman's men were killed, and so the Captain withdrew and continued his voyage of exploration, making only a vague cartographical annotation of his discovery and naming it.

One hundred twenty-seven years later, in 1769, Captain James Cook, the noted British navigator, and Joseph Banks, the eminent naturalist who had been sent by the Royal Society to observe an eclipse from Tahiti, sailed to New Zealand aboard the barque *Endeavour*, circumnavigated the islands, and made maps that have long been admired for their accuracy. Though he at first had some difficulties in making friends with the Maori, Cook established a harmonious relationship with several tribes from which he learned that there was no tradition of Tasman's visit.

Cook's impressions of New Zealand, as recorded in his diaries, were such as to make it appear an extremely valuable discovery. He described its "steep hills covered with prodigious fine woods," producing the straightest, largest, and cleanest trees that Banks had ever seen and "fit for any kind of buildings, and thick enough to make masts for vessels of any size," then continued:

It was the opinion of everyone on board that all sorts of European grain, fruits, plants, etc., would thrive here; in short, was this country settled by an industrious people, they would very soon be supplied not only with necessaries, but many of the luxuries of life. Should it ever become an object of settling this country, the best plan for the first fixing of a colony would be either in the River Thames or the Bay of Islands. [*Journal of Captain James Cook on His Voyages of Discovery.*]

After "displaying the English colours," wrote Cook, "I took formal possession of the place in the name of His Majesty." Then he sailed westward towards New Holland and discovered its eastern coast, naming it New South Wales.

The island that Cook had claimed for England covered just over 100,000 square miles of the finest and most varied landscape in the Pacific, extending almost a thousand miles from the subtropical latitude of the Bay of Islands to the extreme cold of Stewart Island and Invercargill at the southermost extremity of the South Island, and possessed of abundant natural harbors, majestic lakes, reliable watercourses, mountains towering up to 12,500 feet, and verdant plains that provide a congenial setting for almost any human endeavor. The idyllic nature of so much of the country is suggested by the name given to the focal point of Auckland—Mount Eden.

Cook's recommendation that any British settlement should be located at the Bay of Islands was acted upon by the Reverend Samuel Marsden, chaplain of the settlement at Sydney, who in 1814 led a small band of missionaries under the sponsorship of the Church Missionary Society intent upon carrying the Christian message to the Maori tribes. Twelve years later the first attempt at colonization was made by a group of some sixty persons, but the hostility of the natives was thought to be sufficient to preclude peaceful and productive settlement, and all except five of the colony returned either to New South Wales or to Britain. These five prospered, however, as much by supplying masts, spars, deck planks, and sealskins to whalers of French, Spanish, British, Dutch, and American flags, as through the products of their animal husbandry and agriculture. By 1835, the year in which Charles Darwin visited the settlement, wool was first exported from New Zealand.

In 1839, the first settlers sponsored by the New Zealand Company arrived, and they were followed the next year by a large contingent of immigrants under the authority of Captain William Hobson, who was designated Lieutenant-Governor of the Islands of New Zealand, which had been placed under the authority of Queen Victoria by

6

the Treaty of Waitangi in exchange for an assurance of protection of the almost 150,000 Maori against other foreign intervention. But in a matter of five years the Maori Wars, caused by disputes over land tenure with the white settlers, who now numbered about 50,000, started their dreary and bloody twenty-year course. In many respects this aspect of New Zealand settlement resembles the experience of European colonization of North America; it certainly had no paradigm in Australia, where the aboriginal inhabitants followed a nomadic existence, were relatively unsophisticated in the arts of defense and warfare, had smaller tribal units than the Maori, and were of an inferior physique. The Maori fought for his land; the aborigine retreated into the bush to avoid the major perils of confrontation.

In another significant respect white colonization of New Zealand differed from that of Australia: it was a free settlement rather than a convict settlement and was unattended by the stultifying effects of a military oligarchy, a sullen work force, and a controlling bureaucracy located a hemisphere distant. Having to contend with none of the severe natural conditions encountered by the settlers of Virginia, New England, and Botany Bay, encouraged by the entrepreneurial interest of the New Zealand Company, supported by the spiritual and material capital of the Church Missionary Society and its minions, and defended by the British Crown, few colonies can have begun under more auspicious conditions.

The pressures which propelled these nineteenth-century Englishmen into the farther reaches of the Pacific were not those of religious freedom or political toleration. These settlers were the products of the new industrial order, and the forces that encouraged their migration were the same forces that in England produced the nineteenth-century political debates over poor laws, child-labor laws, and the place of organized labor.

The main body of the immigrants who undertook the miserable journey to Britain's farthest colony were working men and women who often possessed few skills and little education. They were not revolutionaries, but working people hoping to find a better life. New Zealand held that promise. Their new land, when compared to Australia, became the more agreeable and well worth the extra days' sailing. It was a land of equable climate, with the bluest of skies and the most luxuriant pasture, containing in its small compass soaring mountain chains and snow fields almost as extensive as Switzerland itself; placid lakes, sublime fiords, and rushing streams alike rich in fish; forests congenial to the animals introduced by Cook, Marsden, and subsequent visitors; boiling pools and gushing geysers; ample and uniform rainfall; tropical and subarctic vegetation. Nowhere was the settler more than eighty miles from the sea, nowhere so isolated as to have to fend entirely for himself against nature, the Maori, or adversity. New Zealand, in fact, seemed to offer the best of all possible worlds. It was remote from the industrial and political problems of the Old World, independent of the primitivism and barbarism of Pacific island communities, protected by the Tasman Sea from the predatory instincts of irrepressible Australian politicians, and yet linked to them and the rest of the world by all the modern means of commerce and communication.

By the end of the nineteenth century both islands were settled, the Maori had been pacified, and a national government was organized. New Zealand quickly and readily accepted its role as a British colony with an agricultural economy profitable to the mother country and local inhabitants alike and felt assured, by the invention of refrigerated shipping, of reasonable prosperity in perpetuity. And so closely did the new nation replicate the old in both social and political life that in 1903 Henry Lloyd entitled his book on New Zealand *Newest England.*

But only too quickly New Zealand discovered that the future was not in its hands. Depression, unemployment, inflation, and recession were beyond its power to control. Peace and tranquility were interrupted by the German presence in Samoa and New Guinea and then by the Boer War, to which a New Zealand contingent was sent in support of the British cause. Yet, so considerable had been its social development and progress that when New Zealand ceased to be a colony and became the Dominion of New Zealand on 26 September, 1907, no motto for its coat of arms could have been more appropriate than the single word *Onward.*

After 1907 the character of the new country began to emerge more clearly. New Zealand was to be a land of equality of opportunity from which the extremes of wealth and poverty were to be excluded, where women enjoyed the right to vote, and where legislation protected the working man from exploitation. With such a prospect for the future, it was a land to attract the notice of idealists like Beatrice and Sidney Webb, who went there to appreciate the egalitarian quality of life and left to deprecate the crudities of colonial manners.

Like Anthony Trollope, Mark Twain, and innumerable other visitors, the Webbs tried to capture the feel of New Zealand, the essence of the national ethos or culture; but their predispositions were such and the occasion so early that it eluded them. Subsequently, it has become somewhat easier to describe, because more frequently and clearly made manifest.

The overriding preoccupation of New Zealand life is with security: social, economic, and political. This tends to inhibit extremism, to discourage radical proposals, to glorify conformity, and to curb those flights of individualism in thought or action that eventually effect substantial cultural innovation or modification. Notwithstanding, nothing approaching the Australian concept of mateship has evolved: in its place there is a cooperative disposition. A sense of partnership substitutes for the fraternal identification that characterizes the mateship of the Australian outback, and this partnership concept is generalized into the pervasive egalitarianism of the nation; in education, in team sports, and in the modest range of incomes. Even when a New Zealander receives a knighthood it does not set him apart from the remainder of the community as it does in Australia or the United Kingdom: it is perhaps best thought of as the New Zealand equivalent of the honorary academic degree in the United States.

The rise of egalitarianism is not easily explained. Certainly it is not simply a result of pronouncement or legislation. In France, where it has been a part of the national mystique for almost two hundred years, it appears to be less a reality of life than in New Zealand. It may be a function of free settlement by a relatively undifferentiated economic class in a natural environment that presented most of the amenities of a comfortable existence and few challenges or catastrophic occurrences to be contended with. No

New Zealander ever had to encounter the hardships of the outback, with its floods, droughts, bush fires, and pestilential vicissitudes; none ever experienced the animosity and acrimony of a community that contained at the same time convicts, marines, emancipists, and free settlers; none had to overcome the calumny, hatred, and strife that are born of racial, national, and religious bigotry.

But if egalitarianism is in part the result of an accommodating environment, it is possibly also accounted for by the absence of folk heroes in New Zealand, where there was no period of exploration and discovery comparable to those in the history of Australia, Canada, South Africa, or the United States; and so New Zealand has no equivalents of Leichhardt, Burke and Wills, Eyre, Stanley, Lewis and Clark, De Soto, or Brigham Young, whose exploits have fed the imagination of generations and created a folklore of individuals of legendary prowess, stamina, willpower, endurance. Only the name of Sir Edmund Hillary approaches the charismatic.

The pre-eminence given to security and egalitarianism is most clearly witnessed in the educational and social systems and by the preference among schoolchildren for employment in government service and the skilled trades. While there is little comprehensive evidence to support the conclusion, personal impressions gained over a number of years suggest that there is a national predisposition against high-risk occupational opportunities in favor of more stolid and certain ones. As a corollary, there is not the widespread interest in stock-market speculation by persons of modest means that is to be observed in the United States and, to a growing extent, in Australia. The innate desire for the excitement that accrues to risk is channeled into socially approved and State-operated racecourse betting and lotteries.

Social life is still largely family-oriented, and the family unit remains tightly knit. A home and its furnishings, a car, and a cottage in the mountains or at the beach are the common material goals, and the home may be surprisingly well supplied with books, records, the electrical and mechanical paraphernalia of modern life, and the trappings of popular culture. When these material goals have been achieved, and the family's children have married, those who are able usually make a pilgrimage to "Home": England, Scotland, or Ireland.

The short stories in Maurice Shadbolt's *The New Zealanders* (1961) and similar anthologies remind us that a day at the beach, a picnic in the country, afternoon tea with the neighbors, a few beers at the local pub, and comparable small pleasures and excursions are still as important an ingredient of New Zealand life as they were almost fifty years ago when Katherine Mansfield recorded them so poignantly. Nightclub life, *haute cuisine*, café society, and the *dolce vita* are equally alien to a society that has seldom been shocked by a Profumo affair, a Mafia scandal, the assassination of a high government official, or sensational examples of corruption, amorality, treason, heresy, or malfeasance. Accordingly, one can empathize with one of Shadbolt's characters who alludes petulantly to "New Zealand, where nothing ever happened."

Like the Australians, New Zealanders place a high premium on leisure time and pursue both recreational sports and avocations with considerable skill and diligence, so that their achievements in international athletic competitions are universally acclaimed and their contributions to other cultural pursuits are likewise quite distinguished. Josef Pieper's contention that leisure is the basis of Western culture is amply borne out in New Zealand, where there are very few full-time professional writers, actors, musicians, artists, sculptors, and critics. But in matters of sporting activities the reverse seems almost as true: some young people seem to regard their regular employment as a means of spacing out the weekend and midweek athletic engagements that they approach with almost passionate frenzy or of providing agreeable companions with whom to discuss the vagaries of wind and water while yachting, the intricacies of batting and bowling in cricket, or the irregularities of a line-out or scrimmage in Rugby football matches. Only conversations and arguments concerning competitive sports seem able to disturb their otherwise genial mien and friendly demeanor.

While football, cricket, sailing, and horse-racing are the most popular spectator sports, cycling, bowling, mountaineering, skiing, horse riding, car racing, and fishing are the principal participator sports, though almost every outdoor activity has its enthusiasts and promoters.

The visitor to New Zealand is likely to agree that the country is small and remote, but beyond that his conclusions are likely to be less definite. He will see it as isolated culturally and spiritually, not only geographically. For him it is a country that was, briefly, at the beginning of the century, a leader in certain kinds of legislation—an international distinction lost almost as quickly as it was gained. It is a country populated over the last hundred years by lower-class Englishmen who have come to uphold Victorian working-class culture as if it were the ultimate achievement of mankind; stuffy, authoritarian, vulgar, and prudish, suspicious of new ideas, or higher education, and of changes in the world outside. It is like a part of some large industrial English city transposed to the countryside. Suspicious of outsiders, foreigners, and strangers, it has maintained its English purity through a variety of stringent immigration laws and regulations which are rarely publicly admitted. In spite of this, it has many of the potential difficulties of any country faced with a large minority population, including a wide range of opinion on the question of race. To the outsider the country is economically and politically insignificant and impotent. It is unknown by most people, even in England, but if they do know of it, they think it only an island somewhere off the coast of Australia.

In architecture, dress, manners, speech, and customs there is a sameness as one moves about the country, a "blandness" as it is referred to locally. There was a time during the 1930's and into the period of the Second World War when immigration from Europe held the promise of increasing diversity; but most modifications have either been lost or absorbed into the local culture. There now appears little prospect of changing the cultural quality of the country through immigration, excluding the possibility of major upheaval. The population at large, the unions in particular, and the government more generally, are convinced that immigration should be limited to those who can adapt themselves readily to the existing community and who will not form ethnic communities of their own. Proponents of this point of view look with alarm at the expe-

12

rience in the United States, and more recently in Australia, when faced with the problems of a multiethnic community.

For the foreseeable future immigration will be limited to persons of northern and western European origin, although in the long run the pressures of international obligations and internal needs may force a change. Should such a day of change arrive, it will only be after the most serious internal resistance. In the absence of a broader view on immigration, the country suffers from a chronic shortage of labor.

Because of restrictive immigration, the minority communities within the country are small and few, except, of course, for the Maori population. For the most part these minorities are in no position, educationally or economically, to contribute to the higher cultural life of the country. Cut off by distance, by cost, or by legislation from overseas contacts, much of their own culture has been lost. Their absorption has also been encouraged through the pressures of a centralized educational system and by the conservatism of a small community resistant to innovation. The result has been rapid adaptation in speech, dress, and manner.

What upsets some New Zealanders and visitors is that there is no way to shake the sense of assurance of well-being; there is no responsible, critical press, and no means of livelihood for serious professional critics, whether of politics or the arts; the population is too small for national publications outside the limits of orthodoxy. The almost total exclusion of women from public life is itself disquieting and anachronistic. This sense of satisfaction may well be fully warranted, but it is unrealistic. There hangs over New Zealand a sense of imminent change. It is impossible to doubt that change is coming; all that can be in question is when and where it will begin and how extensive its consequences will be.

Britain's imperial demise and almost certain membership in the European Economic Community will bring about a fundamental reorientation of New Zealand's economic structure, just as her inability to contribute substantially to the defense of Australia and New Zealand during the Second World War necessitated a basic review of time-honored tenets of defense policy. The exigencies of war dictated an alliance with the United States and showed the probity of joining the Southeast Asia Treaty Organization and the Anzus Pact; the inescapable realities of economic life have already caused New Zealand to reassess its trade relationships vis-à-vis the United States in particular. The degree of their associations in defense and economic matters will be worked out in the coming decade, but there are numerous indices that they are already effective. New Zealand has already adopted a decimal currency based on a dollar; it has selected United States military equipment and commercial jet aircraft; it has attracted American capital for the construction of large tourist hotels; it has supplied materiel and support for the United States Antarctic expeditions and has provided token military support for United States military action in Viet Nam.

Complicating an easy prognostication of New Zealand's future role is the changing picture of Pacific politics: the rise of Asian nationalism, the independence of former island colonies and dependencies, such as Nauru and Western Samoa, and the rapid development of Fiji, Papua-New Guinea, and Tahiti may alter the quiescent atmosphere of the past and necessitate a restudying of late-Victorian plans for a single Australasian nation.

The remoteness so characteristic of New Zealand's past becomes less marked year by year with improvements in international travel and communication and the acceleration of migration from island areas to New Zealand, a condition already apparent in the labor force, where an increasing number of islanders are employed, along with Maori, in skilled and semiskilled occupations. It is difficult to believe that the country can maintain her essentially European culture in the face of this continued immigration when it is combined with a rapid increase in the size of the Maori population. Unlike Hawaii, which has produced an amalgam of cultures and built a modern community within which Polynesian culture forms an integral part, New Zealand has rejected the possibility. Thus, for the Islanders and the Maori, finding a life in New Zealand means that they must become European. In the face of educational and other impediments, a prospect exists somewhere in the future of the country becoming dependent on an unskilled Polynesian labor force. Most New Zealanders reject such a possibility out of hand, but there

14

is a body of evidence that suggests that it is not at all unlikely. If adaptation to these as well as other international needs is to come about, then the transplanted English culture of the past must be modified before too long, yet such a prospect holds little appeal within the country.

What people believe about themselves may be as important in any attempt to discover the national ethos as what they do, for their beliefs serve to give them a sense of national identity and provide motivation for their actions. The New Zealander holds his beliefs about his country with confidence and assurance; he is not quite so certain of his personal image and role, however. As Professor Russel Ward has written in *The Pattern of Australian Culture:*

It seems that the people of similar new countries, much smaller in size or less remote from powerful neighbors, have more difficulty in coming to feel at home in a new land. New Zealanders and Canadians, for instance, tend to define their respective self-images with some difficulty and in negative rather than positive terms. When asked to sketch roughly his national stereotype, the New Zealander usually answers, not with a positive statement that most of his countrymen *are* people of such and such a sort, but with two negatives. "Well, we're not as rough and crude as you Australians, of course. No convicts. We're much more like the English. But we're not really as genteel and formal as the English either. We are something in between."

Whatever there is of British equanimity, complaisance, reserve is balanced by conviviality, adaptability, pragmatism, and good humor. As Kenneth Melvin writes in *New Zealand: The Small Utopia* (1962): "Despite outward appearances we have much in common with the American people, and we covet their understanding no less than their goodwill in our alliance. We with them are part of the New World, though the New Zealander himself is different from the practical-minded Canadian, the volatile Australian, the stubborn South African and the uninhibited American."

To many recent observers the most disconcerting facet of New Zealand life is the general satisfaction with the status quo, the absence of any sense of national purpose, the lack of any real inclination to consider what the nation could become. This transcends mere lack of planning or cavalier disregard for the future: it is fundamentally the absence of the idealism that propelled national policy and individual action for the first one hundred years. Perhaps it is tacit recognition that small nations can no longer plot their destinies independent of the total world political, economic, and social picture. Perhaps it is satisfaction at having achieved those multifarious goals set by the early juggernauts of democratic socialism. Perhaps it is indicative of a quiet reassessment of the past as prelude to the enunciation of new goals. Whatever those goals may be, it is certain that they will have to be stated within the parameters of Australian and United States economic, political, social, military, and cultural influences more than within the traditional British ones.

16

LITERATURE

J. C. REID

WHAT has happened in New Zealand writing is what has happened in various ways in all the lands that have been settled by people of British stock. It has been a matter of trying to establish a separate identity in an environment and under circumstances very different from the old ones, and of shedding or modifying inherited attitudes which have little relevance to the colonial situation. Only as "home" became for New Zealanders the country in which they lived, and not the exile's idealized vision of England, could an indigenous literature begin to grow. Not only were there social ideas to be modified, but older literary models—not always the best—became petrified in the new land and had to be rejected or reseen before a native literature was possible. Early development was hampered, too, by limited opportunities for publication and the lack of a united spirit and national self-awareness in scattered groups of pioneers not yet consolidated into a society. In Australia, with its longer, if more checkered, history, the symptoms of truly native writing were apparent some two generations earlier than in New Zealand.

Writing for publication began with the arrival of planned bodies of colonists from Great Britain before the middle of the nineteenth century and the formal annexation of New Zealand by Britain in 1840. The literate arrivals brought with them the current books from England: Dickens, Carlyle, Tennyson, sermons and essays, and the lesser Victorians, Smiles and Tupper among them. A Pickwick Club, dedicated to spreading the fame of "the inimitable Boz" was formed in Port Nicholson just three months after the arrival of the first New Zealand Company settlers there in 1840. Nevertheless, the earliest literary efforts took a practical form: journalism, pamphlets, diaries, manuals. The useful arts were of prime importance. By one means or another, the land-hungry pioneers gradually acquired most of the country from the Maori and were faced with the tasks of clearing, plowing, establishing pasture, and creating a market in Great Britain for primary produce. In such circumstances, writing was most highly prized when it was most practical and informative.

A further determining factor was the strong Nonconformist element in early New Zealand society, which helped to infuse a Puritan tone into the emergent culture, of which traces still show in aspects of New Zealand legislation (on drink and gambling, for instance) and in the emphasis placed on respectability and decorum. The values of hard work, money-making, and stolid conformity acted as a brake on the raffish habits inherited from the sealers and whalers who had preceded the colonists. But a philosophy which regarded literature as time-wasting and which distrusted the imagination hardly made for an environment within which creative writing could flourish.

The first verse arose out of the celebration of special occasions in the form of topical pieces recited or sung at a "social." As it developed more consciously literary manners, it graduated as a branch of minor Victorian verse, with its post-Keatsian worship of beauty, its vague generalizations, its didacticism, and its sentimentality. So, too, the plays written later in the century belong to the crude tradition of Victorian melodrama and burlesque, and the novels owe more to Theodore Hook and Mrs. Henry Wood than to Dickens and Thackeray.

The lack of any amount of significant writing in nineteenth-

18

century New Zealand may be explained simply by the absence of writers of real talent. Only in flashes did the more "literary" poets of the time produce a line or two that looks like poetry, for the early settlers suffered from a divided sensibility that prevented them from responding creatively to their surroundings. They were exiles whose hearts were still in the Old Country. This inevitable colonial condition was aggravated by the island character of the country and its distance from Europe; these bred a sense of physical isolation leading to a compensatory closer clinging to the image of Mother Britain.

The English literary models, too, of the first writers, with their class values and middle-class ideals, bore little relation to the egalitarian attitudes of the new land. For at least three generations New Zealand writing reflected this dichotomy, a clash between Victorian sensibility and colonial reality. Not unexpectedly, then, much of it shows the author's uncertainty as to his identity and, indeed, as to that of his audience. At the same time, certain characteristics that New Zealanders have come to recognize as part of their national make-up do reveal themselves in early writing, especially the "being torn two ways." Fossilized Victorian concepts, apparent then as now, especially at the local-body level, include a narrow notion of "respectability," a drab sabbatarianism, a conviction that money made is a sign of God's favor, a distaste for controversy about fundamentals, and petty social snobberies. Legacies from the pioneering period are represented in the booze party, the passion for Rugby football and other sports, the prizing of the practical man and the distrust of the intellectual, the desire to get away from it all "into the bush," and the fear of—even contempt for—women, except as sex objects. In some things there is concord, perhaps most notably in the fallacious conviction that New Zealand is "God's Own Country," and that it has "the highest standard of living in the world," meaning, of course, a material standard. While it would be grossly oversimplifying to suggest that the frequent conflict between private morality and public and official morality represents a clash between these two attitudes, there was clearly in New Zealand a split which still to an extent remains, at the class level and elsewhere, between those regarding the country as an outpost of Empire and a temporary home, and those seeing New Zealand as a new beginning.

A rooted distaste for privilege was one of the earliest of the fresh attitudes to show itself. Even though the proclamation of a freer and more independent life in the colony sometimes seems like whistling in the dark, the better writers on occasion proclaim values that have been central to the New Zealand philosophy, whether it be the assertion of the equality of all men by John Barr, the Otago poet; the example of success through work in Alexander Bathgate's novels; the dry humor of F. E. Maning; or the visionary political utopianism of Sir Julius Vogel's novel, *Anno Domini 2000: Or Woman's Destiny*. But the mere presence of these elements does not in itself constitute an indigenous literature.

The first clear signs of writing different from that of exiles in that it came, in the poet James Baxter's words, "from the point of view of one who has grown up in entire acceptance of his environment, truly inhabiting the country," can be found in the 1920's with the New Zealand stories of Katherine Mansfield and the early poems of R. A. K. Mason and A. R. D. Fairburn. But these writers still shared in the moods and used the forms of current English literature, and felt the pull of Europe. It was Katherine Mansfield's returning, in spirit, to her native land after years in Europe that more than anything else in the 1920's gave intimations of the change to come.

The new mood was generated largely by the depression of the 1930's. This economic calamity proved to be a literary catalyst, for it brought together writer and audience; it also jolted men into a sharpened awareness of immediate realities and made them realize that in their own lives and circumstances lay the stuff out of which literature can be made. During the depression years, New Zealand writers found their proper subjects and themselves as well. Third-generation and fourth-generation New Zealanders, they were not yet free from inherited conflicts. Yet they were facing directly for the first time the challenge of their own society and environment and they saw their task as, in Fairburn's words, that of being "willing to partake, internally as well as externally, of the anarchy of life in a new place and, by creative energy, to give that life form and consciousness." Where before there had been scattered, isolated

20

achievements, there was now a substantial corpus of work that could properly be called a literature. There was also an increasing audience for it as readers found in the writings of their fellow-countrymen not only their own feelings and aspirations given significant form, but assurance of further growth.

During the past thirty years this body of writing has continued to grow in scope and diversity. The expansion of local book publishing, the raising of standards of book production by the Caxton Press and other firms, the finding of markets abroad for New Zealand writing, the assistance of the State Literary Fund, the growth of literary criticism, the almost universal literacy, the expansion of population, and the appearance of talented writers—these have all helped in the development of a flourishing contemporary literature.

The poetry of the first sixty years or so makes depressing reading. Its drab landscape is diversified only occasionally by small outcroppings of individuality. Most published volumes represent an attempt to provide a literature to fill a vacuum, a literature based, necessarily, on English models. In the topical vein, some vigorous verse came from the Scots settlement of Otago, written by poets like William Golder and John Barr. Barr's *Poems and Songs* (1861) makes forceful use of the Scottish idiom to celebrate New Zealand freedom as contrasted with the restraints of "home" and to satirize money-grubbing colonists.

These poets were at least concerned with the essential matter of New Zealand living; those who turned to serious themes were dominated by a stilted pseudo-Romantic poetic diction and by the idea that poetry must be elevating and awesome. The most ambitious of these was Alfred Domett, Browning's friend "Waring," who became prime minister in 1862 and made considerable contributions to the country's life. But his *Ranolf and Amohia* (1872), an epic of Anglo-Maori life, hardly ranks as one of them. A diffuse work told in a dead diction, it tries to shape a romantic New Zealand far from the realities of colonial settlements.

The most characteristic and popular poet of his age, however, was Thomas Bracken (1843–1898), Irish immigrant, journalist, member of Parliament, and kindly Bohemian. There were three different and typical writers in Bracken: the snook-cocking fabricator of topical

21

doggerel, the pompous bard sprinkling the earth with clichés, and the crowd-pleasing rhymster with something of Hood's gift for poeticizing the commonplace, as in the popular "Not Understood." In "God Defend New Zealand" he wrote the national song. Yet, despite his wide reputation in the 1880's, none of his books survive in print.

In the 1890's there were some signs of change. The country was attaining a balanced economy, the population and urban life had grown, and a liberal-minded government was introducing progressive legislation. The time seemed ripe for a truly indigenous consciousness and tone in literature. Unhappily, there was not yet a wide enough audience for serious poetry; again, there was no cultural continuity inside the land itself, nor were there many writers of real talent.

The leading figure at the turn of the century was W. Pember Reeves (1857–1932), a New Zealand–born statesman and historian. His poetry, though cultivated and dignified, deals fairly heavily in conventional phrases and imagery. Perhaps his most successful poem is "A Colonist in His Garden," written after he left New Zealand in 1896, finding his colleagues too conservative-minded. A new emphasis is seen in his dramatizing of the cultural split his contemporaries felt, as a debate between his New Zealand self and his English self. For the latter, the country consists of

> Isles nigh as empty as their deep,
> Where men but talk of gold and sheep.

But the former retorts:

> "No art?" Who serves an art more great
> Than we, rough architects of State
> With the old Earth at strife?
>
> "No colour?" On the silent waste,
> In pigments not to be effaced
> We paint the hues of life.

The promise of the nineties was not fulfilled in the next two decades. During these years, New Zealand verse stubbornly maintained its provinciality. In fact, the Boer War and the First World War intensified the sense of loyalty and attachment to Great

Britain. Many New Zealanders prided themselves on being "more English than the English"; a nostalgic conception of Britain meant that Old World standards and manners provided models and norms in poetry. It was inevitable that the New Zealand idiom should have been considered, *ipso facto*, nonpoetic and that images drawn from the local scene should have been self-conscious or illustrative rather than integral parts of the writer's imagination. Arnold Wall (b. 1869), with his gnomic and witty poetry, Edwardian in tone and English in sentiment, and Alan Mulgan (1881–1962), torn between "home" as a cultural Mecca and a deep love for his native land, typify the poets of this time.

It was in the 1920's that signs began to appear of true distinction and individuality. The first volume of R. A. K. Mason, *The Beggar* (1924), was virtually unnoticed. But where most previous poets had been bent upon exploring the relationship between the New Zealander and his environment, in this immature work of Mason (b. 1904) there sounded a new note, the voice of a man determined to make his own private sense out of experience and seeing poetry as a shaped and ordered art. Mason grew to full stature as a poet in the depression years. A Marxist by conviction, he wrote his poems, however, not about social conditions, but out of his own sensibility as it reacted to his times. *No New Thing* (1934) and *This Dark Will Lighten* (1941), in their spare language and taut rhythms, show the influence of Latin poets, of Housman, too, and Beddoes, and in their emphasis upon human suffering, their somberness and skepticism, something of the Georgian reaction against socially directed poetry. They deal not with New Zealand or New Zealanders, but with what it means to be a human being. The voice which speaks of the problems of belief, sex, personal identity, and man's anguish is often harsh, but as it says:

> For my bitter verses are
> sponges steeped in vinegar
> useless to the happy-eyed
> but handy for the crucified.

Mason's refusal to be discursive provided a salutary example to his contemporaries, as his idiosyncratic vision inspired confidence that true poetry could be made in New Zealand.

A. R. D. Fairburn (1904–1957), like Mason an Auckland poet, was a more extroverted and varied writer. He was convinced that the local poet must forsake the emotional security of cultural dependence on Britain to immerse himself in the chaos of New Zealand life and help to impose a new order upon it. *Dominion* (1938), more than any other volume of the day, expresses the whole sense of spiritual and social discontent and the hope for renewal the depression called forth. Other poems by Fairburn are lyrical responses to life and love, affirming a humanist trust in the purity of man's fundamental instincts. No other New Zealand poet has written so much and so variously of kinds of loving. For all Fairburn's repudiation of romantic gestures, he remained a romantic to the end, singing of death with mingled fascination and horror. Another side to him was his irrepressible talent for light verse, half-mocking and half-serious, and for keen-edged satirical slashes at the Pharisees and the publicans alike. An unresolved conflict between the polemicist and the nature-loving humanist sets up a powerful vibration in his best poetry.

Three women contributed to the new assurance of verse in the 1930's. Eileen Duggan (b. 1900) carried the dominant Georgian manner to its furthest point in New Zealand poetry and moved beyond it. Sensitive rather than strong, her work nonetheless shows the result of stern self-discipline, and her Catholic faith and a sincere love of the land charge it with deep feeling. From *Poems* (1924) to the present day, she has gone on developing her own independent statement, moving from her earlier lyricism to a metaphysical manner, tauter and less prone to conventional responses. Mary Ursula Bethell (1874–1945) attempted to convey the essence of her Canterbury landscape in terms of time and eternity, as a Christian acknowledges them. She worked hard at her poetry, avoiding romantic simplicities. Her mind sometimes outstripped her feelings, but she has few local peers in tranquil meditativeness, and she is at times capable of a mystical exaltation like that of the Metaphysicals. The early verse of "Robin Hyde" (Iris Wilkinson, 1906–1939) contains much romantic posturing, but in *Houses by the Sea*, published posthumously, she attained a new depth by turning, like Katherine Mansfield before her, to recall with tender insight her childhood in

Wellington. Free now from literary affectations, these poems recreate a time and a place and the emotion of an adolescent on the threshold of womanhood.

Denis Glover (b. 1912) began in the 1930's as a literary associate of Mason, Fairburn, and Allen Curnow. To some extent he has fostered a public image of a clowning, irreverent, practical Kiwi. But this is, at least partly, a strategy to divert attention from his other personality, the sensitive appreciator of nature and the compassionate singer of misfits and loners. His best work, in *Sings Harry* (1951) and *Arawata Bill* (1953), centers on men who find the open spaces more congenial than cities and embody one of our most durable literary myths, the "man alone." The style is bare, compact; the rhythms, conversational. The poems are rich in empathy and in a special feeling for New Zealand scenes; the apparent simplicity of the forms is the product of skillful control of emotion.

Charles Brasch (b. 1909), who also springs from the 1930's, deploys a talent less robust than that of his contemporaries: solemn, fastidious, aesthetic rather than exciting or firm-centered. His poems early indicated a love-hate relationship with his native land; on the one hand regretting the absence of a sophisticated culture, on the other enamored of its scenery and its Polynesian history. His more recent work reveals a less ambivalent attitude, as if he has found his own point of resolution and sees this reflected in the community at large.

The most noteworthy figure to emerge in this period is Allen Curnow (b. 1911). As a poet of technical resource, intellectual curiosity, and subtlety, he has no contemporary rival. Some of his first verses were satirical, in the manner of Glover and Fairburn, but this mood has been retained, with greater urbanity, only in his overtly light verse. More important is his search for a coherent poetic myth of place and history to make some sort of sense of the New Zealand fact, in volumes significantly entitled *Not in Narrow Seas* (1939) and *Island and Time* (1941). In these he plumbs history, Pacific exploration, and the march of empire for subjects, writing of the paradoxes of the long sea voyage, the hostility of the land, and the character of the new society that feels itself alien. His poems are attempts by a New Zealander to fashion a lasting experience out of his own awareness of his country's past and landscape, finding it "something different, something / Nobody counted on." In his more recent work, the preoccupations have become more personal and the verse more allusive and gnomic; often the themes are self-understanding, the nature of poetic experience, and the problems of being and becoming. Curnow's poetry is always beautifully shaped and governed by what is probably the keenest artistic sensibility possessed by any living New Zealand poet.

His poetic practice and his critical writings have, in conjunction with the criticism of M. H. Holcroft, stressed the character of New Zealand as a remote island, the importance of persistent memories of voyagers and explorers, and the notion of "sundering seas." It was inevitable that a younger generation should, to some degree, react against this. The reaction came in the 1950's most determinedly, if not always coherently, from a Wellington poet, Louis Johnson (b. 1924), who argued that New Zealand poetry should treat not of the problems of being a New Zealander, but of those things that are every man's concern. His own poems are often powerful but rather undisciplined expressions of personal anguish, sexual torment, the loss of innocence. He has matured into a poet of mordant satire and of urban life and domestic concerns. His technique lacks subtlety and his work varies widely in quality, but his voice is an individual one, and in writing of the responses of men and women to everyday living, he has helped to draw the attention of younger poets away from nature themes and other manifestly indigenous poetic statements.

James K. Baxter (b. 1926) stands aloof from both the Curnow and the Johnson points of view. Basically a lyrical poet, he is also a prophet and a rhetor. His strong, if often tormented, moral sense issues not as preaching, but as savage satire or as a fierce concern with truth, integrity, charity. His poems frequently take their origin from an aspect of the land, but pass beyond this to a vision of the human condition, to man as a spiritual being rather than as a social one or an alien settler. His voice is unmistakable, yet it is one that covers a wide range of varying tones. His unusual eloquence, his apocalyptic sense, his technical virtuosity, his ability to fuse the concrete with the metaphysical, are widely recognized, although some have seen in him a dangerous taste for the rhetorical gesture and an adolescent delight in shocking. Baxter is unquestionably the major talent to emerge from the 1940's and is one of the most complex and exciting of New Zealand poets, haunting, challenging, growing in stature with each volume.

Other notable Wellington poets include Alistair Campbell, Hubert Witheford, Patrick Wilson, Ruth Gilbert, Peter Bland, and W. H. Oliver. Campbell's poems blend lyrical and elegiac tones in a delicate, yet firm, celebration of place; W. H. Oliver, a scholar-poet, has a dry wit, a sense of history, and a tightly reined sensibility that allows him to explore the inner heart of his land in taut, unemphatic verse. Charles Doyle, who published first in Wellington, later in Auckland, has repressed earlier poetic gestures in favor of a reconciliation to his adopted land that permits him to treat of domestic themes with irony and affection.

Christchurch, once the center of poetic production, has lost its precedence of recent years. Christchurch poets include Basil Dowling, whose verse is lit with religious feeling and a keen awareness of the physical features of the South Island; William Hart-Smith, whose recent work shows the influence of Australian ballad-type poems; "Paul Henderson" (Ruth France) whose insights make her a sophisticated descendant of earlier more overtly Wordsworthian poets; J. R. Harvey (1889–1958); and Charles Spear (b. 1910). Harvey, whose first book appeared when he was fifty, treats of age, death, mutability, and mature married love. Charged with meditative peace and joy, his poems rise nobly from hard-won simplicities. In his single volume, *Twopence Coloured* (1951), Charles Spear's beautifully exact verse, plumbing European history and scenes and foreign literatures, delicately exploits symbolism in the interests of stoic resignation and the wise acceptance of pain, sacrifice, and change.

Finally, in Auckland, a substantial body of poetry has been produced since the Second World War. It is no more possible to speak of an Auckland school than of a Wellington one, but tentatively it may be suggested that, whereas in the capital city poetry tends to embody a new Romanticism or to be concerned with urban life and social contexts, the dominant Auckland tone is academic or meta-

27

physical. For instance, M. K. Joseph (b. 1914) draws upon a well-stocked and exquisitely precise mind for starting points for poems about the eternal verities, religious faith, time, change, and the nature of being. He is much concerned with the relationship between time and eternity, between art and life, social custom and belief. He is also a gifted parodist and satirist. Another professor-poet, Keith Sinclair (b. 1922), finely captures the distinctive character of the national landscape, writes vigorously of love and marriage, gives rein to a quirky imagination, and meditates upon New Zealand's past.

By contrast, Kendrick Smithyman (b. 1922) owes comparatively little to the New Zealand scene. His work, often complex in its syntax and its pattern of ideas, is academic in its playing with ontological concepts and with questions of identity. The harvest of his strenuous struggling with the outer reaches of spiritual and emotional experience and with problems of artistic form is a poetry giving a new perspective on everyday reality. It well repays being fought through. Smithyman is a dedicated poet and a meticulous craftsman, intensely self-critical; his strange, oddly angled, austerely conceived poems are among the most sophisticated productions of the past twenty years.

For the size of its population, New Zealand has produced an unexpected number of good poets, not all of whom have been mentioned here. New and interesting ones make their debut yearly: recently Gordon Challis; Vincent O'Sullivan; Richard Packer; C. K. Stead, with his sardonic humor and his reanimation of traditional forms; Hone Tuwhare, whose integration of Maori and *pakeha* traditions marks a new development; and Fleur Adcock, with her frank treatment of sexual love.

Seen from this point in time, the major poetic achievement seems to belong to the 1930's, when New Zealand poetry became truly an art and showed a vigor and a drive springing from something deep in the poets' awareness of their land and society. Since that period Baxter, Joseph, and Smithyman, most notably, have maintained the artistic integrity of our poetry, without recourse to sociological theories or philosophies that concern poetry alone. In all their work we recognize the New Zealander's response to the tangible realities of his fellow countrymen and his environment. The current poetic scene, with its overlapping generations, its lively controversies, and the presence of poets who are distinct individuals, shows a fruitful diversity, in which it is futile to seek for hard and fast trends and schools. There is, perhaps, less force, less power, less urgency in New Zealand poetry today; it tends to pick up, a little too easily, the manners and themes of newer British and American poets whose concerns are sometimes only lightly relevant to life in this land; it has, frequently, an adolescent solemnity which can go hand in hand with triviality; it sometimes mistakes the form of poetry for its substance. There is, too, a general absence of real gaiety from New Zealand verse, and a widespread melancholy which, manifest as early as Mason's first poems, has survived the hypothetical joys of a welfare state. Only in older poets like Fairburn and Glover, and an occasional individual like Joseph, is there a consistent sense of life's goodness and the joy as well as of the challenge of being a man.

The first New Zealand novels, almost all written for a British public, shared with pioneering guidebooks the aim of describing and interpreting the new land. When novelists departed from this purpose, it was to exploit the exotic material in exciting adventure tales. Naturally, too, several novels took the form of a first-person account beginning in England, recording the long voyage out, and plunging into varied pioneer experiences. By comparison with the great novels being written in England at that time, New Zealand fiction between 1860 and 1890 is unusually crude, melodramatic, and sub-literary.

The first New Zealand novel, *Taranaki: A Tale of the War* (1861), by Major H. B. Stoney, was of this kind and became the prototype for several tales of Maori War adventures. Not until the end of the century did novelists attempt to get inside the Maori mind or appreciate his culture. Another early fictional pattern, that of the pioneer-family saga, was established by Isabella Aylmer in *Distant Homes* (1862). The experiences of a lone male pioneer constitute the stuff of another group: perhaps the best is Alexander Bathgate's *Waitaruna* (1881), a Presbyterian variant on the idle and industrious apprentices theme, which allows the author to give some authentic pictures of sheep-station life.

No novel of the nineteenth century has any claim to literary worth. When, however, the period of consolidation followed the pioneering era, novelists began to feel that they could write in acceptance of a country with some individual character, which they could criticize and interpret rather than exploit or explain. The pioneering novel virtually disappears in the 1890's. Its last fling is the curious, confused, yet sensitive *Philosopher Dick* (1891), by George Chamier, in which a critical view of New Zealand mores is expressed through the responses of an idealistic young immigrant who comes, after considerable disillusionment, to at least a partial acceptance of the underlying assumptions of colonial life. Oddly formless and overdetailed, *Philosopher Dick* remains interesting for its adumbration of themes and attitudes later to become stock ones in our fiction: the outsider, the need for mateship, the pettiness of small-town life, and a mannered pessimism.

The crusading influence of women in a brash, hard-drinking community showed itself also in the 1890's in several propaganda novels that came out of the associated prohibition and feminist movements, and New Zealand's social and political concerns spawned a clutch of Utopias.

Yet, despite individual achievements of some historical interest, the country up to the First World War had produced no abiding fiction. However, some of the basic themes of a local literature had been hinted at and the habit of writing novels had been well established when William Satchell (1860–1942) arrived—the first novelist with any claim to be taken seriously. Despite creaking dialogue, melodrama, and some sentimentality, Satchell transmitted the genuine feel of the bush country and the gum-lands and their effect upon people. Imperfectly realized, but nevertheless there, is a sense of the power and presence of nature as we know it, of the open spaces, and of the kind of society that has grown up in them.

The First World War acts as a convenient line of division. One effect of this conflict was an intensification of a nascent prewar revolt by the younger generation against many Victorian social and moral conventions. The most mature of those questioning inherited values was Jane Mander (1877–1949). *The Story of a New Zealand River* (1920), set in a Northland timber-milling district, tells of the gradual, painful readjustment of a genteel Englishwoman, married to an uncultured New Zealander, to her new environment. But, in the main, fiction marked time in the 1920's. The outstanding achievement was that of Katherine Mansfield, whose short stories will be discussed later. In any case, she had no immediate effect on our fiction. The novels continued to be provincial in outlook, technically naive or clumsy, and based to a large extent on inferior or outmoded British models.

The economic crisis of the 1930's blew Edwardian gentility in fiction sky-high, focused attention on living issues, and made English subjects and moods appear unreal or irrelevant. Typical of this new mood are the novels of John A. Lee (b. 1891), Labour member of Parliament and one of the architects of the social-welfare policies of the first Labour government elected in 1935. Lee's *Children of the Poor* (1934) and *The Hunted* (1936), in part autobiographical, brought the poverty and squalor of slum life into New Zealand fiction for the first time. Socialist-propagandist in manner, overemphatic and highly colored, they nevertheless have considerable power. Lee's bull-like charge against the polite conventions of New Zealand fiction left them in ruins. The novels of "Robin Hyde" also helped the transformation. *Passport to Hell* (1936) and *Nor the Years Condemn* (1938) convincingly recreate the war years and the postwar and depression periods. In a tour de force, *Check to Your King* (1936), she brought to life Baron Charles de Thierry, who tried to establish himself as Sovereign Chief of New Zealand in the 1830's, and in *The Godwits Fly* (1938) she dramatized the pull of the Old World on New Zealanders. Very much aware of the colonial situation, she sought to reject both the aggressive insularity of her contemporaries and the "dear old home" attitude in order to concentrate on wider human issues.

Perhaps the most significant novel of the 1930's was *Man Alone* (1939), by John Mulgan (1911–1945). In a style reminiscent of Hemingway's, Mulgan expressed the predominant political sentiments of the time and made concrete modern man's dilemma in a bewilderingly divided society. His hero, Johnson, is a full embodiment of the rootless individualist without responsibilities who was to become a literary stereotype: Johnson finally finds his "cause" in

31

the Spanish Civil War. The man alone theme recurs in such books as Erik de Mauny's *The Huntsman in His Career* (1949), Guthrie Wilson's *Strip Jack Naked* (1957), and Gordon Slatter's *A Gun in My Hand* (1959). Although twenty years separate Mulgan's and Slatter's books, the subject matter is in many ways similar: a lone wolf views his society with disillusioned eyes, violence is a predominant element, women are traps for men. Slatter, however, suffuses his story with a strong dash of irony; he rejects violence as a solution and sees the man alone as a disruptive force.

In serious novels after the 1930's, writers found it possible to take New Zealand more for granted, without explanatory local color. Building on the achievements of the decade, more conscious of structure and form, more aware of overseas experiments, with a wider experience of the world, and living in a more stable society, recent novelists have expanded and diversified the areas of fiction. The Second World War, while it stimulated a crop of war novels, had little, if any, direct impact on the main direction of fiction. New Zealand, still small and in the main free from fruitful tensions, is now large enough and varied enough to permit a certain regionalism, as in the novels of Dan Davin, three of which are set in the Southland Irish community, or the treatment of specific social or professional groups, as in the school and university novels of Guthrie Wilson and M. K. Joseph.

The most original talent to flower since 1945 is Janet Frame (b. 1924). Her *Owls Do Cry* (1957) is a truly remarkable novel, which organizes her intuitions about loneliness, spiritual exile, and emotional insecurity through the intricately told story of a family in a small New Zealand town. The elaborate pattern of symbols, poetic devices, and interior monologues recurs in various forms in her later books, set either in New Zealand or Britain, in which she explores children and introverted or unbalanced characters searching for identity and communication with others. Janet Frame is primarily concerned with ultimate values, with issues of life and death, normality and abnormality, with the quest for what is really valuable in the past and the present of the individual, for the true reality, "the genuine treasure."

Ian Cross (b. 1925), another writer of stature, began in 1957 with

The God Boy, a moving study of a thirteen-year-old boy reliving an earlier tragedy in his home and electing a state of youthful rejection. More ambitiously, in *After Anzac Day* (1961), Cross tried to convey an impression of New Zealand's essential character, especially its political and social values, through the consciousnesses of a household involved in seemingly private relationships. The technique is mature and subtle, the sensibility complex and delicate. A large number of New Zealand themes—Maori-*pakeha* relationships, the magnetic appeal of "home," our Puritan traditions, for instance—as well as the meaning of Anzac Day, inherited political clichés of thought, and the Kiwi's notion of his own virility are probed to illuminate the role of the dominant male in our society. In the end, unmistakably New Zealand though the novel is in setting and its premises, it achieves a broader significance in its presentation of maleness and paternity.

Both of these writers raise the question of what, if anything, is distinctively New Zealand about the contemporary novel. It is difficult to say what in the literary sense may be characteristically such about Janet Frame's work. True, the background and characters are usually recognizably of this country, as are such themes as the hollowness and inadequacy of our bourgeois values. But if we distinguish between material and vision we find ourselves in the presence of an idiosyncratic talent that cannot be tied down to tradition or locale. The world in which Janet Frame moves is that of man's mind and heart. This is Ian Cross's world, too. While he works more directly and intimately in *After Anzac Day* with subject matter perhaps fully intelligible in detail only to those who share his environment, he also is bent on dramatizing realities beyond the sociological.

In this universal extension, does anything remain which represents some special contribution from the New Zealand psyche? Have our novelists extended human awareness, revealed new sensibilities, deepened responses, enlarged horizons? Perhaps a glance at recurrent themes may help towards an answer.

One area constantly explored by New Zealand novelists is the mind of the child; sometimes, in Janet Frame's fiction for instance, the child appears as another instance of the outsider in an alien world; sometimes, as epitomizing adjustment or merely growing up. *The God Boy,* James Courage's *The Young Have Secrets* (1954), Roderick Finlayson's *Tidal Creek* (1948), Maurice Shadbolt's *Among the Cinders* (1965), and most delicately, Noel Hilliard's *Power of Joy* (1965), show the persistence of the child's view of reality as a New Zealand subject. This may be explained by saying that the local environment still allows for a Wordsworthian innocent eye; that, lacking rewarding and diverse experiences, our novelists find that their childhood is the one significant area of their lives that they can use with some detachment; that, consciously or unconsciously, our novelists see in childhood an image of New Zealand's own immaturity, or as M. H. Holcroft suggests, they "turn to it in search of completeness, the identity which eludes them in the suburbs where they live today."

Then there is the frequent criticism of the Philistine society, with its materialistic basis, its crudities, its drab functionalism, or of the simplified image of the hard-doing Kiwi joker as epitomized in Barry Crump's *A Good Keen Man* (1960). In Bill Pearson's *Coal Flat* (1963), a solidly socialist-realist book, Frank Sargeson's *Memoirs of a Peon* (1965), Maurice Gee's *The Big Season* (1962), Pat Booth's *Footsteps in the Sea* (1964), and many others, New Zealand's basic values of living and its flattering notion of itself are criticized with varying degrees of irony and skill. Sometimes the criticism is less direct and works by considering the place of the oddity or the individualist in a society that makes little or no allowance for the artist, the eccentric, the nonconformist—as in Maurice Shadbolt's *The Presence of Music* (1967), or *Spinster* (1958) and *Incense to Idols* (1960) of Sylvia Ashton-Warner. Miss Ashton-Warner's novels, written in lush and hectic prose, are romantic and overheated, but in *Spinster,* at least, she comes close to making real the liberating impact of a gifted individualist in her story of a brandy-tippling teacher working to enlarge the sensibilities of her pupils, Maori and *pakeha.* The trouble is that, in the hands of some novelists, the critical attitudes have hardened into clichés: the six-o'clock pub swill, the religion of Rugby, the disdain for creative artists, the male fear of women, the petty snobberies and pathetic imitations of English middle-class customs among them. There is

34

seldom any urbanity in the way novelists describe the defects in New Zealand mores or, save in a writer like Frank Sargeson, a point of view that goes below the surface to anatomize the philosophy sustaining the values criticized. Even in such an interesting novel as Maurice Gee's *A Special Flower* (1965), with its unusually sensitive treatment of married sex and family tensions and its insight into women's minds, the stereotype of the oafish football player intrudes.

In a society with a significant Maori minority, race relations inevitably provide a favorite theme. Contemporary novelists and short-story writers make a much more serious attempt to understand the Maori than their predecessors did. In *Maori Girl* (1960), by Noel Hilliard, the problem of the urbanized Maori is handled with unsentimental realism; Charles Frances's *Johnny Rapana* (1964) less successfully attempts to do the same for a Maori man. Others have tended to sentimentalize the Maori, from the best of motives, no doubt, but also perhaps with a certain amount of the guilt complex New Zealanders harbor about the Maori. The social realities of our society—the fact that the blame is not wholly on the shoulders of the *pakeha*, the need to accept the Maori as a human being without patronizing or leaning over backwards—such considerations are by-passed by writers in particular, in favor of a simplified and romantic emphasis on the Maori virtues of courtesy, personal generosity, and community feeling, so that New Zealand fiction seems sometimes in danger of substituting an overcompensating twentieth-century stereotype for the nineteenth-century one.

The Maori, of course, features prominently in our historical novels, since the Maori Wars provide one of the few substantial deposits of native historical material. Earlier endeavors, like William Satchell's *The Greenstone Door* (1914), offer sentimentalized stock Maori characters; similar conventions mark novels as recent as Leo Fowler's *Brown Conflict* (1959). However, in his Major Williams trilogy, *The Flying Fish* (1964), *The Needle's Eye* (1965), *The Evil Day* (1967), Errol Brathwaite (b. 1924) has found a new way with our history. Despite the authenticity of background and detail, he is concerned with basic moral issues, the effects of war upon men, the nature of violence, the growth of nationhood out of con-

35

flict, the confusion of loyalties that war breeds. The same interest in spiritual and moral problems gives added strength to Brathwaite's *An Affair of Men* (1961), which deals with the Japanese war in the Pacific.

The increasing, if limited, complexity of New Zealand society has permitted the writing of novels set in selected areas of our community life, nearly all critical of the values found there. Examples include M. K. Joseph's *A Pound of Saffron* (1962), examining power politics in the university, Redmond Wallis's *Point of Origin* (1962), concerning snobbery in Christchurch, and Gordon Dryland's *An Absence of Angels* (1965), offering a disenchanted view of local intellectual phonies and pseudo-Bohemians.

From these rough groupings, which are by no means comprehensive, what general conclusions can be drawn? First, although the crusading novel has almost disappeared, New Zealand novelists still have an almost obsessive concern with the structure and character of their society, insofar as it relates to customs, values, and attitudes at least. Their continual self-scrutiny and their anxiety about egalitarian ideals seem to indicate an uncertainty about their own identity as a people: Are we colonists still at heart? Are we a "peasant nation," as Maurice Shadbolt has called us? Are we needlessly concerned with themes that history should quietly have buried? If there is one thing the novelists are seldom in disagreement about, it is that the New Zealand egalitarian philosophy, even in welfare-state circumstances of imposed averageness, is superior to that of class-structured societies, and that this philosophy has bred a special type of man, one who values, sometimes with wry acceptance, comradeship, loyalty to mates and sharing above all else, and respects a class rather than heroes.

It is perhaps because of this pervasive mateship and because sex can be disruptive in society that New Zealand novelists find it hard to write meaningfully of sex. The futile father, the sage mother, the male child responsive to mother—this pattern of Momism runs through much New Zealand fiction from Katherine Mansfield to Ian Cross. Heterosexual relations, when they are treated at all, are usually seen in terms of naive fictional clichés, as if the author were merely going through expected motions without knowing really what it is all about. Many short stories and several novels have an explicitly homosexual strain; it is latent in others. When sex is not ignored, romanticized, or homosexual, as in James Courage's work, it is often abnormal, as in R. H. Morrieson's story of a necrophiliac killer in a small town, *Scarecrow* (1963), or Janet Frame's *The Adaptable Man* (1965), with its mixture of incest and violence. Perhaps all this distrust of normal sex is a reflex from New Zealand's primary Puritan or colonial attitudes, or it may simply represent another suppression of the real personality in the interest of social values conceived in narrower terms than older societies do. Or is it that, in Ian Cross's words, "the modern New Zealand male is a eunuch of twentieth-century socialism"? Whatever the reason, the rarity with which love, sex, and marriage are treated with insight and sensitivity in our fiction, the grave absence of joy in man-woman relationships, is a measure of the still markedly provincial character of our writing.

These lacks illustrate the limited range of experience New Zealand fiction draws upon. Few writers are venturesome, even when they tackle new subject matter. Perhaps New Zealand, with its pragmatism, its doggedly working-class prejudices, is not a society to stretch the imagination; perhaps the work that most of us do does not require enough resource and courage. There is a certain predictability in New Zealand fiction: solid craftsmanship, competent writing, a dash of sensitivity, and one or other of a restricted range of themes, most likely one with a sociological basis. Few novelists have looked sufficiently hard and deep into their own hearts to produce a vision of reality that transcends a nagging concern with aspects of the national image.

While the short story has somewhat fallen out of favor elsewhere, it has remained one of the most widely practiced New Zealand forms, possibly because publication opportunities are greater here than for novels. A few early short stories, such as those by Lady Barker and William Baucke, retain some interest, either as literary equivalents of pioneers' yarns or as attempts to interpret Maori life. Some writers, such as Blanche Baughan, made tentative stabs at a native colloquial style; but it was Katherine Mansfield (Kathleen Beauchamp, 1888–1923) who raised the New Zealand short story to the level of an art and became the first native writer to gain an international reputation. After she left this country forever as a young girl, she remained always somewhat immature and chaotic as a personality, but in her work she was a perfectionist, seeking tirelessly for precision and clarity.

In general, her stories present a swift, penetrating look at a character or a situation. They rely hardly at all upon plot, but heavily upon the creation of atmosphere; the method is impressionistic, catching the innerness of life through the slight things of every day. Concentrating the time span of her stories, she explores the sensations of her characters and miraculously imprisons the transient mood or the stir of evanescent memory. It is this fineness of truth to the more elusive movements of the soul and to the inexpressible apprehensions, especially of children, her sensitive response to tensions in married life and in family life, and her superbly disciplined style, that make her outstanding.

Her ability to relate moods to outward signs by an exact use of imagery sets her characters firmly in the world of things. Her style, refined in her later years to an exceptional purity, became a beautifully supple instrument, delicate yet strong, poetic yet firm. As her health failed, it was her memories of her New Zealand childhood that gave her a center of repose and relief from her burdens. Stories like "At the Bay" and "Prelude," with their intense visualization, their exquisite texture of language, their searching out of the hearts of their characters, and their capturing of the sounds, sights, and smells of the land, remain the country's highest achievement in the short story. Despite attempts to break free from her influence, few later New Zealand writers have escaped her.

Soon after Katherine Mansfield's death a young returned soldier, Frank S. Anthony (1891–1925), brought something new to the short story. His stories, later collected as *Me and Gus* (1938), embody moods and qualities typical of the Kiwi farmer and are told in a vivacious variant of the New Zealand vernacular.

A much more sophisticated use of the New Zealand idiom was made by Frank Sargeson (b. 1903), who refined it for a conscious artistic purpose. He took as his early characters men of the depression days, misfits, rootless workers, failures, solitaries; the general attitude his stories convey is a distaste for the conventions of a bourgeois society, an assertion of the superior quality of life lived true to natural instincts, and a powerful sympathy for nonconformists. His unsentimental realism is in sharp contrast to earlier writers' idealizations.

Many of his stories are first-person narratives; others give the impression of being so. His quest for what is basic in human behavior is allied to his search for what is basic in language. Using as a foundation the flat, unemphatic speech of the average New Zealander, he has created a style in which the emotions and aspirations of largely inarticulate people find expression. In his later stories and his novels, Sargeson has broadened his range of characters and has developed his style in the direction of greater irony, flexibility, and subtlety, at times approaching a Jamesian manner. It is, however, his earlier style and view of life that have had an enduring effect on younger writers. He summed up in prose many of the attitudes of revolt and restlessness the poets of the 1930's also expressed, but his best stories have a relevance that extends beyond their decade. Among writers owing something to his example are A. P. Gaskell, David Ballantyne, and O. E. Middleton. Middleton's understated stories, notably those dealing with children, precisely catch the New Zealand mood and atmosphere.

In Sargeson's early period, Roderick Finlayson (b. 1904) brought a powerful sympathy to the portrayal of the Maori, contrasting what he deems to be the white man's decadence with the Maori's simplicity and dignity. Moving and telling, his stories nevertheless spring from a romantic anarchism that tends to glamourize the Maori.

Since the Second World War, New Zealand short stories have extended their subject matter and intensified their art. Such novelists as Janet Frame, Dan Davin, Noel Hilliard, and James Courage have written fine stories, and although it is now easier than before to have novels published, some writers have continued to give their prime attention to the briefer form. Helen Shaw's *The Orange Tree* (1957) reveals a precise, fastidious sensibility fascinated by old houses and people; Maurice Duggan's *Summer in the Gravel Pit* (1965) offers beautifully wrought stories, sometimes impressionistic, sometimes subtly realistic; Maurice Shadbolt, in three volumes, shows professionalism and a penetrating eye. Despite early traces of slickness, he possesses insights into New Zealand mores, especially as they affect young people, and a stylistic sense that suggest the possibility of a major talent.

New Zealand playwriting has been hampered by the absence of local professional theatre. A handful of New Zealand dramatists, among them Reginald Berkeley, Merton Hodge, Bruce Stewart, and Ted Kavanagh, have had some success in the English commercial theatre, radio, and television. But until recently most of the best work, after the era of Victorian melodramas and burlesques, was done in the one-act form, which amateurs could perform. In the 1930's J. A. S. Coppard (b. 1899), with his experimental, expressionist plays, broke away from polite one-act conventions, but had no immediate successors.

Douglas Stewart (b. 1913), long resident in Australia, embarked upon his own experiments in his excellent poetic radio dramas *The Golden Lover*, a Maori legend, and *The Fire on the Snow* (both 1944), about Scott's Antarctic expedition. His stage plays, notably *Ned Kelly* (1943), which is about the celebrated Australian bushranger, transform colloquial speech into moving dramatic poetry. Also poetic in form is Allen Curnow's *The Axe* (1949), dealing with the clash between Christian and pagan cultures. James Baxter and Frank Sargeson have likewise experimented in the theater. Baxter's *The Wide Open Cage* (1959) ambitiously essays a contemporary tragedy.

More orthodox practitioners include the prolific Claude Evans, Stella Jones, and Bruce Mason. Mason's *The Pohutukawa Tree* (1960), perhaps the best-known New Zealand play, tackles the theme of Maori-*pakeha* relations in dialogue that is true to character.

Generous radio opportunities have brought to light several very competent writers well aware of what is going on in new drama overseas. But in the absence of local television drama and sustained professional theater, New Zealand is a land of largely unpublished and unperformed plays.

Nineteenth-century explorers, missionaries, scientists, and traders all left their records, journals, and histories, but only a few, by their exuberance of personal vision, go beyond the specialist purpose. For instance, E. J. Wakefield's *Adventure in New Zealand* (1845) has a rare ebullience. Its prejudices and its enthusiasm for the new land give it more gusto than the early novels possess. The Maori Wars, too, inspired some interesting narratives, such as Sir John Gorst's *The Maori King* (1864), with its fine portraits of the main actors in the drama.

Rather more skillful writers chronicled the pastoral period. Samuel Butler (1835–1902), who spent five profitable years as a Canterbury sheep farmer, sums up in an easy relaxed style much of the contemporary temper of the country in *A First Year in the Canterbury Settlement* (1863). Lady Barker, who also lived on a Canterbury sheep farm in the 1860's, recorded early New Zealand manners from the point of view of a genteel upper-class Englishwoman, but with unpatronizing understanding, in three delightful books. F. E. Maning's *Old New Zealand* (1863), the most animated and original pioneering record of the century, welding together burlesque, yarning, mock philosophizing, and horrific anecdotes in half-ironical, half-serious style, gives a highly individual appraisal of Maori life and castigates modern "decadence."

History began to assume something of its modern approach in W. Pember Reeves's *The Long White Cloud* (1898), an essay-history of great charm and polish, colored by his radical bias, but cultured, scholarly, and intellectually lively. Since his time, historians, scientists, economists, anthropologists, and others have built up a formidable list of books of quality in their special fields. Few have equalled the literary accomplishment of W. H. Guthrie-Smith (1861–1940), in *Tutira* (1921). This naturalist, scholar, and sheep farmer expanded his original plan to write the story of his sheep station into a complete physical and human history of his own section of New Zealand from early geological times up to and through his own occupancy. The unique combination in him of poet, scientist, artist, and humanist makes his book an intensive study of a particular place, which also contains much that is characteristic of New Zealand as a land and as a community.

The doyen of New Zealand historians, J. C. Beaglehole (b. 1901), celebrated for his edition of Cook's journals; Keith Sinclair, historian of the Maori Wars; W. H. Oliver, Harold Miller, and James Rutherford are among the noted writers of our history, most of them academics. Peter Buck, Gilbert Archey, Andrew Sharp, Roger Duff, Raymond Firth, and Ernest Beaglehole have studied the Maori.

Biography came fairly late as a literary form, but the past fifty years have seen big developments here. Typical of recent trends are Major-General Howard Kippenberger's *Infantry Brigadier* (1949), the excellently written personal story of a brave soldier-scholar; Helen Wilson's *My First Eighty Years* (1951), an account of country life and community service sustained by a robust philosophy of life; E. H. McCormick's *The Expatriate* (1954), an invaluable study of New Zealand's most famous painter, Frances Hodgkins; and *King Dick* (1955) by R. M. Burdon, which skillfully assesses the Liberal prime minister Richard John Seddon. In *Black Beech and Honey-Dew* (1966) Ngaio Marsh (b. 1899), well known for her sophisticated detective stories, has written a reticent autobiography of great charm and delicate flavor.

We find, perhaps, the clearest signs that New Zealand has developed a characteristic literature of its own in the maturation of literary criticism during recent decades. Earlier criticism was thin and sporadic, even in the little magazines in which New Zealand has been so prolific. But in 1940, the country's centennial year, M. H. Holcroft (b. 1902) laid the foundations for contemporary criticism with his book *The Deepening Stream,* followed by two others, the three later published under the collective title of *Discovered Isles* (1951).

In this epoch-making trilogy, Holcroft set himself, as no earlier writer had done, to examine the special nature of critical problems in New Zealand. Anatomizing the national culture, he emphasized the themes of exile, loneliness, and frustration in our literature, and stressing the effect on writing of the bush and of the memory of the immigrants' long voyage from Britain, he found in them basic drives and conditioning factors. A Wordsworthian vision of literature and of the forces of nature operating on the poet is the source of both the strength and weakness of this seminal criticism.

Also important was E. H. McCormick's *Letters and Art in New Zealand* (1940), a work of lightly worn scholarship, the first historical survey, which examined the growth of local literature and painting in close relation to the growth of the community.

The foundations laid by Holcroft and McCormick were rapidly built upon in postwar years, notably by Allen Curnow in his lengthy prefaces to his two anthologies, which have some affinity with Holcroft's essays in their stress upon indigenous elements and the role of landscape in poetry. Among important later critical works are Joan Stevens' *The New Zealand Novel* (1961), M. H. Holcroft's *Islands of Innocence* (1964), a study of childhood themes in New Zealand fiction, and Kendrick Smithyman's *A Way of Saying* (1965), the first book to explore the body of New Zealand verse in search of regional characteristics and emergent neoromantic and academic traits.

Of special importance, too, was the presence of *Landfall*, the literary quarterly established in 1947 by Charles Brasch and edited by him for twenty years. By setting high standards, *Landfall* has done an incalculable amount for critical writing. If it has been sometimes dull, self-consciously superior, and overly aesthetic, it has printed much good prose and poetry and some most acute analyses of our writing and mores. The *New Zealand Poetry Yearbook*, founded in 1952 by Louis Johnson and appearing irregularly since, is less even in the criticism it prints. In general, it shows a hostility to the "myth" of New Zealand literature attributed to Curnow and Holcroft of "a lonely desert island, discovered by navigators and developed by baffled explorers," and emphasizes the need for New Zealand poetry to deal with urban realities and with values common to all modern societies. So far only a handful of full-length studies of individual writers have appeared, among them W. A. Sewell's brilliant monograph *Katherine Mansfield* (1936) and Anthony Alpers' definitive biography of the same writer (1954), Airini Woodhouse's study of Guthrie-Smith (1959), and Phillip Wilson's book on W. A. Satchell, *The Maorilander* (1961).

In the later 1960's, however, New Zealand literary criticism seems to have reached a turning point. Most earlier criticism, that of McCormick, Holcroft, and Curnow, for instance, has had a sociological or historical bias and has been interested in isolating specifically indigenous characteristics. Critics have valued writing for the degree to which it reveals New Zealanders to themselves, depicts their landscapes, expresses their special concerns and dilemmas, helps them in their search for identity, interprets aspects of their life, and chimes in with the working-class or lower-middle-class view of society. A younger generation of critics is beginning to move against these critical preoccupations, to judge New Zealand writing in more purely literary terms, to try to evaluate the kind of human experience it presents, to set it squarely beside world literature and see how it measures up. Inevitably this has meant challenging some basic earlier assumptions: the value and scope of R. A. K. Mason's achievement, the stature of Sargeson, the staying power of Fairburn's verse, the originality and durability of John A. Lee and "Robin Hyde," the "sundering seas" myth as well as the reaction in the 1950's against it—the things, in fact, taken for granted by critics belonging to the same generation as the writers they assessed, sometimes themselves being, under different hats, the writers. The criticism of the previous quarter of a century represented a necessary and salutary phase, and was by no means always confined to the detection of "New Zealandism." But the urge towards a more precisely literary criticism, excluding traditional extra-literary considerations, seems to indicate a new maturity of outlook. At present, little of this work appears in book form, but is to be found in such periodicals as *Comment, Landfall, Mate,* and *New Zealand Listener,* and comes from such writers as C. K. Stead, Terry Sturm, K. O. Arvidson, and P. J. Downey.

When New Zealand literature is viewed in the context of world literature, or even of literature in English, it shows as unmistakably minor. There are some writers who fit easily into the company of the good or moderately good anywhere: except for, perhaps, Katherine Mansfield in her limited sphere, there are no great New Zealand writers, none whose absence would leave a conspicuous gap in literary history. But then the great writer is a rarity. And New Zealand writers have unquestionably enriched the experience of their compatriots.

Our reviewers and critics still refer with pride to the fact that

44

some of our poets have been published by Oxford University Press ("received the accolade of the O.U.P." is the customary phrase), that several novelists have sold well in Britain, that others have had the "distinction" of rave reviews in *Time*, that one or two New Zealand plays have been performed on British television. Irrespective of the merits of the works concerned, the use of such circumstances as a criterion of literary achievement, even sometimes by the writers themselves, indicates an odd dependency.

New Zealand has, in fact, not developed a native literary tradition of its own, comparable with, say, the Australian bush ballads; it has tended to prefer factual writing to imaginative writing; it has produced no poet as considerable as Roy Campbell nor any novelist as remarkable as Patrick White. But in a New Zealand context, writers, for all their complaints about nonacceptance, have created a special place for themselves. This place may be more significant from the sociological than from the literary point of view, in that in our imaginative writing we find the only consistent criticism of our values, often the only articulation of otherwise half-sensed, submerged attitudes towards our environment, physical and social, and the most coherent expression of the spirit of unrest, uncertainty, and insecurity beneath our welfare-state smugness, fake sophistication, and placidity. But the result is that our better novels and poems have a special immediacy for the New Zealand reader.

Sometimes one feels that our writers are hampered by the uniformly unexciting, gray mediocrity of their social environment, in which they are tempted too easily to seek for or to fabricate "causes," and that they often spill their considerable technical skill and sensitivity on unrewarding characters and themes because around them there is no real challenge, no conflict such as America, for instance, provides. Yet even here, the writer can serve a purpose by showing the expense of spirit in a waste of mediocrity. The dilemma of the artist or the unusual personality in a provincial society is not a specifically New Zealand theme, of course, but translated into local terms it can vibrate for us as the same theme in imported works seldom does, and thus plays its part in helping to shape a different kind of national sensibility. Criticism of Philistines, money-grabbing businessmen, petty snobs, muddied oafs is again not peculiarly a New

Zealand occupation; but this may have special significance for us if it is meaningfully related by the writer to our particular awareness of being a social animal. The fact that criticism of this kind widens the gap that already exists in this country between literature and everyday life, however, is one of the matters the younger critics are rightly concerned about.

It comes down to weighing the historical, the topical, the social experience we all share as New Zealanders against the more purely aesthetic experience, the one in which form and vision are fused in a special thing felt and seen that may have its base in the topical but extends beyond it. It becomes a matter, too, of deciding to what extent the moods and attitudes that may seem to be the product of our history and environment are part of the *Angst* which infects so much of modern Western literature. To use as a criterion of worth what is true of this land in this land's terms is to abandon literary values altogether, and to be forced to rank John A. Lee's novels above those of Janet Frame; to concern oneself only with those things that exclude the sociological is possibly to substitute the preferences of a debilitated aestheticism or a precious academicism for the moral and human considerations that literary evaluations ignore at their peril. In assessing contemporary works—and virtually all New Zealand literature worth talking about is recent—it is always difficult to decide, in those which clearly have qualities above the ordinary, how far one's attitude toward them is influenced by factors which are really irrelevant to literature. There is obviously a value in books and poems that interpret New Zealanders to themselves and play some part in modifying the national consciousness. But ultimately the quality and achievements of New Zealand literature must be determined, not by the presence or absence of recognizable, indigenous characteristics, but by the talent and vision of its writers.

With a modest accomplishment behind us and a contemporary scene full of activity, diversity, and potential, an appropriate conclusion to an interim report might be an attempt to sum up what seems to be distinctive in New Zealand writing as a whole. New Zealand literature smacks strongly of secular humanism, one aspect of which shows as a romantic vision of men, less as individuals in the fullest sense than as they conform to or depart from certain virtues deemed special to the proletariat or a "noble savage" ideal. It has a generous quantity of compassion, but it is frequently sentimental, especially about the underdogs of both races. It has, in its powerfully egalitarian bias, a distaste for privilege (except, seemingly, as it applies to the artist); it is anti-urban and believes that "getting away from it all" purifies the soul. (Male writers distrust women, seeing them as bedmates, mothers, or snares; female writers tend to favor the "male as spoilt child" attitude.) It is profoundly ambiguous in its attitude towards Britain and British middle-class traditions and values; both Britain and America, in fact, seem equally repellent and attractive to New Zealand writers. It is stubbornly narcissistic; even when it turns away from the usual literary image of New Zealand, it continues to search in new waters for its own face. It wavers between a chauvinistic acceptance of social, literary, and historical myths and a despairing quest for fresh ones. It is convinced that true realism is of the social kind; it is timid in the face of tragedy, which it tends to process into melodrama, but it knows, and will at times seek for, tragedy's purgative power. It is brash, overrefined, clumsy, mannered, urban, peasant, arrogant, humble, confident, bewildered, neurotic, extroverted. In a modern welfare state, with no grave social or political problems, it is all too frequently melancholy, hagridden, sad, testy, unsure of itself. But it has had, from the 1930's, a slight but persistent strain of self-mockery, now deepening into a wit not without urbanity; it is steadily maturing in craftsmanship and in the sophistication of its art. It is also beginning to doff the mantle of the prophet, the sage, the visionary, and to be more conscious that, in poetry at least, what is said is how it is said; human relationships as such are slowly occupying more and more writers of talent. Perhaps it is a measure of what is happening in our literature that an increasing number of New Zealand writers wish to be accepted simply as poets, novelists, and dramatists without the national modifier.

BIBLIOGRAPHY

Baxter, James K. *Aspects of Poetry in New Zealand*. Christchurch, 1967.
Holcroft, M. H. *Discovered Isles*. Christchurch, 1950.
——. *Islands of Innocence*. Wellington, 1964.

McCormick, E. H. *New Zealand Literature: A Survey*. London, 1959.
Reid, J. C. *Creative Writing in New Zealand: A Brief Critical History*. Auckland, 1946.
Smithyman, Kendrick. *A Way of Saying*. Auckland, 1965.
Stevens, Joan. *The New Zealand Novel, 1860–1960*. Wellington, 1961.

Anthologies

Chapman, Robert, and Jonathan Bennett, eds. *Anthology of New Zealand Verse*. London, 1956.
Curnow, Allen, ed. *The Penguin Book of New Zealand Verse*. Harmondsworth, 1960.
Doyle, Charles, ed. *Recent Poetry in New Zealand*. Auckland, 1965.
Reid, J. C., ed. *A Book of New Zealand*. London, 1964.
Stead, C. K., ed. *New Zealand Short Stories*. Oxford, 1966.
Thomson, John, ed. *Five New Zealand Plays*. Auckland, 1962.

SOCIAL INSTITUTIONS

D. A. HANSEN

ALMOST from birth, New Zealand has been something special among nations. In many ways consciously fashioned after England, similar in cultural heritage to Australia, Canada, and the United States, New Zealand has met and solved its problems—problems similar to those which confront any emerging nation—in ways unique and often inspiring. In little more than one hundred years it has developed a way of living and an arrangement of economy, politics, and government which brings into unusual compatibility varied individual and collective interests. The New Zealand solution is by no means perfect, but it is unusually successful; it is not complete, but it is pervasive; it is not altogether stable or consistent —there are still inequities in income, life chances, and social power —but neither is it stagnant.

As in most modern nations, at the heart of New Zealand society is the government, legislating, adjudicating, and administering. Affairs of state have grown exceptionally diverse in New Zealand, and

49

today few other democracies present such extensive social welfare and economic socialism. The popular influence and control of the national centralized government are to be found everywhere in New Zealand, and the influence continues to grow.

New Zealand is not unusual in its centralization of state control, however, for successful moves toward democratic socialism have been made in many countries. What makes the New Zealand case rather special is the unusually easy relationship of the government to those it governs, serves, and directs, and on whose compliance or subservience it depends. How is it that such a harmonious and productive relationship has developed in New Zealand, when in other countries the continuing growth of centralized bureaucracy is often viewed uneasily and interpreted as government interference, as a threat to individual freedom and dignity? That is the concern of this essay, which focuses not on the political and economic character of New Zealand government, but rather on the relationship of that government to the individual citizen, on the values supporting that relationship, and on some special problems and potentials it involves.

In New Zealand the transition to centralized government, collective economy, and social welfare continues to be made smoothly and with apparent popularity. The transition, however, is not something of recent origin; rather, it is seen almost from the beginning in colonial New Zealand. When the first colony of New Zealand Company settlers reached Port Nicholson in 1840, they found a country in which the ways of life they had learned in their homelands were inadequate, in which the forms of agriculture and commerce, of education and government appropriate to the complex and well-established societies of the British Isles were only partially applicable. However abundant the land promised to be, however pleasant the climate, the settlers had to solve problems they had never faced before: problems of staying alive, of developing agriculture and commerce, and of building an economy; problems of socialization, of rearing their children in a new land where life was unsettled; problems of social control, of winning and maintaining order and consensus in a situation that offered few guidelines.

50

Such problems were not greatly different in type from those faced in many other nations, yet it is a fair guess that another people—say, if Japanese or Serbs had colonized New Zealand—would have reacted to them in quite different ways. Why did early New Zealanders act as they did, and how were these actions important to contemporary New Zealand?

Problems which face the people of a nation may be solved, or evaded, in many ways. In great part, however, the response is determined by two things. One is the solutions that the people have accumulated in meeting past problems, large and small. These solutions may be considered ways of life or the social institutions of the country, which act rather like blueprints, offering individuals and groups guidelines or prescriptions for ways to act. In New Zealand these blueprints were brought primarily from the British Isles. But many of the tendencies to act in British ways, to follow British institutions, were soon discarded in favor of others more appropriate and effective in the colonial situation.

The other major determinant of responses to new problems is the basic values that are shared widely throughout the society or community. It is difficult to exaggerate the influence of such values. A nation whose peoples are fiercely equalitarian and freedom-loving, who honor individual dignity, and whose cultural heroes are men of wisdom, compassion, and understanding will respond to challenges quite differently from a nation that seeks national power and collective strength, and whose cultural heroes are the statesman and the military genius.

It would be most unfair to represent New Zealand as a whole cloth, evenly woven, in which individuals all act alike, all subscribe to the same values, all accept and live in a single pattern of life; hundreds of patterns of life exist in New Zealand. But it is instructive and revealing to identify those few ways of life and solutions to collective problems that are predominant in the great part of the population. In these terms, we can think of New Zealand society as individual men, women, and children, each living his own personal life and holding his own personal values and commitments, yet facing problems in common with others, bound together by generally shared solutions and basic values.

51

PATTERN OF NEW ZEALAND CULTURE

To gain even a preliminary insight into the contemporary relationship of the New Zealander to his government, it is essential to consider three interacting components; the problems that have beset New Zealand through its history, the predispositions (ways of life, blueprints, or social institutions) with which New Zealanders have met these problems, and the basic values that support these predispositions. For, as initial problems were met, new dispositions formed for meeting future problems, and slowly, the unique New Zealand character developed, residing not only in written laws and recorded words, but also (and more importantly) in the minds and emotions of the men who made up the emerging nation, influencing their decisions in periods of stress, helping to determine their actions and the developing character of the nation they were building. Existing scholarship does not allow complete and final description of these developments in New Zealand. Over the years, however, documents have been filed and studies developed which afford at least preliminary insights.

In attempting to understand the easy and comfortable relationship of the individual New Zealander to his government, it is important to remember that New Zealand was born during the early maturity of the Industrial Revolution, when major technological, social, and political innovations were an expected part of life in many nations of the world. From the very first years of colonial life, the idea of controlled political management was evident, for the early planners had heeded well the unsystematic and haphazard colonization of other countries, and had benefited from these lessons. Moving to a new and untamed land, it was apparent to the settlers that they could not take the institutions from industrialized and complex societies and transplant them intact in the wilderness. But even their contemporary colonial and frontier societies offered only partial lessons for these settlers, who, for one thing, lived in isolation not only from other parts of the world, but also from other parts of their mountain-ribbed and slender country.

Geography alone could have thwarted the early attempts to establish, in the Act of 1852, a government system that was in part modeled after American federalism, providing not only for a central government but for provincial authorities as well. Mountains

52

and miles did their part to make this system inefficient and were more than aided by men not able or willing to cope responsibly with the continuing problems they faced. In a little time interprovincial struggles over trade and disease control sapped the strength of the local bodies. Faced with special problems and plagued with irresponsibility or foolishness, some authorities began to borrow money indiscriminately, leading to the loss by all provinces of their credit rating and to a ban on provincial borrowing from foreign interests. In the face of the continuing costs of their provincial systems, local authorities were willing and even eager to look to the central government for help.

The central government proved effective in dealing with Maori uprisings, and inevitably its activities expanded to other services: laying railways, establishing communications, building bridges and roads. These were essential to the growth of both province and nation, but required far more coordination and funds than could be offered by the bickering and undernourished provinces. When the provincial system finally and completely collapsed in 1874, few mourned its passing, and few resisted the rapid expansion of centralized activity under Prime Minister Vogel in the decade following 1869, even when the central government took responsibility for education in the 1877 National Education Act. The first wave of social experimentation ran its course with only token opposition and only muffled complaint.

The next great wave, which led observers in distant nations to herald the experiments and even to predict the birth of a new Utopia, came as the new century neared. By the time the Liberals left office in 1912, the influence of the central government was to be felt in almost every phase of life, and the contemporary relationship of individual to state in New Zealand had been solidly established. Since that time little has happened to contest the essential relationship; only in occasional periods of strife and discomfort have individual New Zealanders resisted or deeply resented their government.

Part of the reason for this tranquil relationship, then, may be that central control was established early and generally accepted as the only reasonable course at that time. Faced with the necessities of meeting the problems of a new nation, possessing only limited resources, hoping to effectively compete with overseas producers who were mechanized, tantalized with the offerings of technological innovations that could meet their demanding problems, lacking the funds and manpower to do the job, colonists readily looked to the central government. They could do little else. Their problems demanded solutions, and the Industrial Revolution had developed means—highly expensive means—for achieving those solutions, means which only the central government was able to employ.

But that is only part of the story. It alone does not explain why the cries against government services were so muted. It is often the case that an individual, a community, a province, or a nation is forced by circumstances to accept the aid of a stronger organization. But it is also often the case that the aid is resented, that further aid is resisted, that fears of *de facto* fetters develop. In New Zealand these themes can be seen, but only barely. Why were they not more pronounced?

Once again the time and place of the birth of New Zealand offer partial answer, for New Zealanders did not have to fight against unyielding authority; they likewise suffered few periods of frustration and agitation for overdue governmental revisions. In relationships with England, other colonies had blazed the way, allowing New Zealand an easy and safe journey to independence. Indeed, in 1852, when the New Zealand population still numbered only 27,000, the British Crown granted the small colony representation, and three years later, with little concerted effort by the colonists, the Crown agreed that its ministers should be responsible to the representatives New Zealanders themselves had elected. Virtually before they could agitate for revision, could feel and resent an oppressive weight of Crown government, the colonials were offered a revision.

Similarly, when a crucial situation could have developed toward the end of the century, the New Zealand government moved before concerted agitation had a chance to develop. In emerging nations there comes a time when the major concerns of government shift from distribution of land to distribution of wealth and produce. In this transition a populist movement is likely to develop;

the unlanded farmers can no longer expect to win their own land, for little is left to be won, and the underprivileged urban workers become articulate in their demands for greater shares of the wealth. The responses of government to these changing forces are crucial in the development of a nation and can in great part set the stamp not only of government activity, but of the essential relationship of man to man for generations to come. At this point in its history, the New Zealand government responded admirably.

Great credit for the social innovations in the Liberal administration, beginning in 1891, must certainly go to a few sensitive and alert leaders. The role of these individuals can be overemphasized, however, for the terms of innovation had been set long before the Liberals began their twenty-one-year term. Earlier unmistakable and continuing tendencies of New Zealanders toward social services were crucial to the successes of Richard Seddon and his colleagues. Also crucial was the fact that middle-class leadership in the New Zealand legislature began to move toward enfranchisement almost before the seeds of agitation had begun to develop among urban laborers and unlanded farmers. Experiences of other countries indicate that if the legislature had not moved as it did, conflict and strife would have resulted sooner or later, creating wounds and memories that might even today disturb the relationships of individual to government and of individual to individual. In part, the success of New Zealand in making the critical transition not only successfully, but almost brilliantly, can be explained by various circumstances of population and historical time.

For one thing, the ruling elite had never been able to entrench firmly during New Zealand's short history prior to the Liberal cabinet. For New Zealand was also born in a time of enfranchisement, of peaceful social revolution, in which elite rule was being challenged from country to country in the Western world. As New Zealand was being settled, the unenfranchised in other countries were pushing for reform. Even Britain, in the Act of 1867, established precedent for the case of the unenfranchised. In 1879 a New Zealand act was introduced to permit any man of twenty-one years of age or over to vote if he had dwelt in the colony for one year and in his electoral precinct for six months. Although a property qualification was retained, and although a man of property could vote more than once (in each district in which he owned property), this single Act greatly broadened the base of enfranchisement.

More was to come, and come quickly. In 1889, under the leadership of Gray, the Liberal party won a further victory, establishing the principle of "one man, one vote." With these two enactments the stage was set for the Liberal victory in 1890. Liberal representatives were elected by narrow majorities in districts where, under the old system, they would have been defeated. After this victory, New Zealand moved rapidly toward full enfranchisement of virtually all adult male citizens, and soon of females.

Thus, in New Zealand legitimacy of the government has never been a real issue. Only small minorities and a few dissidents have questioned that the established New Zealand government had a right to govern them; themes of revolt and overthrow of the Crown authority or of the elected government are noticeably rare in the nation's history, even during the comparatively peaceful riots in times of depression. This does not mean that there has been complete consensus on the matters of what the government has done and what the government should do. But in New Zealand conflict over social and political issues has rarely reached the point of violent strife. Acrimonious debate and public cries of despair are on record, but for the most part dispute in the great matters of state and economy have been settled before the conflict could reach major proportions, and in such ways that few individuals and groups of any power have been left discontent to the point of either despair or rebellion.

But this explanation, too, is only partial. For one thing, it has ignored the evidence that many early New Zealanders held beliefs opposed to the spread of centralized government; early immigrants had brought from their native British Isles a political ideology which supported laissez-faire economics and encouraged distrust of government intervention in private matters. It has been suggested above that in New Zealand such ideologies quickly gave way in the face of exigencies that could be successfully met only by centralized government. This interpretation, however, leaves unanswered a major question: Why was there not more objection, more open political conflict, more cries of despair and discomfort, more serious effort to defend laissez-faire doctrines? It could be argued that the doctrines failed in New Zealand because they were inappropriate to the problems of the colony, which from a position of geographic isolation was attempting to break into well-established and competitive world markets; a controlled economy in New Zealand was an historic necessity. However appealing, such an argument does not account for the ease with which the doctrines were compromised and abandoned.

This type of argument also provides at best but a partial answer to a related question: Why did early New Zealand leaders act as they did? Why the willingness of the already landed, of the well-off, to extend social welfare and to allow, even encourage, enfranchisement? To argue "historical inevitability" is inadequate (however probable it may be that the populist movement would have eventually overcome any resistance by an entrenched, ruling elite), for the middle-class leadership almost willingly moved toward reform, even before demands had grown unavoidable. A more complete explanation might be developed from the suggestion that laissez faire and the doctrine of government by an elite was all but contradictory to the basic values of early settlers. It could be argued that uncommon values played a role from the beginning in New Zealand, that early settlers did not share the values which were dominant in their countries of origin, but held special ideals and ideas about the nature of man and his relation to his fellow man, of equality, freedom, and individual dignity—ideas and ideals which had been perhaps no more than unnurtured seeds in distant homelands, but which quickly sprouted and pushed roots deeply into the soil of a new country.

It is often remarked that the development of New Zealand democracy derived heavily from the particularly intense feeling of settlers for equality and liberty. The remark appears to be valid, but can be easily misinterpreted, for in New Zealand these values have taken on a somewhat unusual character. As in Australia and the United States, an anti-elitism apparently was carried by settlers to New Zealand in reaction to the class-dominated structures of their native England. As in these other colonies, many early New Zealanders resisted efforts of government officials and other settlers to establish any sort of social distinctions and privileges based on position and likely to pass on by birth. Even today in each of these countries equality and liberty are the most ubiquitous of values. In each of these countries, however, the concepts have developed special meaning.

In fundamental ways, individual freedom and equality are uneasy companions. For centuries, democracies have shown that the two can exist together; yet they exist in some tension, and to the present time no nation has succeeded in bringing to full flower both qualities. In the United States, the fierce dedication to individual liberty (encouraged, some say, by a deeply rooted Protestant ethic, and stimulated by a seemingly limitless frontier and by historical exigencies unknown in New Zealand) contributed to a lesser emphasis on equality. Liberty—freedom from restraint and the imposition of power—has been the dominant value in the United States from earliest colonial days. "It is a Statue of Liberty which greets the visitors sailing toward Manhattan Island," Leslie Lipson wrote in *The Politics of Equality: New Zealand's Adventures in Democracy* (1948). "In New Zealand, if any sculptural allegory were to be placed at the approaches of Auckland or Wellington harbor, it would assuredly be a Statue of Equality. For equalitarianism is there regarded as the core of the democratic doctrine."

It appears fair to say that in comparison with England and the United States, and even Australia, New Zealand has most actively and consistently emphasized equalitarianism. Little more than thirty years after the first colony settled in New Zealand, even conservative politicians were pushing for and encouraging measures to assure equality; already, by the 1870's, free and compulsory education and state-financed universities had been established. Efforts were made to create opportunities especially for the common man, most significantly in the Industrial Conciliation and Arbitration Act of 1894, which founded one of the most dramatic contributions New Zealand has made to conceptions of humanitarian democracy: a compulsory system of state arbitration aimed at preventing class conflict by insuring the workers an adequate share of the national

58

wealth even as it assured adequate incentive to the employer. Since the early days of the Second World War, state programs of taxation and social security have sought to extend this equalization by redistributing the income.[1] Although these dramatic measures have not been completely successful, even the most severe critic must confess that in New Zealand neither extremes of wealth nor wretchedness are commonly seen.

The special quality of New Zealand equalitarianism, however, is suggested by the often decried tendency of the New Zealander to distrust success, to tear down the striver or anyone who has achieved too much. The stress on equalitarianism is seen in the distrust of conferring honor on anyone in a position of influence; all men must be reduced to a common level. This lack of desire to show respect to persons of authority has earned New Zealanders in their military campaigns the reputation of being in constant disorder and disrespectful to ranking officers.

The special flavor of New Zealand equalitarianism and liberty is also indicated in the tendency of the individual to relate to his fellow men in ways somewhat different from those of individuals in other countries. Even compared to Britain and the United States, in New Zealand individuals tend to evaluate each other as "whole" persons rather than as players of specialized roles, and tend to emphasize an individual's personal qualities rather than the reflected glory of the money or power he possesses. Such tendencies may reflect basic differences in pervasive value orientations; within the context of such relations, equalitarianism is broadened from an ideal of *equal opportunity* to an ideal of *equality in all aspects of life.* Not only should one person not inherit greater life chances than another; none should be allowed to accumulate a great deal more than another through his own efforts or luck. Exceptional performances or capacities are deprecated by both individuals in a

[1] Whether this end has been achieved is difficult to establish, although consensus is that it has. Westrate, however, unable to prove or disprove the idea, emphasized that the government's efforts more equally to distribute income may be behind certain undesirable features of the New Zealand economy, such as the binding balance-of-payments deficit, which results in import restriction and exchange control (C. Westrate, *Portrait of a Mixed Economy: New Zealand* [Wellington, 1959], pp. 202–213).

59

relationship. Added to this, New Zealanders evidence unusual tendencies, compared to other Anglo-American peoples, to forgo individual pleasures for the benefit of the group. This is not to say that individual New Zealanders are selfless, but only that compared to people of other English-speaking countries they are highly solicitous of friends and others, and of the needs of and desires of their fellow New Zealanders, as is emphasized in the comaraderie of "cobbers" and the easy, outgoing friendliness of even males to one another.[2] Such relationships are far more apparent in New Zealand than in England; they go far to characterize equalitarianism in New Zealand, and especially the attitude toward individual achievement and success.

This attitude shows in the educational system, where a high standard of mediocrity seems to be the goal for all children. Excellence in academics is suspect, especially below the university level, where, for example, training programs to identify especially talented children and teach them separately have met with strong resistance and criticism. The fault is not with the educators alone, as Melvin suggests:

Our school system, for instance, has little power to inculcate a greater respect for standards of performance, for learning, taste, intelligence, and excellence than the community as a whole really feel. We but delude ourselves if we expect the educational system to maintain our ideals of achievement that the community as a whole has abandoned or never held. The need for people of superior imagination, training and drive

---

[2] Those acquainted with the work of Talcott Parsons will recognize his pattern variables in these statements. Parsons also suggests that relationships be characterized on the degree of emotional expression generally allowed (Talcott Parsons, *The Social System* [Glencoe, Illinois, 1951], pp. 58–67). Using these variables S. M. Lipset compared Australia, England, Canada, and the United States on types of relations of individuals to one another and to the collectivity. Lipset suggests that these orientations reflect values which have influenced the formation of the unique form of democracy in each nation. He also suggested that similarities in basic values and historical experience have made Australia and the United States more like one another than like either Canada or England: the similarities override the influence of Australia's continuing contact with England, and Canada's relatively intimate contact with the United States (S. M. Lipset, *The First New Nation* [New York, 1963]).

is much greater than we can supply, but New Zealand too often gives the impression that we have been so persuaded that all God's chillun must have shoes, that we think they've all got the same-size feet.[3]

As the concept of equality has developed from an idea of equal opportunity to the idea that men should be equal in all phases of life at all ages, in rewards as well as opportunities, so the concept of individual freedom has taken on a special character. New Zealanders have from the beginning had to pay little for their liberty, rarely have had to suffer undesired exercise of power and control. The result has been that there is less concern in New Zealand with the freedom *to do*, which has so heavily dominated the development of American political systems and is in many ways antithetical to the idea of equality. In New Zealand the concept of freedom, however jealously guarded, is more limited. It implies a freedom *from:* freedom from want, freedom from hunger, freedom from external danger, freedom from manipulation. In the very pursuit and success of equality lies a lessened demand for freedom of individual opportunity, for to reduce inequality through legislation and civil service necessitates forbidding as many actions as are required and permitted. In Lipson's words, "Socialism becomes harmonized with democracy by a system of rationing liberties and by imposing upon the State the duty of adjusting the ration." New Zealanders have, it seems, tended to equalize liberties.

It has already been suggested that this development holds some danger for the vitality and future economic and political welfare of New Zealand; for, compared with other Western countries, it is a nation in which success is little honored and individual achievement is not highly stimulated. This means, for one thing, that it is not only possible, but probable, that New Zealand will continue to lose many of its talented and productive individuals whose activities, whether selfish or selfless, are so important to the growth of contemporary economies. The emphasis on national programs to assure

[3] K. Melvin, *New Zealand: The Small Utopia* (Auckland, 1962), p. 50. It should be noted that similar attitudes have been popular at times in the other Anglo-American countries, including the more liberty-oriented United States.

equality and security of human dignity, then, are admirable and desirable in many ways, but they do pose problems.

If any single question about the easy relation of individual and government is critical in New Zealand today, however, it is this: Have enough controls been put on the centralized power to assure the continuing liberty of the individual New Zealander? It cannot be denied that New Zealand today enjoys both abundance of equality and security of dignity, but the dangers of the condition cannot be ignored. They are tied to the problems of exercising political differences in a democracy.

The constant threat to peoples governed by a powerful, centralized authority is that they will lose their voice in the affairs of state. As the activities of the government grow, its power grows, and through the expanding intricacies of bureaucracy, it is less and less accessible to the individual citizens and organizations. The growth of centralized power in any complex nation today is not merely a matter of legislation emanating from one particular location. It is also a matter of the growth of administrative bureaucracy, for every piece of legislation is followed by some provision for its administration, usually delegated to the existing civil service.

In a polity such as New Zealand, the danger is not that selfish despots will seize control; rather it is that in pursuit of national welfare the possibilities of effective expression of political differences may be reduced. For prime example, a vital economy requires efficiency and predictability in both government and commerce; yet free and open political disagreement results in at least temporary inefficiency and some uncertainty about future policy. Quite simply, the more persons involved in political decisions, the less the political efficiency.

The problem is essentially one of assuring the consensus necessary to the operation of a rational and effective bureaucracy, and at the same time allowing for disagreement, cleavage, and conflict between persons and groups of various interests. Without the former, there can be no effective operation of modern government or economy; without the latter, there is no democracy and but little hope for individual freedom.

62

SOCIAL INSTITUTIONS

The traditional solution to this problem is not only to centralize decision-making, but also to assure that all groups and factions have a direct or indirect part in decisions and administration. The latter is achieved by giving voice to the diverse clubs, organizations, and institutes on a local level, not only through political lobbying, but through opportunity to present their opinions and attitudes on limited and specific subjects, or on the sweeping tendencies of government. Thus, even organizations so far removed from political activity as a Society for the Advancement of Compost, or the Plunkett Society, might be politically important: though their activities are non-political, when political questions related to their specialities arise, their ideas, their desires, and their programs theoretically are taken into consideration by the politician, the legislator, and, hence, the civil servant.

Among the most politically relevant of such organizations, of course, are the political parties. Because of its system of representation, strong tendencies are built into New Zealand to develop and maintain a two-party system, in which splinter parties have limited opportunity to grow to real power: if a third party is to gain major power, one of the two must fail. Continuing cleavage or controlled conflict between the two major political parties, then, is a major vehicle for maintaining individual liberty in a democracy such as New Zealand's.

Students of politics in other countries have long analyzed differences in characteristics of the supporters of various parties. The assumption is that, if labor, for example, votes for one party and management for another, voice is being given to differences in vested attitudes. Through the history of New Zealand politics the split between rural and urban voters has been noticeable, though it is far from clear that the split is based simply on the rural policies of the parties.[4] Today, it appears that religious differences play a minor role in politics, but economic differences are related most dramatically to party vote. It is rather ironic that in New Zealand, where the claim is so often heard that no real social classes exist, it

[4] See R. Chapman, W. Jackson, and A. Mitchell, *New Zealand Politics in Action* (London, 1962).

appears that laboring and more privileged individuals may vote along class lines more consistently than in the United States, Australia, and even Britain.[5]

The effects of contemporary tendencies in New Zealand government on this political cleavage, on the exercise of legitimate disagreement, are crucial. The spread of bureaucracy often tends to homogenize political attitudes; when governmental bureaucracy employs nearly one-fourth of all workers, as in New Zealand, the homogenization can become politically important. Once again, the problem is not nearly so crucial in New Zealand as it could be, for the civil service, though under ministerial control, has been fairly independent of the prevailing political power. Nonetheless, bureaucracy implies conservatism and a tendency to resist change of existing authority; similarly, it implies strong pressures on existing authority to maintain conservative programs. The effect of this is notable, for it suggests the unintended creation of power, the influence of political decision by the existing bureaucracy.

The possible influence of such a situation is evidenced in the similar tendency of political parties toward conservatism. Each party must orient its policies and programs toward the existing bureaucracy; each is heavily influenced by the power of this theoretically apolitical body. Other organizations dedicated to political aims (even those that, like the Compost Society, are interested in only a limited spread of government activity) are similarly conditioned by the existing bureaucracy as well as by the ruling legislative powers. In short, the voice of the people, the opportunity to express popular and unpopular ideas and demands through local groups and political parties, is strongly influenced not only by the acitivities of elected representatives, but also by the civil ser-

[5] It must be cautioned that evidence on New Zealand political cleavage is extremely limited. Mitchell's study of Dunedin Central in 1960 indicates the same tendency as was suggested by Milne's study of Wellington Central in 1957. In the context of Alford's discussion of political cleavage in England, the United States, Canada, and Australia, these studies suggest that occupational level in New Zealand is closely related to political vote (A. Mitchell, "Dunedin Central," *Political Science*, XIV [1962]; R. S. Milne, "Voting in Wellington Central, 1957," *Political Science*, X, [1958]; R. R. Alford, *Party and Society* [Chicago, 1963]).

vice. The result, barring crisis, is further homogenization of ideas and programs, a type of conservatism that leads to a stability envied by nations torn by internal strife, but which is dangerous in a rapidly changing world that demands imaginative flexibility of a nation.

The situation deserves close attention from students of government, politics, and society in New Zealand. Even today the cleavage between parties may be deceptive, for whatever the class and occupational difference between voters for the various parties, the policies and programs of these parties are not highly different from one another. Does this mean that the individual special interest of the voters and supporters of one party, or both, are not to be satisfied in party programs? Are the parties and the government unresponsive to the needs and desires of their supporters? Or is it possible that the government programs and policies are, at least roughly, adequate to the needs and desires of all potentially potent New Zealand voters, regardless of their income and social position? Today even those complaints which are voiced are rather mild and easily released through a splinter party such as Social Credit. Does this reflect a lack of interest or sensitivity of New Zealanders to their political and social needs?

The observable political homogenization in New Zealand may indeed be a critical problem, but it is also possible that it represents an emerging solution to an old dilemma: the apparent incompatibility between political consensus based on the satisfaction of the diverse desires of the people, and the establishment of the efficiency and predictability necessary to a vital economy.

In New Zealand, as elsewhere, it is theoretically possible that the traditional defense of the individual through the contest of political factions, each dedicated to the ideology of a special class, religion, or geographical voting block, can be replaced by a more homogeneous, less strife-ridden cleavage—if each faction, each party, is committed to pervasive moral standards based on some conception of individual dignity.

In spite of the bickering, vaudeville-type performances offered by the Parliament, in spite of the often-decried mediocrity of many government officials and leaders, individual integrity and commitment to an unwritten yet pervasive social ethic appear dominant in New Zealand politics, legislation, and civil service, just as they appear dominant in most phases of New Zealand life. This dominance is belied by many actions and may be uneasily doubted by many New Zealanders who have never left their home shores. When compared with other nations, however, New Zealand appears not only homogeneous in political attitudes and social activities; beneath these appear to lie strong moral commitments, their existence masked by their pervasiveness and hidden by their own nature. For these moral commitments appear as orientations which are less demanding than restraining, involving less a commitment to *do*, to achieve for the nation, than a commitment to *not* violate accepted standards and practices, to not impose unduly on individual privacy and dignity. This orientation often makes officials, in meeting problems, appear pragmatic, and even opportunistic. If it is opportunism, however, it may well be strictly controlled by pervasive moral commitments—accepted as a part of the general scheme of life, almost unrecognized—quietly, powerfully urging New Zealanders, whether political leaders or private citizens, to act in ways that support the structures of their democracy.[6]

The emotional depths of New Zealand democracy, the nature of the values of the individual and the social integrity so evident in New Zealand, are difficult to fathom. A few preliminary efforts have been made here, but they are clearly inadequate. It is apparent

[6] Wisdom and commitment may be seen in the efforts of the government to assure the freedom from political influence via mass communications and education. In many respects, the Television Commission is a model for other highly developed democracies to follow, its political inadequacies far overshadowed by its strengths. Many argue that the Commission, as it stands, is entirely adequate to the maintenance of a free and responsible TV press. One major flaw, however, is generally overlooked: the Commission, though responsible from day to day only to itself, can be directed to alter its programming through written communication from the Minister of Broadcasting. It is obvious that in working democracies some control over irresponsibility must be maintained, if for no other reason than national security. But in a democracy such as New Zealand, far from free of structures which could one day threaten individual freedom, free and socially responsible media are crucial. The less vulnerable the media to either the threat of manipulation or the actual (however indirect) exercise of control by an individual prime minister or other politically oriented leader, the more resilient the system.

to anyone who is at all familiar with New Zealand, however, that some such values exist and are widely shared; it is apparent that they operate not only in legislation and political decision, but even in the relationship of individual New Zealanders one to another. These values, basic and pervasive, are in part the product of a unique history and, once formed, have turned about and helped to shape that history. Offering stability to check the license of the liberal, and ideals to counteract the conservative's resistance to change, they have helped to form the character of the nation and its special form of democracy.

BIBLIOGRAPHY

Brasch, Charles, ed. *Landfall Country*. Christchurch, 1962.

Chapman, R., W. Jackson, and A. Mitchell. *New Zealand Politics in Action*. London, 1962.

Lipson, Leslie. *The Politics of Equality: New Zealand's Adventures in Democracy*. Chicago, 1948.

Melvin, K. *New Zealand: The Small Utopia*. Auckland, 1962.

Polaschek, R. J. *Government Administration in New Zealand*. Wellington, 1958.

Webb, L. C. *Government in New Zealand*. Wellington, 1940.

Westrate, C. *Portrait of a Mixed Economy: New Zealand*. Wellington, 1959.

POLITICS

AUSTIN MITCHELL

TO be the Britain of the southern seas is the boast of New Zealand's citizens and the bane of her political scientists. The heritage is clear: the great majority of the population is of British origin or descent. The institutions—electoral, political, and administrative—are largely inherited from, or modeled on, Britain's. The political pattern, with two parties of Right and Left, is the same. Linked by an economic umbilical cord, Britain and New Zealand have shared the same series of broad economic fluctuations which create the mood of politics; from interwar depression, through reform and wartime recovery, to the uncertain affluence of the 1950's and 1960's. Even the political histories demonstrate striking similarities: Liberal decline, Labour rise; wartime coalitions; coalitions and doctors' mandates in 1931. A tendency to see New Zealand as Britain writ small, and to view her politics in British terms, is hardly surprising, therefore.

Yet it is unfortunate. The similar institutions operate in a context of size, society, geography, economy, and attitudes very different from those of Britain. This environment transforms the essence; a different tortoise inhabits the shell of similarity. Small size softens the harsh outline and the impersonal nature of mass democracy with an intimacy unattainable elsewhere. Politics are more personal, direct, and immediate, and politicians are more reluctant to expose themselves or take bold stands. An egalitarian society and the absence of any elitist commitment bring the parties closer together and give politics and administration a different tone and personnel. The importance of the small centers of population and that almost-federal balance between four more-or-less-equal main centers, which is only now breaking down with the sprawling growth of Auckland, both prevent metropolitan domination, strengthen the impact of localism and of the pork barrel, and give a small-town atmosphere to politics. The economic situation gears politics to fluctuations overseas and supplements a class pattern of party allegiance by an urban-rural divergence.

New Zealand attitudes influence both the pattern of politics and institutional arrangements. Imported ideologies have not exercised any substantial influence, and local substitutes have hardly developed. The attitude to ideas and ideologies has, for the most part, been one of skepticism: Does it work? is a more important question than Is it right? Differences between the parties are due to conditioning rather than ideology. Where ideas are influential, a healthy respect for the practical dilutes them in eclectic fashion rather than treating them as pure essences. This situation is complemented by a young country's lack both of any pervading tradition and of the institutions, such as Church or Oxbridge, which sustain it. National attitudes to the State and its institutions can only be compared to the New Zealander's attitude to his house. Far from being an organic growth which must be treated with awe and touched with respect or, alternatively, a perfectly planned monument which can be improved by following abstract plans, the State can be changed at will, redecorated, and periodically extended. And as in the case of the house, the New Zealander can carry out any alterations himself, without benefit of tradesmen, architects, or elaborate plans. New Zealand's are the politics of pragmatism.

If pragmatism, flexibility, and independence have characterized the treatment of the machinery of government and politics, the processes of adjustment have been only intermittent. Change has resulted from accumulating pressures rather than continuous adjustment or planning ahead. So long as institutions function with reasonable efficiency, they are left untouched. When they break down, when the need for modification becomes obvious, or when material dissatisfactions develop and the good life is imperiled, the response is to change things. New Zealand politicians, administrators, and businessmen share with the population at large a common desire for a quiet life, born partly of the conditioning educational process, partly of prosperity, and partly of a reluctance to disturb things, which is inevitable in an intimate, small community. Only when the quiet and well-being of the community are endangered does it respond. Then it does so in pragmatic and undoctrinaire fashion.

In terms of standard of living and social capital, New Zealand is a developed country, one of that small number of "advanced" westernized communities in which political democracy has taken firm roots. Nevertheless, the Dominion has a one-crop economy, depending essentially on grass, which in turn sustains about nine-tenths of her exports. Mineral resources are few, industry is newly developing behind high protective barriers, and the potential of agricultural development is not fully tapped. New Zealand is a developing country still. Its politics for much of the last century can only be viewed as the politics of development.

The first phase of politics saw national unity weak and the province a natural unit in a colony where communication between scattered settlements was slow and difficult. The pattern was recognized in a semifederal constitutional system, but it continued even after the provinces had been abolished in 1876. At the center, politics were, and remained, a system of balancing among provincial groups. Four large provinces, Auckland, Wellington, Canterbury, and Otago, constituted the nuclei of parliamentary coalitions and oppositions, while the minor provinces plied for hire. The main pattern of alliance was the provinces at the geographical extremities against Canterbury and Wellington, each union with a periphery of minor makeweights, but a whole series of permutations were possible as the provinces competed for shares of the development pie. The result was instability as coalitions were formed and broken. Ministries were short-lived: half the administrations up to 1890 lasted for less than a year. Nevertheless, the competition sustained national unity at a time when such a concept was an accidental one. New Zealand remained a unit before communications and the emergence of a national economy turned her into a unity.

Within the politics of factionalism new groupings slowly emerged as new issues such as protection, poverty, class conflict, land aggregation, and political reform created new poles of unity that gradually submerged the provincial ones. Self-conscious liberals or radicals, differing in the degree and the vintage of their liberalism, and still split by provincial competition, began to feel themselves in a measure distinct from unspoken conservatives, whose attitudes were the product of a gentry tradition, a laissez-faire philosophy, and the instincts of vested interest. In 1890 the deepening impact of a sustained depression set politics on this new course. The Atkinson Ministry of 1887 to 1890 had turned to conditioned reflexes of economy and deflation. This and the depression fused labor discontents with the grievances of the landless and the small settler into the first colony-wide movement of protest. Strikes and agitation developed and took political form in a swelling of discontent against the incumbent administration at the election. The colony had, for the first time, moved as one nation. The result was to fuse a clique of parliamentary liberals into a party with backing and impetus provided by the discontent in the country at large.

The Liberal party's response to the problems of depression was influenced by imported ideologies such as single-tax theories, socialist ideas, and collectivist attitudes, but was basically pragmatic: the system was not working and had to be improved. Previous administrations had not hesitated to use the power of the State, the only agency with really powerful leverage in a small colony. The problems of increasing and educating the population, developing communications, raising money in London, providing a trustee to handle estates, or bringing down insurance rates had been resolved by state-assisted immigration, by free, compulsory, and secular education, by state-owned railways, by government loans, and by the creation of the Public Trustee and the Government Life Office. The Liberal response was in the same vein, only on a different scale. For urban labor the Conciliation and Arbitration Act created a framework allowing more equal competition with capital and deliberately encouraging the trade-union movement. For the poor, legislation against sweating and the old-age pension scheme provided minimal measures which were not much behind diffident expectations. As for the landless and the countryside, their demands were conceded in full by a graduated land tax, advances to settlers, measures against land aggregation, and a small number of public relations victories such as the purchase and subdivision of the vast Cheviot estate.

The 1890's was the key decade of Liberal legislation. The formula was the use of the power of the State, however minimally, to solve the pressing and immediate problems which the electorate had forced on the attention of the politicians. From that time, gratitude for services rendered, the myth of the Liberal revolution, was in itself a key to power, but it was less important than others. Overseas prices rose and prospects revived. Refrigerated transport and the rapid development of the North Island dairy industry spread the prosperity among a class of small farmers. The party that John Ballance had associated with self-reliance soon found that the politics of development were the politics of borrowing on a large scale in London and channeling the money through works and loans into the electorate. Development and the promise of development were the bases of Liberal success.

From the politics of factionalism New Zealand had moved into a period of one-party dominance. Opposition was disunited, leaderless, dispirited, and without any clear or acceptable alternative: indeed, in 1901 it was actually disbanded. To the government there gravitated all those who benefited, or hoped to benefit, from the *status quo*. The Liberal party thus brought together supporters of the sale of the freehold on Crown lands, those advocating the leasehold tenure, urban business interests, labor representatives, and farmers both old and newly established. Its vote was similarly distributed, drawing principally from the working-class areas of the towns and the newly developing areas of the countryside. Outside the Liberal party salvation was in short supply: as one member later put it, "the Liberal platform has for many years been a very good one to get elected on." Inside the party, unity was maintained by deference to "King Dick" Seddon and later to Sir Joseph Ward, by the lure of public works, and by the government's tolerance of candid friends who could speak and even vote haphazardly, provided they would support the administration on no-confidence motions. The balance of the party was conservative, but its left wing preferred it to any alternative, and the opposition was too inflexible to be a practical possibility. The first phase of national politics, therefore, was a *de facto* one-party state.

The breakdown came with the emergence of divergent interests. Urbanization was proceeding apace, the economy was becoming more complex, the general response to depression disappeared, and the common hope for development pointed in divergent directions.[1] It became increasingly difficult to hold the Liberal coalition together. Sir Joseph Ward tried to do so by a legislative holiday, which avoided broaching problems, and by practically suspending party meetings: keeping the troops together by keeping them apart. This inability to deliver the desired goods accelerated the organization of a new, rural-based conservative grouping in the Reform party, the opponent of Liberal patronage and champion of the freehold tenure. On the Left, labor groups, disenchanted with the paucity of favorable legislation, concerned by a new tendency of the Arbitration Court to incline towards the employers, and hit by new economic uncertainty, began to organize independently. The Liberal high point was the 1905 election; 1908 saw an erosion of the Liberal vote as abstention increased and was the prelude to a 1911 transfer of support to Labour and Reform. This transfer was sufficient to bring down the government when, in 1912, it was deserted by sufficient independents and fringe supporters to bring the Reform party to power.

The pattern of New Zealand politics was now more complex. In

[1] The urban population, as measured by the population of towns and boroughs, rose as a proportion of the total: 1881—40 per cent; 1901—46 per cent; 1911—50 per cent; 1921—56 per cent; 1936—59 per cent; 1961—66 per cent.

place of the one-party pattern a multiparty system had emerged, with Reform, Liberal, and (first two, then one) Labour parties. Here was a more "modern" system. The two new parties based themselves on divergent nationwide interests, while the Liberals, a relic of the past, sought unavailingly for middle ground. This three-party system was the key to Reform's long tenure of office. Without an electoral majority over its two rivals, it stayed in power from 1912 to 1928, largely because of the split vote.

The new government was only a degree more conservative than the old, for the balance of the Liberal party had been rural and conservative: indeed, some Liberals pulled on the new uniform and liked the fit. The only substantial difference was that the Reform party could act, where the Liberals had been restricted by their own heterogeneity. Reform's inclinations came out chiefly when it had to act on the basis of instinct, as in 1912–1913, when it faced strikes in the mines and on the docks. For the rest, its path was that of the conservative pragmatist. The freehold was sold at low cost to the farmers. The desire for efficiency produced a public-service reform which cut the bureaucracy off from political patronage. In the 1920's the response to economic uncertainties was to introduce market regulation through the establishment of a series of producer boards, the first step towards controlled marketing.

Renewed economic uncertainty and the exhaustion of Reform brought a revived Liberal party, misleadingly renamed the United party, to power in 1928. The party had the same leader, Sir Joseph Ward, and the same policy, massive development financed by a £70,000,000 loan. But the circumstances had changed with depression and unemployment, and the United party had no solution, save the stock orthodoxies of retrenchment and deflation, a policy which the Reform party was prepared to support, so the two joined in coalition in 1931 and soon took the name of National party. The new grouping was conservative in its approach and instincts, though this did not prevent the Minister of Finance, J. G. Coates, from experimenting with more unorthodox solutions by creating the Reserve Bank and the Mortgage Corporation, introducing a number of reforms in agriculture and taking control of the exchange rates.

74

POLITICS

The depression of the 1930's set the future pattern of New Zealand politics. The electorate was now restricted in its choice between Labour and National. Parties which had emerged from the interest-group chrysalis were soon based on a broad and nationwide class division. Labour's ideology had originally been that of socialism and the class war, its base the mining areas and the working-class core of the main centers. To expand beyond this base and become a major party it had been compelled in the course of the 1920's to modify its program, to talk more of welfare and less of socialism, and to drop nationalization of the land. Depression accelerated this process by concentrating attention on immediate problems and on the relief of suffering rather than distant Red dawns. The election platform of 1935, *Labour's Plan*, was a policy of stimulating purchasing power, alleviating distress by fighting unemployment, insulating the economy from overseas fluctuations, and satisfying the farmer by guaranteeing his prices against short-term fluctuations. Trade-union Keynesianism was the economic policy and humanitarianism the social policy. By 1935 the bitterness produced by the depression and delayed recovery drove new supporters into the Labour ranks, and the old 1890 coalition of urban worker and small farmer was temporarily revived, thus facilitating Labour's rise. At the same time there were enough desertions from the coalition party to defeat that government and place Labour in a position to implement its program.

The modern New Zealand economic and social system was planned in reaction to the experience of the depression and built by the Labour party in its fourteen years of power. Construction proceeded pragmatically as a series of responses to the existing and emerging problems. The welfare net was sewn up and raised higher by increased pensions, by family allowances, and by social security. After 1938 the economy was insulated by import licensing and exchange control. Government spending through public works, restoration of wages and benefits cut by the preceding government, and increased unemployment benefits were used to prime the economy. All this might or might not have worked. Labour was, however, supremely lucky, for its accession to power coincided with a recovery in overseas prices, so that the myth of a Labour-inspired recovery could sustain the party for two decades. Without the recovery, however, which was already in progress by 1935, the measures taken might well have produced only an inflation and a depletion of overseas reserves. Even with the economic revival, these two contingencies had developed by 1938 and overseas loans were becoming difficult to renegotiate.

The war alone solved the problem of unemployment and provided the final boost to recovery. At the same time it created new problems to which Labour again responded in pragmatic fashion. Stabilization, through control of prices and wages, became the new policy; a system which did keep down the cost of living. Yet, taken with other wartime restrictions and the postwar shortages, this new framework of controls, and the obvious weariness (moral and physical) of a party too long in office, produced the inevitable electoral reaction. In 1949, Labour lost office to a revived National party.

Flexibility was the key to the National party's rise to power. In 1938 it had expected to win simply by rallying the anti-Labour forces and pointing to the dangers of Labour's programs, but its massive defeat showed the need for a new policy. A new leader, Sidney Holland, whose bounce and bumptiousness were indispensable to a party in the doldrums, led the party away from a stand-pat opposition to Labour and toward acceptance of the reforms the new government had initiated. Better administration of the *status quo* became its promise, but not its performance after 1949, for it seized power greedily and made a series of blunders as it learned to handle the complex machine of government. A doctrinaire opposition to controls and a buoyant enthusiasm for private enterprise caused initial problems as subsidies were cut, decontrolled prices rose, and increases in imports caused employment problems. Yet experience showed the limits of economic and electoral maneuver, and the latter part of the period in office became a phase of pragmatism as the party adjusted itself to administrative realities. A very few state enterprises were sold to New Zealand's unenterprising entrepreneurs, but the great majority were retained, as was the broad structure of social welfare and economic controls. The party that went out of office in 1957 was a far more sober, realistic, and zestless party than the one that had come in eight years before.

The brief second government of an unrejuvenated Labour party allowed Walter Nash to gratify his own ambition to gain power as prime minister and his party to extend the welfare framework by increasing family allowances and pensions, by permitting capitalization of the family allowance for house purchase, and by making school textbooks free. Like National, Labour learned in office; the party became increasingly identified with a new policy, a rapid industrialization designed to conserve overseas funds and maintain full employment. Yet, since the accession to power had coincided with a serious downturn in overseas earnings, the tough deflationary measures and the rapid reimposition of import controls which were Labour's solutions incurred such unpopularity that in 1960 the party lost office to National. As before, National accepted almost completely the changes made by Labour. Better administration of the *status quo* was again its policy, and substantially its performance, for this time the party was less inclined to tinker, and circumstances gave it less freedom to do so. But imperceptibly both parties changed in the early sixties with new circumstances and new parliamentary personnel. Welfare had been the dominant concern of the 1930's, controls of the 1940's, and decontrol in the 1950's, with a sudden retrenchment at the end when the uncertainty of affluence suddenly became obvious. With this warning and the example of other countries to underline the point, growth became the major preoccupation of both government and opposition. Renewed economic difficulties in 1967 served to heighten this concern.

The postwar pattern of New Zealand politics has been one of narrow differences between the parties. Class-based parties cannot be far apart in an egalitarian community. An electorate which is basically contented and affluent, and which believes, with partial justification, that New Zealand's standard of living and social welfare legislation lead the world, does not provide support for widely differing policies. The doctrinaires of Right and Left, concerned to import a New Jerusalem, have dwindled to futility, for extremism requires distress for sustenance. The precarious economic tightrope that any New Zealand government walks restricts its range of action very severely. Networks of alliances and dependence for defense on Britain and the United States make a small power unable to act independently in foreign policy. Since the 1930's, too, the major social problems have been eliminated, allowing the range of minor problems and partial dissatisfactions to dominate the political scene. In response the parties have moved closer together. They have also supplemented their old roles as parties representing different viewpoints by adding a new American one, that of political shells, receptacles for issues and mediators for pressure groups.

If political similarities strike the visitor, and if a section of New Zealanders is apt to complain of the politics of Tweedledum and Tweedledee, most of the community show no inclination to regard differences between the parties as nonexistent. Election surveys demonstrate that voting habits are essentially the same as those in other countries with a similar political system. Most people can distinguish between the two parties in terms both of image and of actual policies. Most of the electorate identify, however tenuously, with one of the two main parties, and political allegiances are just as permanent as they are overseas. While the high voting turnout, fluctuating around 90 per cent, may in part be due to higher average educational levels and a sense of civic duty rather than to high partisanship, any measure of political interest does indicate that average interest in, and average levels of information about, New Zealand politics are higher than in comparable systems overseas. Further, the proportion of "changers" has in no opinion survey been more than one-seventh of the electorate, a proportion much the same as overseas and one which would surely be higher if the parties were viewed as essentially the same. The third-party vote for Social Credit is also low, settling in recent elections around 8 per cent, an indication that the safety-valve function that third parties perform, however esoteric their doctrine, is not greatly in demand. Only in 1966, with an electoral stalemate between the two main parties and unusually complex issues, did Social Credit improve its situation and win 14 per cent of the vote.

In voting, most New Zealanders divide themselves with judicious nicety along the lines of self-interest. Labour is essentially a working-class party and an urban grouping, receiving its main support from the less-well-off areas, new and old, in the main centers and from the Maori, who are mainly a lower-status group. It does reach up the scale to attract a substantial support from the white-collar workers who are not economically better off than the manual workers and, to a less extent, from lower professionals and business groups. Labour also reaches out from the main centers to win a number, rising and falling with victory and defeat, of the secondary centers.

National is more of a residual party, winning support from those higher up the occupational scale, from the better-off suburbs, from the smaller centers, and from the rural areas. It straddles those interests of town and country which in Australia are represented by two different parties. The result of this division of society, a class voting pattern superimposed on a rural-urban division, is a very even division of the vote.

Parties based on such divisions will inevitably differ in their policies, since each will pay particular attention to its own section of the community: all sections are equal, but some are more equal than others. The same social division, a quiet and undemonstrative acceptance of "us" and "them," is seen in an exaggerated degree in the individual memberships of the two parties. It is also visible in their parliamentary teams. Labour's parliamentarians are drawn mainly from the manual-worker, trade-union-secretary group (nearly one-third of the party at present), from the lower professional levels of teacher and minor public servant, or from employees in business. National's members are nearly all from a more substantial section of the community: over half are farmers; most of the rest are lawyers, accountants, or company directors. The class war is continued, but several rungs higher up the social ladder on each side. These differences of social background guarantee that each set of members of Parliament has had a different life experience and will approach problems from a different point of view. Equally, each party is responsive to different interest groups— Labour to the trade unions (nearly two-thirds of which are affiliated with the party), National to the business and importing interests and to the farming organizations. Each party is therefore being tugged in a different direction, with the tug being more effective when the party is in opposition than when it is in power. In power a party usually responds only partially, though it can hardly remain completely unresponsive, and sometimes the responses can be spectacular, as when the National party at the behest of importing and soft-goods interests canceled the contract for the Nelson cotton mill.

Parties which differ in background and in the sort of company they keep inevitably differ in their policy emphasis. The area of common ground is wide—it is bound to be so in a society as well integrated as New Zealand— but this simply means that the parties plow the unsettled edges of the plot more vigorously. And where settlement is to be extended, each would pioneer in a different direction. Traditionally the impetus for improvement and extension of the social-welfare structure comes from Labour: National accepts, even keeps up to date, but rarely initiates. Both parties proclaim willingness to reduce taxation, but National's preoccupation is the more real, and its method tends to be the reduction of direct tax rates and of death duties. Labour would favor raising income and similar tax exemptions and is somewhat deafer to the pleas of the widows and orphans who alone appear to be affected by death duties. Labour is readier to raise money by taxation; it fought the Second World War largely on this basis, and in economic difficulties such as those of 1958 it has resorted to remedial taxation. National, on the other hand, prefers credit squeezes for crises and lacks Labour's puritanical distaste for borrowing overseas. Both parties proclaim their concern with development, but Labour would emphasize industry and protect it by import licensing; National is preoccupied with agricultural expansion and conceding substantial incentives to farmers. In each case development is by cooperation with private enterprise, but National's penchant is to keep the State's influence, though not necessarily its contribution, to a minimum; Labour would measure the influence by the contribution. National's steel industry is to be privately controlled; Labour would specify partnership, just as, in the construction field, it would extend the Ministry of Works to the maximum while National would delegate more to private contractors and consultants.

Attitudes to the State also produce a different approach to administrative problems, Labour favoring direct department control, National leaning toward the more independent corporation. Indeed, constitutional innovations have in the main come from National—the abolition of the second chamber, the creation of the ombudsman to protect individual rights, the proposal for a bill of rights, and the extensive reform of the administrative structure after the Royal Commission of 1962. Labour's efforts concentrate on the economic and social sphere, and the finer details of the institutions are not as important to it as the attitudes of the party in control. Externally, too, differences of attitude emerge. Though both are tied up to the American alliance, National's allegiance is the more wholehearted and uncritical, while Labour has a more genuine sympathy for the Third World and for a safely effete and increasingly irrelevant Britain.

All these differences are variations on a common theme, a different conditioning producing diverging responses to problems and differing preoccupations. They are not absolute differences. Yet they are adequate to sustain the party system, to maintain a level of public interest that, though low-key and lacking in passionate involvement, is continuous and well informed, and to prevent the disgruntlement and negativism inevitable on the margins of any party system swelling to an appreciable size. In a society as homogeneous and uniform as New Zealand, this is the most that can be asked. In a political system based on maintaining a choice between two competing teams of leaders so that the government can be periodically displaced and free criticism maintained, it is more than enough. Such a system would still work effectively and maintain the people's right to choose the government even if the parties were identical in their policies.

It is appropriate to a country whose politics are essentially practical and utilitarian that pragmatism should not be hindered by the restraints of a written constitution. The Dominion does have a Constitution Act of 1852, with eighteen clauses still in force, as well as constitutional lawyers who write and lecture on an entity called The New Zealand Constitution. Yet a constitution, in the sense of a body of rules and conventions within which the institutions operate and by which they are limited, does not exist. For a country without a written constitution, the word either means all—the institutions and the way they operate—or nothing at all. New Zealanders have not really decided on their semantic preference, for the problem is a pressing one only to those on the Right who would restrict the scope of left-wing pragmatism by introducing a written document. For practical purposes New Zealanders talk of a constitution and yet act as if none existed—and none does.

Constitutional formalities are of little concern to the New Zealander because of his shrewd concern with the realities of power and with practical rather than theoretical problems. This same concern has led to the elimination or relegation of the formal and traditional institutions. The second chamber continued to exist practically unnoticed, its attendance low, its influence slight, its basic role to serve as a source of patronage, until a government could finally be bothered to abolish it in 1950. The governor general, though formally exercising for the Queen the powers of the British monarchy, in fact has no influence because of his lack of information and his brief quinquennial tenure. An amiable figurehead, he has only a symbolic and honorific importance; his term is mostly spent moving in leisurely fashion around a pleasant social backwater, saying the things that people like to hear but seldom act on. Similarly, the Executive Council, the formal instrument of government, is simply a meeting of the cabinet wearing different suits and sitting with the governor; a necessary chore which can, on occasions, be fitted in during the cabinet's lunch adjournment.

The same practical attitude is shown to the central myths of the constitution. Ministerial responsibility, treated almost as a fetish in Britain, is viewed in far more commonsense fashion in New Zealand. It hardly featured as an argument against the creation of the ombudsman, who is allowed to seek advice given by departments to their political heads in a way that would hardly be tolerated in Britain. Similarly, cabinet ministers have been prepared to share their responsibility for formulation of legislation with caucus and its committees. Individual responsibility has been viewed in equally sensible terms: unless a minister has been shown to be directly and personally at fault, as Sir Apirana Ngata was in 1934, he has been graciously prepared to accept responsibility for departmental errors and inadequacies while strenuously refusing any blame. If there is a convention on this subject, it is that of not resigning. Collective responsibility has been more important, but ministers occasionally break collective cabinet ranks behind the closed doors of the party caucus, make private views clear privately, hint at them in Parliament, and occasionally excuse individual inadequacies as the result of the cabinet's failure to accept their views, or their own failure to persuade it.

Departmental anonymity means little in a country where public servants are one of the few available sources of opinion and expert information. Departmental heads and other public servants are prepared to appear and speak publicly, even on television, and have never observed a very clear distinction between publication of their own views, of departmental attitudes, and of ministerially sanctioned policy. At an extreme the views of a departmental head such as Dr. Sutch, the former Secretary for Industries and Commerce, can become better known than those of his ministers. Finally, abstract concepts such as civil liberties have little practical influence. New Zealanders have been prepared in emergency, such as war or the 1951 wharf strike, or in special cases such as action against the drug traffic, to concede very sweeping powers to the executive. Infringements of normally accepted standards of police, departmental, or security service behavior have excited comparatively little interest. In part this is because of a reluctance to exaggerate instances out of all proportion. There is also a tendency to emphasize human rather than theoretical considerations. In part, too, it is an instinctive trust in the goodwill and the reasonable attitudes of the people who exercise the powers. Actual powers are not as important as the type of person exercising them, and a very high state of trust characterizes the New Zealander's attitude to his government, his officials, and his state.

With such practical preoccupations it follows that the political machine will be simple and straightforward. In basic outline it is a system of government by party. A first-past-the-post electoral system of single-member constituencies effectively restricts choice to two parties, while the basic social division of the democratic class war is uncomplicated by vertical divisions of race, religion, or region which could provide bases for minor parties. Democracy, therefore, consists essentially of the power to choose, at regular triennial intervals, between two political parties. The majority party governs for three years, controlling the institutions of state and pushing its program through Parliament by using the party majority. The other party opposes, criticizing the actions of the government and stating its alternatives so that at the end of the three-year period the people will be able to make an informed choice on the basis of the two cases presented to it.

In such a system Parliament can neither frustrate the will of the government (since it is dominated by the majority party), nor change the administration (since this choice has effectively been transferred to the electorate). It has three other roles. First, it must check the machinery of administration through parliamentary questions, committee inquiries, and the activities of the individual members of Parliament as minor ombudsmen in their own electorates. Second, it passes and checks legislation, scrutinizing it and occasionally making minor changes. Third, it carries on a continuous public discussion of the activities and decisions of the government, constituting in this capacity a national adult education center where the cases for and against each piece of legislation, each action, each party are put. Typically, New Zealand has done what Britain has been too inflexible to do in recognizing the essential nature of parliamentary debate as a sham fight for the benefit of the people by broadcasting parliamentary proceedings so that they may in fact reach those whom they are intended to inform.

The governing party controls power through the ministers acting in an individual capacity in charge of their departments and united in their collective embodiment of cabinet. There all the threads come together. Cabinet is the supreme committee in a system of government by committee; it is the controlling nucleus of the ruling party, the supreme policy-making body and the top coordinator. Cabinet government is a genuine reality in New Zealand, where parties move as teams, not through individual initiatives, and where small size allows a wide range of decisions to be taken collectively. This makes the cabinet powerful, makes it the central mystery of government, and a body of which the Public Service stands in awe. Yet cabinet can be restrained by the back-benchers of the same party assembled in caucus, for parliamentary parties, never bigger than fifty since the war, are intimate groupings. The votes of these backbenchers must be secured if legislation is to pass the House, and they constitute a counter-weight to the departments and a guide to public opinion. For all these reasons ministers are anxious to consult caucus, which can—and does—change legislation, modify policies, and even drop bills. New Zealand has recognized the logic of government by party in turning caucus into an effective first chamber and party into a team cooperation between ministers and backbenchers—the political forwards and backs.

The political framework is straightforward. The machinery of government it controls is complex: a full machinery of state for a population that is still under three millions. Characteristically, the pattern of development has been one of higgledy-piggledy growth, with two major bursts of reforming in 1891–1898 and 1935–1946 and with intermittent developments in between. The State has accepted new functions willingly and performed them in whatever fashion seemed most convenient at the time, whether by the creation of new departments, corporations, or boards, by the addition of new functions to existing departments, or by a compromise arrangement with voluntary or business interests. Principles of consistency have hardly applied, since very similar functions have been exercised in different fashions; trading roles have been played by departments, administrative ones by commissions, and others (such as operation of broadcasting and railways) have been shunted back and forth between the corporation and the depart-mental types of structure. Nor were the forces working towards amalgamation and rationalization of functions powerful, since no consistent superintending eye has been maintained. Reshuffles and rationalizations have been rare and have often resulted from a mistaken desire for economy rather than the search for efficiency. The reason for this failure is almost a question of national attitudes. Further condensation of departments and corporations would have

85

to be the result of some over-all scheme of relating functions. Abstract perfection is hardly alluring to a New Zealand government when present realities work reasonably well. Always "well enough" is left alone when "better" is hypothetical.

Haphazard growth has left a total of forty departments, ranging in size from the sprawling Department of Works to the tiny law draftsman's office and arranged in a fluctuating hierarchy of power and influence from Treasury down to Marine. Taken with the corporations, boards, and other agencies, this machine presents a real problem of coordination. All seventeen cabinet ministers carry more than one department; cabinet and its nine standing subcommittees struggle bravely, and departments maintain a large number of coordinating committees for specific purposes. In addition, the main control agencies, Treasury, Works, and State Services Commission, in descending order of importance, provide common services and control functions in their respective fields of finance, works priorities, and staffing. All this machinery is sufficient for most practical purposes, but inadequacies do still occur. The concentration on professional skills rather than generalized training does create a lack of political sophistication, and the fragmentation of the system does at times create the appearance of a series of bureaucracies rather than of one common public service. Yet the remedy might be worse than the disease if it created an English administrative class, picked out largely on entry, trained from the first for decision-making (on the assumption that minds untutored in anything else are clear for decisions), and constituted from it the top layer of cream in every departmental cake. Egalitarianism demands promotion largely by seniority up separate professional and clerical ladders and provision for rights of appeal. Any elite within the Public Service emerges through rising from the ranks. Its only common bond is that of working in the same huge organization. Its status is accidental, depending on the department a man is in as much as on his ability and position.

The steady increase in the number of departments is symbolic of the growth in the power of the central government. The role of local government has remained comparatively static: indeed, in recent decades local authorities have tended to lose functions.

There are no serious proposals to add new ones. The test has been the usual pragmatic one: By whom can the various functions and services that the electorate demands best be provided? In the early period, with bad communications and a scattered population, the answer was the province, the one natural unit of local government that has ever emerged in New Zealand. A little later in the century the answer was the State. It alone had size and stature; it could do things really efficiently and maintain uniform standards and equal treatment. The role of the central government expanded while that of local government remained static, until today the territorial units handle only such functions as refuse collections and sewage disposal, road building, electricity and water supply, vehicle licensing and testing, parks and reserves.

Moreover, local government was soon involved in a vicious circle. Without important functions it became hardly worth the trouble to reform. Without reform new functions could not be added. The early units of counties, boroughs, and cities were for the most part too small and unrealistic, particularly when effective communications developed, population expanded, and the settlement pattern shifted. Even with some slight progress towards amalgamation in the twentieth century, there are still 272 territorial units in the Dominion today, mostly too small, mostly unrealistic in their boundaries: only 30 per cent of the population of the Auckland urban area actually lives in the city of Auckland, and the rest is administered by thirty-one other territorial authorities. New functions, deemed appropriate for local control, have been handed, as they emerged, not to the existing and unrealistic territorial units, but to specially created elective *ad hoc* authorities such as Power Boards, Rabbit Boards, Harbor Boards, Hospital Boards, Education Boards, Transport Boards, Catchment Boards, or Drainage Boards. The total number of these separate authorities is now 431. This brings the total number of elective offices in local government to around ten thousand: too many for efficiency, but enough to diffuse responsibility widely and cater to that craving for the trappings of status and recognition which is endemic in an egalitarian society. Labels may talk even louder than wealth.

The number of *ad hoc* authorities creates another vicious circle.

Rationalization and efficiency demand both the amalgamation of territorial authorities to create new and more realistic units, and the merging of some of the *ad hoc* authorities into a strengthened territorial system. Only reform of this type can secure economies of scale, provide reasonable career prospects for local government officers, and turn local government into a realistic entity with adequate powers and hence likely to hold the attention and interest of the property-tax payers. In fact, nothing can be done because the present system establishes a whole series of vested interests—councilors and board members with the enormous dignity their threatened officers confer, and ratepayers who may well be benefiting from lower property taxes than neighbors with whom they would amalgamate. The interests are not numerous, but they are vociferous and entrenched: most proposals for amalgamations are rejected by the bodies concerned and defeated at the polls, even though the turnout is uniformly low. This has reduced the Local Government Commission, fighting the good fight with very little might, to impotence. Even though the local authorities could not carry on without centrally provided finance, Parliament itself declines to step in to offset the impotence of local government. The political reward is small, and the political difficulties and outcry are considerable. Also, local government as an organized entity, through the counties and the municipal associations, has proved assiduous and skilled at lobbying the central government and blocking interference. It may even be better at this than at its job of governing locally. Hence, except for the creation of the Auckland Regional Authority to take over various functions from *ad hoc* authorities in the Auckland area, nothing has been done. This is a situation wholly explicable in terms of national attitudes. Schemes of reform are abstract and their benefits are not immediate, while the present system works well enough and its faults can hardly be weighed quantitatively. Half-sleeping dogs need not be disturbed, however much their posture needs correcting.

Local and central government share the common characteristic of responsiveness to public opinion. Leadership by an elite has never been an acceptable principle in a country where one man is as good as another. Politicians have viewed their role as that of responding to public demands rather than leading. In a country where the public has not been fragmented by class, public opinion is one, rather than many, and hence stronger. An electorate of only 1,410,000 makes politics more personal, and the eighty-four members of Parliament, each representing only 17,000 people and each living in his electorate, are more accessible and open to special requests. A political balance which has been very even since the war, with both major parties winning a few points under 50 per cent of the vote, and each within 4 per cent of the other, also helps to create an excessive caution. Moreover, politicians and administrators naturally incline to a quiet life and to steering clear of trouble. Sensitivity to public opinion is therefore a conditioned reflex. Government is genuinely for the people and by their likes, and the referendum, a favorite device of politicians anxious to abdicate responsibility, is not infrequently used. Leadership in New Zealand is essentially a matter of mediating popular demands and finding the national consensus. The prime minister is the national chairman, the great conciliator, the man of the people voicing the views of the people.

Direct public influence is supplemented by indirect influence through pressure groups. A society largely middle class, versed in self-help, highly educated and with leisure to spare, has proliferated voluntary and sectional organizations. New Zealanders wear many hats as voters; business, farm, or professional organization members; parent-teacher association activists; unionists; Plunket mothers; organic composters; choral group members, and so on to hydra-like proportions. Politics, therefore, becomes a conflict between innumerable pressure-group bureaucracies, each representing more or less inactive members. Characteristically, governments and administrators have responded to this situation in flexible fashion. The leaders of the pressure groups, the interest groups, and of the interested parties—anyone, in short, whose independent operations might cause trouble or disturb equanimity—are either readily consulted or have actually been integrated into the system. This gives them an investment in the *status quo* through influence, status, and privileged channels of communication, but turns them into buffers between government and their own membership. Not only do interested groups have the traditional opportunity for

89

making representations on legislation through parliamentary select committees, but each department of government has its clientele of interested bodies which it will consult as a matter of course, formally or informally.

This development is found in other countries, but New Zealand differs both in degree and type, for the process goes further and the interests have been brought into the process of administration. Unions and employers are brought together with the State in the arbitration system; producers have to work with it in the great marketing boards; users, local bodies, and government share control of the road program through the National Roads Board; and the Returned Servicemen's Association was not only brought into the rehabilitation machinery, but also into the government during the war. Even the prime minister has had his advisory committee of business and farm interests. The examples could be multiplied indefinitely: many of the two thousand or so committees involved in administering New Zealand perform this same "consult and capture" function, while the one field where indicative planning has emerged, the Agricultural Production Council, is essentially the same. The principle is clear. Governments have cunningly integrated potential oppositions into the system, thus ensuring its continued legitimacy and stilling discontent. As the politics of issues fade, the politics of negotiation take their place. The quiet life has become institutionalized.

In highly industrialized countries major issues of class conflict can dominate politics. In countries where ideologies and traditions clash, issues of principle can come to the fore. In countries where a sophisticated elite controls power, politics can be argued in terms of coherent viewpoints. But New Zealand depends primarily on agriculture, is pragmatic, and distrusts abstract ideas and systems. Hence politics are inevitably dominated by economic and welfare questions and the jostling for interest-group and sectional advantage. These are the real stuff of politics, as well as the predominant preoccupations of the machinery of government and administration. This situation is as inevitable as it is distasteful to people more skilled at disguising interests as principles.

New Zealand's economic institutions and welfare legislation have been evolved in response to three basic pressures. The electorate is one with high expectations, a people who came from Britain initially to improve their position, and who have become used to a high and steadily improving standard of living. Governments who fail to live up to these expectations by allowing the standard of living to decline or stagnate, even though the circumstances have been beyond their control, are promptly punished by the electorate, as the governments of Atkinson, Coates, Forbes, Holland, and Nash all found in their turn. In the politics of great expectations no excuses are valid. At the same time, New Zealand's economic position is extremely delicate, dependent as she is on a very narrow range of exports and subject to the fluctuations of primary-produce prices. Since these changes affect all sections of the community, most of the political patterns and the fluctuations in the good life are dictated from outside. Finally, New Zealand shares with the Third World the problem of development. She must face it without those advantages of a large market or substantial mineral resources which have encouraged private enterprise and overseas capital to develop the United States and Australia.

All three pressures work in the same direction: intervention by the State, which alone can satisfy the demand for the good life, protect from the cruel world outside, and develop the country, either by using the stick and carrot on private enterprise, or by going ahead on its own. To turn to the State in this way is a perfectly natural development. In a small community where politics is intimate and retains some of the characteristics of face-to-face days, the State is not an alien abstraction in some remote and unsympathetic capital. It is the community in action. Very few groups can complain about the power of the State without being hypercritical, for very few groups fail to benefit from its activities or to turn to it when faced with problems. Also, the fears of dictatorship and domination seem remote and hypothetical, whereas the problems are real and pressing, and the State is the obvious means of tackling them. Functions and responsibilities have, therefore, been added to the State as the need arose and not in response to any particular ideology. The final result is a government that employs one in five in the work force, costs 10 per cent of the gross national product to administer, spends a third of the gross national product in central and local government administration and capital works, and is concerned in every aspect of the national life.

In the economic sphere it has intervened in many ways. It carries on or participates in a wide range of functions through various channels. Departments like Works and Railways provide services under direct ministerial control, while corporations like National Airways or New Zealand Broadcasting provide a more independent and semicommercial organization. In some fields, such as railways and betting, the State has a monopoly; in others, such as air service, it preponderates. In some areas its trading bodies, the Bank of New Zealand, the Government Life Insurance, and the State Fire Insurance Offices, compete with private enterprise; in others the State cooperates with it, as in the Tasman Pulp and Paper company. In certain spheres it has compelled those involved to organize themselves and work with it, as in the dozen producer boards, councils, and committees. In such products as meat, wool, fruit, eggs, and honey, these organizations control marketing and maintain uniform, and in some cases guaranteed, prices. Here are a series of independent empires over which the government has only a very indirect control and which, indeed, act as pressure groups on it.

In addition the State has a wide controlling function in the economy. Overseas funds problems have led to the erection of an elaborate framework of exchange control, import licensing, and tariff protection behind which a growing range of industries has developed, producing at comparatively high cost for the limited New Zealand market. In return for the protection it provides, the State, as in the mercantilism of old, demands the right to regulate price and in some cases quality. In fact, even consumer protection, elsewhere the function of voluntary organizations, has been handled by a government-supported organization, only recently made independent.

Perhaps the best indication of the role of the State is the trade-union movement, for unionism has been practically its creation. Compulsory arbitration first sustained it, and still does, by compelling the workers to organize into unions in order to get the benefits of the system. Compulsory unionism, enacted in 1936, made unionism all-pervading, which it still remains under a system of unqualified preference to unionists. Finally, the Labour government brought most unions together into a collective organization, the Federation of Labour, which today unites some 300,000 workers, a third of the labor force. In a country where scattered population, small units of production, and a lack of heavy industry have conspired to keep unionism naturally weak, the State has stepped in to redress the balance. It has, in so doing, created a framework in which the naturally strong unions in freezing works, wharves, driving, and mines are prevented from utilizing their strength to the maximum by the inhibitions on striking and the deregistration penalties attending independent action. They are tied to the capitalist system, and when they have tried to break out of the limits of this system, as in 1951, the power of the State has been brought in to break them. On the other hand, members of unions in fields where the movement is not naturally strong cannot be exploited by the employers and can move up behind the stronger leaders. The result of the system is a narrower range of earnings, a lower rate of strikes, and a union movement more hidebound and less vigorous than in most developed countries.

In social services the State plays a major role based, in the main, on the flat-rate social security taxation of $7\frac{1}{2}$ per cent of income. The State provides universal superannuation, old-age pensions, family allowances for each child, unemployment benefits for that minuscule number who find themselves out of work, sickness benefits, free pharmaceutical prescriptions, free hospital care, and a flat-rate fee to doctors to reduce the cost of their services. Yet the structure of social security of which New Zealand is so rightly proud is a structure erected in the 1930's and 1940's that has only been tinkered with and slightly extended since. Indeed, in hospital and school construction it has been allowed to lag badly. Other countries have crept ahead, relating their benefits to standard of living rather than to ordained minima. Economies that are expanding more rapidly can afford to devote more to welfare, without

93

feeling this a heavy burden in the way New Zealand feels the 10 per cent of her gross national expenditure that she devotes to welfare and, until 1967, to food subsidies.

Further weaknesses are also evident. In the main, resources are devoted to a blanket coverage because of a national penchant for equality and a reluctance to discriminate by means tests. Thus, resources are not always applied fully to those they would benefit most. More could be done in crucial areas for the same sum of money. New Zealand has dealt well enough with the old basic problems of poverty, distress, and unemployment. Remaining problems are both complex and partial, needing coordinated research work to discover and assess, and yielding no great electoral bonus in their solution. As a result, the problems of Maori drift to the towns, Maori education, illegitimacy, poverty among sections of old people, psychological disturbances, vocational guidance, mental health, and urban redevelopment are not being effectively tackled. In all these fields New Zealand lags well behind other countries, for pragmatism tends to falter when problems are partial or are not pressing.

Voluntary effort fills some of the gaps, setting conspicuously good levels of child care through the stolid but effective Plunket Society and in kindergartens and play centers, though intervening with more dubious effect in the care of older people. Yet the very fact that problems are left to such effort is an indication, in New Zealand conditions, that they are not considered to be of the first rank of importance. In any case, private effort on a voluntary basis can never have as wide-reaching and as uniform an effect as state activity: middle-class sections are more likely to run such organizations and more likely to use and benefit from many of their services than are the manual workers.

The economic and social system that has grown out of all these developments is frequently described as socialist, justifying a description of New Zealand as the land of the long pink cloud. Such capsule thinking ignores a whole series of more relevant factors. Far from being socialist, the electorate would not recognize or understand an ideology if it bumped into one in the polling booth. In practice, the population is essentially, though instinctively, con-

94

servative, being reluctant to change unless compelled by practical necessities. Socialist theories played little part in the evolution of the system, practical solutions to difficulties a great deal. The growth of the system has been haphazard and unplanned, as its present state demonstrates. On the economic side, the functions are negative rather than positive: to control and restrain, not to plan and organize. The welfare structure is designed to satisfy broad social needs, not to provide a complete and integrated system. Humanitarian pragmatism could be regarded as socialism only by *Time*-think. Indeed, real socialism probably demands a greater willingness to direct and organize pressure groups and to take firm stands against them than New Zealand democracy has yet manifested. Full employment, maintained from 1940 to 1967, has probably done more than the welfare state to form New Zealand attitudes.

Practical responses to difficulties have produced impressive results in New Zealand, where democracy has responded brilliantly to major crises such as wars and depressions. The simple and effective political system has won almost universal acceptance and legitimacy and now controls an economic and administrative system that is complex but efficient and effective in achieving the intended purposes. The country has developed a humane and effective welfare system that successfully prevents individuals and groups falling far below a rather uniform standard of living.

There is no reason to believe that the national flair for improvisation in the face of difficulties is likely to fail in the future. There is, however, some reason to believe that its successes will be more limited than they have been in the past, since the scope for improvization may well be less. New Zealand has attained pre-eminent success in the amateur league, but its prospects among the professionals are less certain—and most advanced states must now be accounted professional.

Pragmatic responses have in the past come, often belatedly, to pressing problems. The prick of discontent has been the indispensable spur to action. Where it has not existed, problems have been postponed or left to solve themselves. Now, however, even with current market uncertainties, the days of the obvious and deep-seated problem appear to have passed. Future responses may have to be to partial difficulties. They may even have to be anticipatory moves against problems yet to emerge. Neither New Zealand democracy nor New Zealand politicians have shown themselves adept in these fields. The system is not necessarily as rational or as efficient as it could be. Planning, rationalizing, and coordinating are skills of a higher order than a quick grasp of the practical.

Moreover, the problems of the future will be rather different. New Zealand politicians have tackled economic and welfare problems and the work of interest-reconciliation very well. With respect to moral problems or problems concerned with the quality of life generally, they have shown themselves timid and all too often ill-informed. Perhaps the prolonged inability to modify the world's most improbable licensing laws was the clearest indication of this. The failure occurs because the politicians have never thought of themselves as trained or selected to lead. Nor has the electorate encouraged them to take any other attitude. It has been quick to rebuff any delusion among politicians that they could be anything more than ordinary men writ large.

Given the intimacy of New Zealand democracy and its close dependence on public opinion, pressure for change has usually come from a public demand produced by real dissatisfactions. Changes unacceptable to that public have tended not to be made. In the future, however, this motive power may well be weaker, the brakes stronger. A sustained belief that New Zealand is God's Own Country leading a world both unconscious of and ungrateful for being led, an isolation that conceals the advances made in other countries, and a press and broadcasting system dedicated to praising façades rather than inquiring behind them, all combine to still pressures for change.

As administration becomes more complex and sophisticated, and the issues it faces less clear-cut, so the system becomes more remote from and less readily understood by, the great mass of the population. Even Parliament finds itself increasingly unable to inquire into, control, or understand the machine and tends to sidetrack itself into party squabbles. A public roughly conversant with the system, such as has existed in the past, can hardly be expected in the future. On the contrary, there may well be a growing alienation based on incomprehension. The divergence must compel the politician and administrator, hitherto used to responding to broad indications of public demand, to act on their own, as well as in the dark.

New men may be as necessary as new skills. New Zealand democracy has fought a long rear-guard action against the emergence of an elite which is, and traditionally has been, associated with privilege. It has insisted on politicians who do not stand out from ordinary mortals. It has looked to the man of general knowledge and skill at improvisation rather than the specialist with his limited perspective. The nation's destiny has been to export first-class brains and would-be specialists, and import second-class brains and tradesmen. The skills of the economist, the scientist, the planner, and the specialized administrator are in depressingly short supply. Today the increasing sophistication of the machine and of its problems creates an increasing role for the expert and the specialist and possibly an emerging function for an elite to control them. A nation that has relied on a practical flair to change and improve its governmental house on a do-it-yourself basis may find in the future that the work has to be delegated to the glazier, the plumber, and the carpenter, all supervised by an appointed architect.

BIBLIOGRAPHY

Chapman, R. M., et al. New Zealand Politics in Action. Oxford, 1962.
——, ed. Ends and Means in New Zealand Politics. Auckland, 1962.
——, ed. Studies of a Small Democracy. Auckland, 1963.
Lipson, L. The Politics of Equality. Chicago, 1948.
Milne, R. S. Political Parties in New Zealand. Oxford, 1966.
Mitchell, Austin. Government by Party. Christchurch, 1966.
——. Politics and People in New Zealand. Christchurch, 1967.
Oliver, W. H. A History of New Zealand. London, 1960.
Scott, K. J. The New Zealand Constitution. Oxford, 1962.
Sutch, W. B. The Quest for Security in New Zealand. Oxford, 1966.

EDUCATION

KENNETH MELVIN

The colonisation of New Zealand would provide the finest opportunity
that ever occurred to see what might be done for society by universal
education.

E. G. WAKEFIELD and J. WARD, *The British Colonisation of New Zealand*
(1837)

IT is a truism that education is social theory in action. New Zealand's pursuit of universal education is a direct reflection of a deep
conviction that equality of opportunity is the very core of democratic doctrine, and in practical terms this means equality of educational opportunity.

In the United States, where the cardinal doctrine appears to be
that of individual liberty more than collective equality, the characteristic national sentiment is expressed in the Jeffersonian maxim,
"That government is best which governs least." New Zealand
disagrees. By the end of the nineteenth century it had enacted the

98

most far-reaching social legislation in the world, and by the 1930's it had become one of the noteworthy welfare states among the Western nations. Today it would be difficult to find a more completely planned and specifically state-regulated representative democracy. Central to this broad social purpose has been the national system of public education.

The vexing problem of preserving democratic liberties under pervasive governmental direction has thus been approached not only by a particular legislative order, but also by reposing a somewhat naïve faith in popular education as both the catalyst of the open society and the basic artifact of personal fulfilment. The English oligarchy and the American plutocracy have no counterpart in the New Zealand democracy. In essence, there has been a combination of free enterprise and state socialism designed to provide a commonwealth in which equality of educational opportunity will hold the balance between freedom and order, individual and society, person and person, European and Maori, labor and capital, and between the political parties. The whole apparatus of government has been applied in an operative code for egalitarian race relations, politics, social organization, and public education.

In the four main sectors of effective democracy—political, economic, social, and educational—it is probable that New Zealand exhibits as much equality as most other nations. Parliament is multiparty and monocameral; there is no written constitution requiring tortuous court interpretations; the community is not class-structured by arbitrary impediment; there has been no extinction of private enterprise; government redistributes the national income through universal social security; and national education from kindergarten through university is the direct responsibility of the State.

New Zealand views Great Britain, by contrast, as a political democracy offering some measure of economic democracy but no comparable degree of either social or educational equality and the United States as a political and educational democracy in which social and economic organization are even more equivocal. These generalizations and oversimplifications are offered not in order to affect for New Zealand some utopian ideal, nor to pretend that it is

99

the sole alembic of effective democracy. Rather, by grace of circumstance and political management, New Zealand has created a social order more consistently egalitarian than that of either of the paramount English-speaking nations. If educational opportunity be admitted as the criterion of the open society, then New Zealand's provision of free, public, universal schooling from five to nineteen years of age for every person who seeks it, and university education which is virtually free to all who qualify for it, seems to constitute a rare achievement in both individual opportunity and social equality.

The centrality of public education in the New Zealand democracy was implicit from the early years of the colony, when there was a highly individual disposition of the loci of power. As the first nation to enact universal adult enfranchisement,[1] New Zealand set about the systematic abatement of the mischief of social class and a closed political order, the legislative moderation of finance capitalism by means of fiscal policies, the protection of home and familial life against personal misfortune by public responsibility, civil liberties guaranteed uniformly to both races by a sovereign judiciary, the separation of Church and State in public education, and the full warranty of individual freedom of conscience. From the passing of the foundational Education Act of 1877, popular education became the social escalator, but till the turn of the century secondary schooling remained the privilege of the few. In 1936 continuing adolescent education was seen as not only the natural right of all normal youth, but also the key to the economic viability of the redistributive society then being instituted. As New Zealand embarked upon its major welfare programs through national reconstruction after the depression, it was obvious enough that the economic surplus necessary for their maintenance could accrue only from new levels of wealth production by an increasingly educated populace. Extended schooling had long been accepted as a direct state responsibility: the government of the day now declared the principle that educational expenditure was different from all other

---

[1] New Zealand introduced universal adult male suffrage in 1879 and added the female franchise on equal terms in 1893, being anticipated in the latter provision only by the state of Wyoming.

forms of expenditure and as an investment in human capital it merited priority in the multiplying complex of public services. During the past thirty years, national education has become more than a social and economic utility and has in fact been accorded primacy as the general inspirer of the whole human situation.

Secondary education for all was instituted in 1936 by the removal of all selective procedures, academic tests as well as socio-economic barriers, and was fully effected in 1944 by the raising of the school-leaving age to fifteen years. In 1964 one-quarter of the total population of New Zealand was undergoing formal education (one of the highest proportions in the world), and three-quarters of the school constituency now voluntarily remains well beyond the statutory terminal age. It may be wrong to attribute national prosperity to the degree of public education (though a high correlation appears to exist throughout the world between these two factors), but the fact remains that New Zealand is third in rank order of per capita gross national product, being exceeded in this only by the United States and Canada. New Zealanders could attribute their standard of life and national culture to the provision which permits no child to suffer serious educational deprivation. By his natural endowment and individual application, every New Zealand youth largely determines his own place in the community.

To interpret one's own national system of education in such roseate hues is perhaps to incur the charge that this is but the indigen with Chauvin at his elbow, magnifying the commonplace into the significant and the significant into the momentous. But the educational expenditure of over sixty million pounds in 1964–1965 for a total population of under three million people is by no means contemptible. Education is everywhere a voracious feeder, and in New Zealand it feels no shame in its demands for more and more for the sake of everything else. This small nation might reasonably congratulate itself on having universalized a human right which in all previous history has been partial, rationed, and discriminatory. Higher education for all is an invention of the twentieth century, has yet to yield its full harvest, and tempts the conclusion that upon it depends the whole human enterprise. It is thus that enlarging public education is thought of in the prevailing humanistic sentiment of New Zealand, where it takes on something of the mystique of a secular religion.

The adoption of a centralized source of finance was the decisive element in the 1877 Act and ever since has had the profoundest influence upon public education. The power of the purse is possibly at its strongest when it is the public purse disposable by popular will. Not that these implications were fully understood at the time of the Act. The national education system which then began as the most fully decentralized in the British Empire, within seventy years and under pressure of financial responsibility had become the most centralized in the British Commonwealth. In this it affords a notable exception to the generalization that democracies characteristically choose local educational control in order to offset central bureaucracy. The Education Act of 1914 secured the final transfer of effective governance of the public schools from local education authorities to a central department, leaving the boards as expending agents of closely supervised annual grants by parliamentary vote, and school committees as trustees of only trivial responsibility. The seventy-clause Education Bill of 1964, with its consolidated body of directive and disciplinary regulations, demonstrated the extent and degree of centralized power that has accumulated through at least forty-three amendments to educational law during the past fifty years.

This sustained and insistent drive for unification of public education drew its initial strength from the defaults and disarray of local control; and the achievements of centralized provision and direction have been quite spectacular. They have also tended to obscure the measure of uniformity and conformity imposed upon education, which may best be regarded as an organism which is instinct with individual difference. In the view of some educators, Leviathan now bestrides the New Zealand scene, fostering a complacent mediocrity engendered by the vices of its democratic virtues: universalism, excessive egalitarianism, and a certain distaste for intellectualism. It is possible to present a disturbing picture of national sameness of mind and attitude induced in large part by a monolithic public school system in which the Department prescribes the

102

form of provision; determines the constitution and function of local administration; controls the inspectorate; supplies the textbooks and regulates the curricula; conducts the certification of both pupils and teachers; promulgates the regulations which govern teachers' colleges, the staffing of schools, and the salaries of teachers; and enrols more than four-fifths of the nation's youth within its benevolent domain. For all that, in the New Zealand experience such centralization of authority is less troublesome and more efficient than the multiple, disparate, and disjunctive local systems that it replaced, and under which the accidents of regional resource determined the type and quality of education that a citizen received. In fact, the education system permits greater freedom to both teacher and pupil than is customarily exercised by either; departmental policy operates without discrimination as to race, religion, or financial estate of those within its charge.

Since 1939 the trends in education in New Zealand have been toward a more flexible school and class organization; a fuller recognition of individual differences among children; a study of subject matter that has real meaning for children; complete acceptance of the idea of free post-primary education for all; better provision for handicapped children; and developments in the field of advanced technical education to meet the needs arising from the expansion and diversification of industry.

Such unexceptionable objectives may be common to all advanced societies: what is uncommon in the New Zealand scene is the high degree to which they have been actualized. As a people averse to the doctrinaire and incorrigibly pragmatic in social practice, New Zealanders would generally think of educational organization in terms of Pope's couplet: "For forms of government let fools contest; / Whate'er is best administer'd is best."

It is easy to show that the best minds in common school receive insufficient intellectual stimulus and sustenance, perhaps by reason of their dispersion throughout the undifferentiated intake whose general standards tend to be those of the median half. It is possible to argue that comprehensive education operates to the neglect of this highly gifted minority, and that in its preoccupation with the many, it inhibits the excellence of the few. It is true that New

103

Zealand has not developed meritocratic principles as it well might in a context markedly less prone to the demonstrable distortions of educational purpose such principles exhibit in class-organized communities. In any case, there is too little understanding of education as a consummatory satisfaction and too general misuse of it as a mere ladder to material advantage. New Zealand culture appears to be shallow, amateur, and improvisatory. But it seems captious to rail at universal non-selective schooling for failing to bring the whole nation to standards of excellence that by definition are the qualities of exclusive elites. This, indeed, is to rebuke the doves and let the ravens go. New Zealand has a fixed indisposition to return to a system in which the segregated education of the intellectually gifted honors the doctrine "to him that hath shall be given," and becomes an agency for the cultivation of academic intellectualism unmoderated by essential sociality. The old system produced several world-renowned scholars, including Dr. A. H. Macdonald, the classicist, of Clare College, Cambridge; Dr. Desmond Pacey, the historian of Canadian literature, of the University of New Brunswick; the late Professor F. W. W. Rhodes, of the University of Rangoon, who first classified the numerous Burmese languages; and Lord Rutherford, the nuclear physicist. Indications are that the new educational philosophy will be no less productive of such scholars. New Zealand appears to act on the assumption that it is more democratic to raise steadily the average levels of public enlightenment than to foster individual ascendancy by educational privilege. Although equality of opportunity in any absolute sense is probably unattainable, centralized resource and responsibility have given New Zealand a closer approximation to full educational opportunity than is provided by most other nations.

The New Zealand cultural pattern may indeed demonstrate that social determinism tends to subdue rather than sustain creative individuality. Perhaps the worst thing about it is its aesthetic undistinction, its too general contentment with the moderately gifted, the moderately intelligent, the moderately motivated, and the moderately effective educational product. However, those who hold that the democratization of education has degraded human aspiration, impoverished scholarship, and devalued the educational currency may be left to their task of proof. In a welfare society singularly free from overpopulation, unemployment, organized crime, or extremes of wealth or poverty, the national regularity of thought, attitude, and conduct may be a modest price to pay for security and prosperity, and all things considered, no more than a desirable degree of social control.

New Zealand's social theory as applied to national education was enunciated in 1939 in a government policy statement and has ever since shaped firmly the country's educational aims:

> The Government's objective, broadly expressed, is that every person, whatever his level of academic ability, whether he be rich or poor, whether he live in town or country, has a right to a free education of the kind for which he is best fitted, and to the fullest extent of his powers.

The educational history of the last thirty years is a record of development calculated to achieve this objective.

The first free kindergarten in New Zealand was opened in Dunedin in 1889, initiating a program of voluntary association and philanthropic finance which for the next half-century was to be confined chiefly to the main centers of population. In 1942 the central government instituted grants to kindergarten student-teachers, and in 1949 accepted responsibility for the cost of sites and buildings for teacher-training centers specializing in preschool education. Since 1948 the salaries of kindergarten teachers and full-time training-center staff have been paid by the Department of Education. Where a community raises local finance for the purchase of land, buildings, and initial equipment for free kindergartens, it may receive a government subsidy of two dollars for every one that is so donated. Thus, a certain initiative remains for local effort under strong official encouragement for this extension of national education.

Nursery play centers are a more recent innovation, relying upon parental involvement in the conduct of supervised play activities among preschool children. Such centers receive a small annual maintenance grant from the government where required standards of equipment are met.

The significance of this emphasis on preschool education in New

Zealand is that it is not fostered as a welfare organization, a mitigator of slum conditions, and a corrective to underprivileged conditions. As national welfare programs have served the revolution of rising expectations and brought the country into advanced social provision, preschool education has won its strength because it satisfies the small child's need for developmental activities in companionship with his age-peers beyond the limited creative resources of even good homes. Here, perhaps more than in most other branches of public education, qualitative criteria have not been modified by mass intake. The carry-over of this function of play and developmental tasks into the infant classes of the primary schools helps make the latter as efficient as they are.

The earlier maturation of child and youth in an advanced society leads naturally to the downward extension of educational activities, rendering obsolete many of the concepts of readiness which date from Comenius, if not from Quintilian. New Zealand thus conducts broadcast programs for preschool children in country districts, serving individual homes, maternal groups, and community development in preschool activities even where no kindergartens or play centers as yet exist. Overseas educationists have described the system as "a dream come true" and "second to none anywhere in the world." New Zealand's gratification seems warranted by the literature of the World Organization for Early Childhood Education.

At the age of five the New Zealand child may (and by seven must) enrol at a primary school, either state or private, unless the parent can satisfy a magistrate that the child is receiving an adequate schooling by some other means. The average primary school pupil passes through the infant classes and the first four standards in a little over six years: the further two years within the primary system are spent either at the same school or by transfer to an intermediate school or an intermediate department attached to a secondary school. Geographical location will be a determining factor between these three alternatives, and changes recommended by the Currie Commission will tend to integrate the intermediate stage with secondary rather than primary education, leading to experimentation with Forms I to VI schools serving this purpose.

EDUCATION

At present, most pupils embark upon secondary education at the age of thirteen-plus, entering the Third Form of post-primary school for their first encounter with the traditional foreign languages and mathematics of the secondary curriculum. Under the present transitional plan, secondary studies will commence earlier, at eleven-plus, in both the intermediate schools and the new, expanded secondary schools. There are no selection procedures for secondary schooling in New Zealand, and the common high school ensures no marked differences between schools, courses, quality of teachers, or administrative pattern.

For the great part of a century the primary curriculum has not changed materially in form, though of course there have been great changes in content and teaching methods. Character training, English, arithmetic, geography, history, arts and crafts, nature study, physical education, and music were the main subject areas defined by the 1877 Act, and these remain substantially today's curriculum. Textbooks are provided free in all schools, both state and private, thereby facilitating the constant modernization of the syllabus of instruction. Individual schools have wide discretion in their choice of such free textbooks.

Because the Education Act of 1877 made the primary school curriculum the responsibility of the central Department of Education, the syllabus of instruction maintains a commonalty of aim and purpose throughout the two thousand public primary schools, which, enrolling some 375,000 children, are supervised by the central and district inspectorate and guided by continuous curriculum revision committees. The smallest primary schools may have no more than half a dozen pupils, the largest between 800 and 850, but more than half enrol between 25 and 200. Of recent years, geography and history have been interrelated in a syllabus of social studies, drawing and handwork have been merged in more liberal programs of arts and crafts, including handwork in metal and wood, and music has been broadened to include instrumental as well as choral work. In a typical week in Form II (about the age of twelve-plus) time allotted to the various subjects and activities is akin to current practice in England and North America and is almost the same as the program suggested for senior classes in

Scottish primary schools. It is noteworthy that over half of the school week is devoted to English and arithmetic, the two tender areas for critics of modern education who affect to find deliberate and malign neglect of these core areas.

In the primary syllabus of instruction in English the emphasis is upon sincerity of expression rather than formal regularity dictated by artificial imitation of past models; in arithmetic, upon the understanding of concepts of number rather than rote learning by mechanical drill: in short, upon the use rather than inert knowledge of the basic tools of the learning process. By "sincerity of expression" in the English language is meant freedom from the old bondage to the examination essay as a formal exercise; history and geography as social studies are liberalized from the narrow, descriptive, and unrelated cataloguing of items; and arts and crafts seek creative imagination rather than reproductive techniques. Everywhere there is a determined effort to avoid training in stereotypes; understanding of meaning is the quest that distinguishes the schools of today from those of thirty or forty years ago. This implies a realistic emphasis upon the fundamental processes of learning in application to the common life. The principles were enunciated as long ago as 1944, and practice to date has been directed to these objectives: (a) standards are fundamental to education no less in the newer subjects than in the old tool subjects; (b) the tool subjects must be stripped of inessentials and then taught with complete thoroughness; (c) hard work cannot and should not be eliminated from true education, but it should be on tasks that have a meaning for the child; (d) there is nothing incompatible between good standards in the tool subjects and full acceptance of modern tendencies.

In 1958, following some criticism of standards of work being achieved in the three R's, a national report was presented by the Department in conjunction with the New Zealand Council for Educational Research. Its broad conclusions on a comparative basis were as follows: In English reading standards were higher than ever before, especially in respect to grasp of meaning. In silent reading the attainments of New Zealand children appeared to be "considerably higher" than those of British and Australian children;

in oral English there was clear superiority to previous generations in confidence and fluency, though there had not been the same improvement in the quality of diction. Written English reflected the same advance, age for age, and class for class; and in spelling the average standard seemed to be much the same as in the past. In arithmetic the average attainment had remained stable for thirty years, at standards much the same as those of British and Australian children of the same age, but probably higher than those of the standardized London group.

Promotion in New Zealand primary schools has traditionally been by annual "standard" examinations, but in recent times progress through the primary school has been by classes and as an age group rather than by differential intellectual attainment. School discipline is mild, aimed at a bond of warmth and understanding rather than repressive authoritarianism. Fear is no longer the predominant factor, nor punishment the spur to learning, and it can reasonably be held that over the last thirty years the New Zealand primary school has come closely to the interpersonal relations of Vittorino's "*la giacosa*." Material provision and environmental surroundings in the newer schools built during this period have reached parity with the best primary schools of other advanced nations. Old school buildings still exist; classes are chronically overlarge, and under the continuing shortage of teachers number as high as fifty, though the norm is probably nearer forty-five. The agreed optimum is thirty-five, with thirty as the ultimate target.

All in all, the primary school system represents the most successful sector of national education, though it remains a matter of opinion whether this is because of or despite much closer regulation than obtains at higher levels.

In 1964 there were some 37,000 pupils enrolled in intermediate education, either at separate two-year schools or within intermediate departments of post-primary schools. Since in 1963 fewer than half of all pupils in Forms I and II were enrolled in intermediate schools or departments some forty years after their introduction, the Currie Commission recommended fundamental changes in intermediate education. The very nature of the intermediate school is that it draws its Forms I and II pupils from surrounding primary schools and therefore encounters a numerical limitation in the size of the community it seeks to serve. All intermediate schools are urban, but not all towns can have them, since in order to operate effectively they must have at least a four-form entry. Rural areas have thus stayed the progress of this sector of national education by their inability to contribute the necessary intermediate intake. Furthermore, when the abolition of the entrance test for secondary education brought almost the entire primary constituency into the secondary schools, the intermediate stage was no longer required to provide a terminal course for school-leavers.

There is wide agreement as to the desirability of a transition from the primary school system at an average age of eleven-plus, and it is very commonly at this stage that overseas systems transfer pupils to secondary studies. In recommending that this plan be adopted in New Zealand, the Currie Commission proposed that Forms I and II in all district high schools be added to the secondary departments of these schools, and the secondary departments be translated as far as possible into Forms I to VI secondary schools. A further recommendation was that the present system of intermediate schools in the cities and towns be extended, and that such schools be renamed junior high schools. Thus both town and country pupils would secure the advantages of earlier commencement upon secondary studies, the latter by an arrangement that circumvents the limitations imposed by scattered population. In the proposed pattern, six-year primary schools will serve the five to eleven-plus age group, with eight-year schools confined to remoter country areas; junior high schools will enrol the eleven-plus to thirteen-plus sector in cities, large towns, and thickly settled country districts; and the secondary schools will be of two organizational types, Forms III to VI schools as at present; Forms I to VI schools will be developed in a number of slow-growing country schools. Where district high schools remain, they would be of a single type, with their secondary departments ranging from Form I to Form V or VI as may be determined by their smaller constituency.

In all this there is a determined reach for a common educational highway for all normal youth with no basic differences of provi-

110

sion as between town and country schools despite their differences of size.

New Zealand has no taste for the traditional English tripartite secondary system with its selection of pupils by academic examination for different types of school varying greatly in quality, prestige, and provision. Such an arrangement is regarded by New Zealand educators as being undemocratic in its rationing of educational opportunity according to examination results taken too early to be sound indicators of future interest, ability, or attainment. The introduction of intermediate education was thus an attempt to follow the American pattern of the junior high school for an orientation and self-discovery period, from which pupils might choose within any of the comprehensive multicourse high schools a secondary program best suited to their needs and interests.

To this end, ability-grouping and streaming practices operate in the intermediate stage; there are specialist teachers enabling a start to be made upon secondary subjects with ease of transfer from course to course; and consolidated provision is made for equipment, libraries, and workshops at standards not possible throughout the primary schools. Club activities in weaving, bookcraft, radio, Junior Red Cross, drama, instrumental music, science, and first-aid are fairly common in intermediate schools, and there are electives in aesthetic subjects—literature, art, and music—as part of the introduction to secondary studies. Some educators have held that three or even four years would be a better orientation period, but this has not found favor because it would tend to make the intermediate stage terminal for school-leavers instead of contributory to secondary studies.

In its development of a state system of universal post-primary education, New Zealand had to integrate a variety of institutions, but by gradual assimilation to a common purpose, these post-primary schools have become generically "secondary" schools, differing only in the bias of their courses. Broadly speaking, New Zealand relies upon the common high school, comprehensive in intake and multicourse in curriculum. All secondary schools in the state system operate under individual boards of governors or boards of managers, prepare their pupils for the same external

111

examinations, and are sufficiently alike in their syllabuses of instruction to accommodate pupil transfer from district to district. All are required to teach during the first two years the common core subjects: English, social studies, science, mathematics, arts and crafts, music, and physical education. This is followed in general pattern by some specialization through optional studies for the School Certificate and still further specialization for university entrance, which is attainable either by internal accreditation or external examination.

A full secondary course occupies five years, the School Certificate examination being offered at the end of the third year, Endorsed School Certificate in the fourth year, and the Higher School Certificate in the fifth. University entrance is gained normally by boys at the end of the fourth year, and by girls a year later, and all who so qualify are entitled to free tuition at a university. The Higher School Certificate carries in addition a bursary at the university. In 1900, only 7 per cent of youth continued from primary to post-primary school; by 1964 the figure was 98 per cent, reflecting the national determination to provide secondary schooling for all normal adolescents. In the universalizing of secondary studies it has been necessary to emancipate the curriculum from the severely scholastic, academic matriculation objective, heavily weighted with one or two foreign languages, mathematics, and at least one specialized science. But as late as 1940 nearly three-quarters of all secondary pupils were still pursuing the university entrance course, though less than 10 per cent proceeded to the university. The revised School Certificate syllabus of 1945 established the core requirements with a selection from over thirty electives designed to serve individual interest and purpose. The core studies occupy more than three-fifths of the first year, with diminishing amounts of time in succeeding years.

Within wide limits, the secondary schools are free to specify the content of their core studies and activities, and at all times are expected to adapt their offerings and methods of teaching to individual need; both intensive academic specialization and narrow vocational training have been eliminated from the lower school in the quest for a sound general education during at least the first two years. Among the extracurricular activities, sports take pride of place, the national school games being Rugby football, cricket, and hockey (basketball for girls), with well-organized inter-secondary-school carnivals of swimming and athletics in the larger cities. Aesthetic interests find engagement in drama groups, music clubs, school orchestras, hobby groups, debating, public speaking, and natural history clubs. In short, the pattern of secondary school emphases is much the same as in Australia, North America, and Great Britain.

Subject to certain zoning requirements in larger cities, parents are free to choose for their child the school and course deemed most desirable and suitable; some 17 per cent of school-attenders (both primary and post-primary) are conveyed at public cost; and the Department of Education is responsible for the vocational guidance of secondary pupils, both as to choice of school courses and career, on the basis of accumulated school records and diagnostic tests. A typical academic course consists of English, mathematics, physics, chemistry, and biology; or English, French, history, geography, and Latin or biology. A typical general course would be English, French or mathematics, general science, history, and geography. The commercial courses embrace such subjects as bookkeeping, shorthand and typing, and commercial practice; the home-life courses include homecraft and clothing; the boys' technical courses offer woodwork, engineering workshop, and technical drawing; and rural courses emphasize agriculture or horticulture, animal husbandry, and dairying. Within the course of his choice the secondary pupil is likely to be streamed according to ability, and curriculum enrichment and limited acceleration seek to provide stimulus for the intellectually gifted.

Annual promotion up to the fifth form (third year) is normally automatic, and because the School Certificate is the first external test of ability and attainment in the whole primary and secondary complex, it can be argued that pupils do not have sufficient examination experience to acquit themselves adequately. The majority of secondary teachers are university graduates, and the remainder are generally qualified and trained teachers of nonacademic subjects: homecraft, physical education, woodwork, metalwork, and commercial subjects.

One-third of the boys leaving secondary schools enter apprenticeships; for many of them, technical classes are mandatory for the next three years. Since 1949 the New Zealand Trades Certification Board, in conjunction with the Education Department, has administered a system of examinations covering some twenty-five trades. Increasingly, the School Certificate is required as a prerequisite to apprenticeship, and the Technical Correspondence School enrols about two in every five apprentices. From the apprentice schemes in some of the larger technical high schools, part-time students may take professional courses in engineering, architecture, and accountancy. Under the Act of 1958, the Technicians' Certification Authority prescribes courses and syllabuses and conducts examinations for a number of occupational groups: engineering technicians and draftsmen, building, chemical, and plant-biology technicians, and so on. Whether such studies be regarded as extensions of secondary education or as tertiary studies, there has in recent years been a strong development at the tertiary level in the creation of the Central Institute of Technology, which now includes senior schools such as the one of pharmacy. That such developments have not transpired earlier is because the New Zealand economy is not highly industrialized, so that apprenticeship training and the preparation of technicians have tended to be a no man's land uncoordinated within any over-all plan. It has been the determination to remove trade training from the secondary stage in favor of general education and prevocational studies, which has left apprenticeship training an outrider to the national system. Burgeoning industrial development is forcing upon it a pattern of further integration.

Since 1961 a Certificate of Education has been granted to those candidates who, though not successful in qualifying for School Certificate, perform creditably in some subjects of the examination. It certifies three years' post-primary education and indicates the degree of success in each subject under four grades. This proliferation of certificates at the secondary stage takes its rise from the wide range of abilities and interests of the universal intake and in the desire to provide a variety of qualifications which will leave no major group of youth unserved.

Although the sexes are about evenly represented in New Zealand

114

schools, they are quite disproportionately involved in higher education. A larger number of girls leave secondary school at the statutory release-age of fifteen years, and of those who remain to qualify for higher school certificate or university entrance (10 per cent as compared with 20 per cent of boys) dropout reduces female students at the universities to only one-quarter of the total enrolments. Analysis of the destinations of school-leavers reveals that 7 per cent go to teachers' colleges, and only 3 per cent enrol at universities.

This raises the sociological question whether contemplated employment molds the type and extent of female education, or the reverse. The post-primary elective courses taken by girls suggest that the former is more the case, with the inference that these feminine fugitives from learning do not find sufficient attraction in higher education to offset the high wages and salaries generally available in a society rejoicing in overemployment. For example, stenographers and skilled female bookkeepers or machine operators command some of the highest salaries in the world of the nonprofessional woman and 30 per cent of school girls follow a commercial course.

New Zealand honors the philosophy that every child, regardless of sex, should receive the same broad general education, and that girls ought not to be constrained into school courses that commit too many too early to nonintellectual roles for women. But the actualities demonstrate that feminine emancipation in New Zealand means earning capacity rather than educational advancement, and girls themselves, or their parents, or the community at large tacitly regard higher education for females as being of considerably less importance than for males. This role-expectation appears to be a consequence of a society which offers too narrow a range of employment opportunities for professional women, is reluctant to honor the principle of equal pay, is distinctly cool toward the service of women on juries or as justices of the peace, and is quite unready to send to Parliament a due proportion of educated women.

Primary-school teaching is one sphere in which women take their due part (perhaps half the total number, whereas in most other countries women teachers form the great majority); but it falls to 36 per cent in secondary schools, 34 per cent in teachers' colleges, and 10 per cent in the universities (chiefly in junior positions). This statistical fade reveals a distortion of national educational purpose and conspires against the fuller development of the other half of the human capital.

Yet coeducation exists at all stages of the national system. All public primary and Maori schools, all intermediate schools, and some private schools teach boys and girls together. At post-primary level four-fifths of state schools are coeducational, and single-sex institutions are chiefly private. At the teachers' colleges and universities there is, of course, no segregation of the sexes. Some educators are of the opinion that the education of girls in New Zealand will not improve in duration and depth until to the existing advantages of coeducation—pooled teaching resources and greater sociality—are added firm expectation of parity in achievement between the sexes and firmer prescription of the academic courses which best serve the joint intellectual adventure.

New Zealand affords the rare spectacle of a European community which confers more equality of educational opportunity upon its 8 per cent racial minority than the Maori people are prepared to accept. It is a matter of history that native schools and widespread Maori literacy preceded any provision for the education of the British settlers, an advantage largely lost during the Maori Wars of the 1860's, which could have but one ending—defeat of the hostile tribes, the humiliation and demoralization of a proud and noble people, and lingering mutual resentments in which the common denominator was the question of title to lands. But from that melancholy period emerged the social conscience which subsequently sought expiation in more enlightened policies of legislative protection for a race that faced extinction. As an unthreatened majority, the Europeans could increasingly afford to be both liberal-minded and financially generous to the displaced Maori, for whom in any case an estimated four million acres remain in occupation or trust and to whose interests governmental solicitude directs itself with particular sensitivity.

In what the nation generally regards as the only equitable solution of race relations, the Maori people have been offered progressive integration through full equality before the law, equal access to the common schools or to special Maori schools of their own choice, and higher education on terms that are more liberal than those available to European youth. In this century a small number of Maori leaders have taken full advantage of these provisions and found their place with friendly acceptance in national life. In the political sphere they have become ministers of state who have earned the accolade of knighthood, and a few Maori are to be found in the learned professions. But the policy of educational integration has been widely suspect among the native people as meaning assimilation and extinction of their own traditions. The *pakeha* community can only regard this as a quarrel between the Maori and civilization itself, and no longer feels a sense of guilt in confrontation with arrested development which is so largely of Maori choice. In short, despite the persistent efforts of academic meliorists to indict the European community, the Maori himself is too generally an unwilling partner in the education enterprise, and therefore a reluctant contributor to national progress, rather than its victim.

All this seems to be the more reproachable because the Maori has always been regarded by anthropologists as among the superior aboriginals of the Pacific littoral, and psychologists have found no great gulf between the races in respect to intelligence, character, physical qualities, or social potential. Sociologists, however, document a marked difference in attitude toward the acquisitive society. The Maori is not notably ambitious, shares few of the normal Western drives and motivations toward acquisition of goods, and despite considerable urbanization and ample employment opportunities, declines to become an organization man. In this there may be a sound value system, but it is difficult to see how the noble savage can withstand the synergic pattern of human history or remain aloof from the forces of social development in our time and place. The point of immediate reference is the indifference of the Maori people to the higher education which is freely available to them and which would be the natural corrective to so many of the disabilities under which they live and labor. New Zealand has simply found it impossible to solve biracial problems by legislation or by proffered educational opportunity.

Every New Zealander who desires due place must subject himself to the disciplines of education, sustained work habits, and social adaptation. It is neither desirable nor possible to grant the Maori miraculous exemption from these exactions; yet not a little of the public discussion of the problem of acculturation proceeds upon this unrealistic expectation. It is no tribute to the quality of the native race to argue that some different basis of attainment ought to be devised for it. As the Currie Commission observed, "The ultimate future of Maori culture and language lies not with the intervening European, nor with institutions such as the school, but entirely with the Maori himself, in the Maori home and the habits of the Maori family."

Nevertheless, the stubborn fact remains that since the Maori people will not or can not solve their own problems by the means provided, the emphasis upon greater inducements to education grows more insistent. The Maori Education Foundation, established in 1960, claims that all needs for special educational facilities for the native race would disappear if the lack of all-round intellectual growth in the Maori child's early years could be overcome. Then he would commence school on equal terms of mental development and enter upon full subsequent educational opportunity. It is of course in the preschool years that he acquires his first concepts of language under familial conditions very different from those of his European counterpart. He tends to master neither his own nor the English language, a default which dogs him for the rest of his life. All authorities seem to be agreed that extended preschool education must be provided through Maori kindergartens, play centers, and nursery classes attached to primary schools. The first of these relies on active parental interest, the second on active parental participation; and it is precisely this identification of Maori families with the education of their children which is so generally lacking.

There is no imposed segregation in national education, and over 70 per cent of Maori children do in fact attend the public primary schools, 20 per cent the special Maori schools in rural regions, and 6 per cent the registered private schools. The Maori language is taught in all Maori district high schools, but these enrol only about two thousand pupils. It is not an exact language, lacks a substantial literature, is retained chiefly for sentimental reasons, and can not serve the communications of the scientific age. Yet it has been admitted as a subject for both School Certificate and university entrance, and may be offered as a degree unit in at least two universities. The language of instruction in Maori schools is English, but their cultural background is acknowledged in the teaching of native arts and crafts, songs, legends, and history. Many Maori schools are so well equipped as to function as community centers, with model cottages, laundries, woodwork and cookery rooms. Although there is more liberal scholarship aid per capita for Maori than for non-Maori pupils, the statistics show no commensurate result.

Over 90 per cent of all Maori youth receive some secondary education, but whereas one in 185 Europeans is a university student, the Maori statistic is one in 1,540. Yet 60 per cent of the Maori people are under the age of twenty-one years as compared with 40 per cent for non-Maori. This is the acculturation stress in the contemporary Maori community. It is because the Maori is going nowhere in particular, not even forward into his own educational development, that his racial inertia is not correctable by paternalism in educational and social provision.

Perhaps the most promising corrective to the apparent stalemate in Maori educational development lies in the fact that over a thousand Maori have been trained for the teaching services in a thrust for more fundamental means of preserving racial identity whilst augmenting the woefully scant numbers who desire to correct the pattern-gravitation of their people into unskilled or semiskilled occupations. That there remain areas of problem rather than areas of principle is significant and offers grounds for optimism. Where there are no legal barriers and few antipathies, increased educational effort from preschool years through university remains the hope of the Maori race.

Since prejudice cannot be removed by legislation, the only effective means of eliminating it is through education in the broader sense of the term; and it is precisely in his failure to respond to

119

the invitation to learning that the Maori defaults from the effort which would undoubtedly remove many of his admitted social disabilities. There is in New Zealand no such gross problem as is manifest in the United States with its agonized civil rights programs; in South African *apartheid* with its enforced segregation and denial of human rights to the colored majority; in Canada with its acerbic inter-European racial hostility; in Britain with its violent episodes involving colored immigrants; or in Australia with its intractable problem of an unassimilable aboriginal racial remnant. To make such comparisons is not to adopt some pharisaical pose; it is merely to state a factual situation which seems to be as egalitarian and enlightened as may be found in this imperfect world.

In New Zealand the term "special education" does not refer to particular provision for the highly gifted, but rather to the kind of schooling found necessary for children with marked physical, mental, or educational disabilities. Nowhere is the prevailing egalitarianism more evident than in this sentimental order of values whereby New Zealand has long entertained the heresy that the gifted teach themselves. This dubious doctrine has led to considerable neglect of natural elites and the denial of justice to those whose particular giftedness merits special cultivation because it accelerates the progress of society.

Apart from the many services instituted during the past twenty years, some special schools and classes arose in the previous century. The first school for the deaf was founded in 1880, a school linked with the New Zealand Institute for the Blind. The first special classes for backward children were set up towards the end of the First World War, hospital classes under the control of education boards originated in 1919, and the schools at health camps were instituted in the mid-thirties. Only where it is beyond the capacity of the ordinary school to care effectively for a handicapped child is a separate school provided. And even where the handicap is severe the service remains under the Ministry of Education. Therefore children classified in New Zealand as "intellectually handicapped" (those who are moderately subnormal in mentality in terms of the World Health Report on mentally subnormal children) attend occupation centers conducted by local education boards and receive their schooling under common auspices. Only one per cent of the total school enrolment is receiving special education at public primary schools by reason of defective vision, hearing, speech, physique, intellect, or emotional relationships.

In England there has been the contrary tendency to segregate such children, often under the control of the health rather than the educational authorities; but in New Zealand many retarded pupils of "mildly subnormal" level who are reasonably well adjusted and make due progress are quite deliberately retained in regular classes for normal social relations and group development. All this requires particular teacher preparation in catering for individual differences among children. If there is one chief theme in New Zealand teacher training for the primary service it is child study, analysis of abilities and disabilities, and methodology suited to this span of interest and attainment.

The State Psychological Service supports both home and school; it recruits psychologists from trained teachers with the standard academic requirement of a master's degree in education or psychology. A psychological examination is one of the requirements for admission to special classes for mentally backward children, occupational centers for the intellectually handicapped, cerebral palsy schools, remedial reading clinics, classes for the partially sighted, and schools and classes for the deaf. It is also a chief means for determining the individual educational needs of these "walking wounded."

Educable rurally domiciled children are often enrolled in the Correspondence School; some are treated in the residential units, and all receive guidance and encouragement from visiting teachers.

Throughout the past ninety years the education of deaf children has been confined almost exclusively to special schools for the deaf, of which the majority of members have been boarders. The reasons for this unusual degree of segregation arise partly from history, partly from geography, and partly from the inherent difficulty of teaching deaf children.

The Foundation for the Blind is the controlling authority of the national School for the Blind, but the full cost of the education of the children is met by the Department of Education. No public charity receives greater public financial support than the annual Braille Week conducted by the Foundation for the continued expansion of its residential units and their amenities.

In its operation of these special services, the Department of Education cooperates closely with voluntary agencies and boards, the Children's Health Camps Federation, the Foundation for the Blind, the League for the Hard-of-Hearing, and the state Departments of Health and of Justice. The extension of such services to smaller towns and rural areas, the expanding school constituency, and increased concern for maladjusted pupils are forces requiring increased professional oversight and teacher specialization throughout this area of personal handicaps.

It is New Zealand's claim to have equalized educational provision and opportunity as between rural and urban children more closely than most other countries. This has been achieved by the consolidation of smaller rural schools, the development of larger district schools with comparable equipment and specialized teaching, free transport services, and boarding allowances for those pupils required to live away from their home. The public service through development of free transport services is indicated by the fact that some 18 per cent of the total school constituency now receive this form of assistance, chiefly through bus services operated by the Department of Education itself or under contract to education boards. In more remote areas where there is no organized public transport, grants are made by the Department to parents for the conveyance of their children to school by car. There are even a few residual cases where horseback allowance is still payable!

Yet another facet of national education for which New Zealand has some claim to distinction is its Correspondence School, which for over forty years has given tuition to children and youth in rural areas and those unable regularly to attend school by reason of protracted illness or other causes. The broad syllabus of both primary and secondary stages is handled by correspondence lessons, together with certain specialties available in the public schools. A corporate spirit among these isolated pupils is encouraged by the Correspondence School badge and uniform, daily radio lessons,

122

club activities, a printed magazine, exhibitions of creative work, and Parent Association projects. Itinerant teachers visit pupils in their homes during the first term of each school year, and resident teachers also offer periodic visitation. In addition, residential schools are conducted each year for correspondence pupils, providing further group activities and intensive tutorial assistance in subjects not well served by correspondence tuition. Part-time enrolments in the Correspondence School include pupils of post-primary schools seeking specialized instruction which their own schools may not provide; and at tertiary levels, youths in employment, teachers undergoing in-service training, inmates of Department of Justice institutions, officers of government departments, and others unable to attend organized evening classes.

For some thirty years the state system has operated centers for vocational guidance throughout the country, serving the regional school networks in both the choice of school courses and careers. Vocational guidance officers in the main population areas act in conjunction with headmasters and careers advisers in the schools, and with cooperating industrial and commercial organizations in what is essentially an advisory service.

Professor Albert Morris has reported that New Zealand has one of the world's lowest recorded rates of youthful delinquency, though it is well enough known that delinquency statistics can provide only the roughest index of such morbidity. For example, the records of appearance before the juvenile courts do not register the cases dismissed, withdrawn, or discharged; the tables do not distinguish between serious offences and venial breaches of traffic and other minor regulations; and recidivism tends further to obfuscate the total pattern. In short, official statistics are prone to cloak a situation which may be more, or less, serious than they indicate. With these provisos, it can be said that the incidence of court appearances for various types of offences appears to have remained relatively stable in New Zealand over the past twenty-five years. The prevention of juvenile misbehavior is an integral part of school aims and receives constant and positive support in their character-training and moral-education. New Zealand's reliance upon ethical secularism in the public schools rather than upon religious instruction by an approved syllabus requires particular attention to the general school environment, atmosphere, and *esprit de corps*. That these factors are effective is suggested by the fact that even in the adolescent years when the delinquency rate is higher than at other times, the proportion of young New Zealanders in trouble with the juvenile courts is somewhere between one and two per cent of the age group. Although the youth population is about evenly divided between the sexes, delinquent boys outnumber delinquent girls by about ten to one, and the rate for Maori offenders is some three-and-a-half times as great as that for Europeans and includes a higher proportion of repeat-offenders.

In New Zealand the general pattern is for delinquency to appear after school years, so that, as the Currie Commission concluded, the public school system appears to be a positive agency of control and possibly of prevention. In the familiar world pattern it is an urban rather than a rural problem, but in New Zealand it remains relatively static rather than exacerbating, chiefly because of the relatively stable context of home and school. Statistics maintained from 1934 onward by the Child Welfare Division of the Department of Education indicate that consistently throughout these many years over 99 per cent of the age group from seven to seventeen years were uninvolved in any detected offence which involved a court appearance. That the New Zealand welfare services are so universal and so closely administered tends to render undetected delinquency relatively rare.

Since 1959, New Zealand has had a juvenile crime prevention section of the police force, charged with the detection of incipient misconduct; but here again close cooperation with child welfare officers of the Department of Education ensures that less serious offenders are dealt with apart from court action. No newspaper is permitted to publish the names of children appearing before the children's courts, nor to detail proceedings likely to identify the child. Children requiring institutional care and presenting behavioral or personality problems beyond the management of most ordinary foster parents are entrusted to "family homes," which are private houses, owned by the Child Welfare Division and conducted by selected married couples. But New Zealand educators are firmly persuaded that the normal classroom life of the school affords the most natural environment for all save the most grievously handicapped to grow into adaptation and acceptance among their fellows.

In 1962 the long-standing system of financial assistance for students entering upon a university course was further liberalized into a three-fold pattern of tuition bursaries, tuition-and-allowances bursaries, and bursaries for those essaying a master's degree. In general, the first two types of financial aid are tenable for a period not exceeding five years, though they may be extended for an additional year under special circumstances. Master's bursaries are tenable for one year only. They are tenable for full-time study in any recognized course at a university. Where the student is obliged to live away from home in order to attend university, he may also qualify for a boarding allowance.

When it is remembered that all these awards are by qualifying and not by competition, it is clear that New Zealand makes higher education available on most generous terms: over half of all university students receive free tuition. But all bursaries require the holder to pass a prescribed minimum of examinations; a bursary suspended for failure in examinations can be resumed only after the student establishes the requisite performance, and failure in two successive years leads to cancellation of the award. What might otherwise be treated as a student bonanza is thus responsibly administered on a fair basis of continuing accomplishment. Few if any other countries provide so amply for university education at public charge.

Since 1944 a system of partial accrediting for entry to university studies has been in uneasy operation as a compromise between the equally unsatisfactory alternatives of complete reliance upon either external or internal examination. Certain approved secondary schools may accredit their pupils for matriculation after satisfactory completion of a four-year course of studies; those not so accredited may sit the external examination conducted by the Universities Entrance Board, which represents the universities, the secondary schools, and the Department of Education. The obvious vagaries of this dual system of entry are generally accepted as a lesser evil than the old procedure by which the external matriculation examination held in thrall both secondary curriculum and general educational objectives. Nor does research indicate that the principle of accrediting generally admits to the universities those who would be excluded by sole reliance upon external examination.

Only about 10 per cent of secondary-school graduates proceed to matriculate at the universities, and less than half this number obtain a first degree within three to five years. Few more than half of the university enrolments are full-time scholars, a disbalance relict of the earlier exclusiveness of higher education. Despite all financial assistance to full-time studies and a shortage of graduates in most disciplines, the high wage-structure continues to tempt students to the pursuit of the best of both worlds. This tacit coercion of university purpose is a prime example of the persistence of social practices long after need for and justification of them has been removed. Defenders of this typical New Zealand tradition seem to be untroubled by the law of diminishing returns and quote quite impressive statistics to show that both part-timers and late-arrivers not uncommonly bring to their studies a stronger motivation and greater maturity which yield more enduring results from their degree studies.

During the 1960's the university system has evolved from the original foundation of the federal University of New Zealand with constituent regional colleges, into a congeries of separate and autonomous universities, six in number, and enjoying parity of status and esteem. In general they are alike in respect to faculties of arts, science, law, music, and commerce, differing in their special national schools allocated specifically to avoid wasteful duplication. There were in 1966 single national schools of medicine, dentistry, architecture, veterinary science, home science, physical education, and public administration and social science; two national schools of fine arts and of agricultural science; and there was a second medical school in the planning stage. University finance from the central exchequer is provided in quinquennial grants to each institution, the University Grants Committee instituted by an Act of 1960 being advisor to the government regarding the parliamentary

126

appropriations for these purposes. Massive building and expansion programs are in process in all university centers, the broad pattern of which was recommended by the 1959 Committee on New Zealand Universities under the chairmanship of Sir David Hughes Parry of the University of London.

By the Universities Act of 1961 a new Universities Entrance Board was set up to maintain common education standards for admission to the universities. The chief responsibility of its Curriculum Committee is to maintain parity of academic standards and to facilitate the transfer of students between universities. In final examinations for both first and higher degrees, the long-established practice of mutual assessment of results continues between universities.

Upwards of eight thousand students are in full-time training at the nine teachers' colleges. More than a quarter of this enrolment, while attached to the colleges, were attending university as full-time students preparing for the teaching service. About three-quarters of the remainder were training for primary teaching. Nearly all students preparing for the post-primary service are university graduates. For the past thirty years the normal course of training for primary teachers has been two years at a teachers' college followed by a year as a probationary assistant attached to a public school. Third-year studentships, entitling selected trainees to an extra year's study in lieu of the probationary year, have been available to those desiring to specialize in certain fields, and a limited number have been permitted to spend most of the third year of training on full-time university studies. But throughout that third of a century New Zealand has been painfully aware of the deficiencies of its teacher preparation programs, and successive Commissions and Consultative Committees have been unanimous in recommending closer relations between teachers' colleges and the universities, with courses of greater duration and depth for all teachers in training, both primary and secondary. The government, committed in principle to extending the course for primary teachers to three years, set up a National Advisory Council on the Training of Teachers, which in 1964 issued its first two reports, shortening the time scale recommended by the Commission on

Education in 1962 and indicating that the first teachers' colleges in the conversion sequence might be operating the three-year course in 1966. This has now been instituted. Thereafter, further colleges are sequentially to effect the program; by 1970 the transition should be complete, with two additional teachers' colleges planned for that date.

Currently the universities have been invited by the University Grants Committee to submit proposals for instituting either Institutes or Schools of Education which may integrate teachers' colleges with universities in joint conduct of teacher preparation. It has long been New Zealand's experience that even with the most generous financial assistance to teacher trainees the nation suffers from a chronic shortage of teachers, the necessity to dilute entry qualifications, and inability to achieve fully professional quality.

The centralizing tendency in New Zealand education has led to the full integration of adult education within the orbit of the universities, which have recently been made responsible for conducting this activity in a two-tiered system of internal and external studies financed largely from public funds nominated for this purpose by the University Grants Committee. What had hitherto been an autonomous educational service under regional councils of adult education has thus become a university extension service. The new Act of 1963 represented a complete reversal of former policy. Both the Education Amendment Act of 1938 and its revision in 1947 reflected the view that the objections to university control were so many and so substantial as to require independent direction of adult education. There had long been representation for the universities on the regional councils of adult education, but the nature and content of studies differed so markedly as to yield little concert of purpose. The new policy of university extension services is to raise existing adult courses to more mature standards and to institute new studies suited to university sponsorship. It will take some years to reshape the existing pattern of adult education and to establish the departments of university extension on terms of parity with other departments in the crucial matter of finances.

It seems clear that under university auspices, adult education will move toward studies of higher intellectual content, retaining cer-

128

tain courses in strong public demand, but delegating the less-academic interests to different agencies. The need for refresher courses to refurbish the professional knowledge of graduates seeking employment can well be met by university extension work, and many professional organizations are already doing this sort of thing on their own behalf. Not a little of this effort must duplicate university lectures and be economically wasteful. This shift of emphasis bespeaks a changing concept of adult education from the earlier role of the Workers' Education Association as an agency of social reform or as a leisure activity with vague cultural overtones. The purpose appears now to be to make it increasingly a professional branch of higher education. Once again the educational pattern reflects the incidence of the social service state upon its institutional forms. With the disappearance of the underprivileged groups and the educationally deprived adult seeking second-chance instruction, the role of the university is being stressed in further education.

It is true that in an age of mass communication the conventional packaged courses and discussion material of adult education have tended to fall out of public favor. The Community Arts Service as promoter of country tours by musical groups and art exhibitions is less needed, for other agencies have gradually taken over this entrepreneurial role. But the friends of adult education will know the continuing value and importance of resident rural tutors in promoting local group activities in music, drama, arts and crafts, and home science. In the centripetal tendency of New Zealand education there is danger to the role of voluntary association in community life, so that what is needed is not some grandiloquent program of academic studies so much as streamlined, modernized adult courses. It would certainly be precipitate to dismiss indiscriminately the established pattern of popular contributions from library services, art galleries, technical high schools, and various government departments.

Unless much that is of continuing value is to be lost, the university extension departments must retain the grass-roots relationships they inherit, however they may seek to revivify them by cross-fertilization. The educational needs of countrywomen, for instance,

129

simply cannot be met by formal university lectures; Maori adult education remains at an essentially elementary level of homecraft, housewifery, health and hygiene, and family care; leadership conferences, courses in business management and industrial efficiency must be devised at more practical levels than academic degree courses; and it is by no means clear that university staffs have as yet a lively appreciation of the fuller implications of the differences between their traditional intramural and their new extramural extension responsibilities. The characteristics of university studies are teaching in depth, progressive specialization, and research. The distinctive features of adult education have been consumer-demand, *ad hoc* courses dependent upon response for their continuance, studies in breadth rather than depth, deference to rural interests, and peripatetic instructors. The newer emphasis in New Zealand —formal refresher studies for graduates—will naturally appeal more to the universities since this is basically postgraduate instruction within familiar orbits. The judicious selection and elevation of part-time leisure courses will constitute a real test of the new university extension structure. Whether learner-demand can be conditioned into conformity with university emphases remains to be shown.

The most astonishing default in New Zealand education is the neglect of speech training and basic communication in the mother tongue as a cultural skill which so largely determines the usefulness of most other qualifications. Nor in the universities does speech education receive any attention comparable to that of the American pattern wherein there are academic professors of speech, full departments of communication, and provision for majoring in speech for degrees. New Zealand assumes that everybody save the grossly handicapped acquires all necessary skills in English by the simple process of youthful imitation. In teachers' colleges something is done to set standards in spoken English; there are lectures in phonetics, and students may participate in drama, oral interpretation, debating, and public speaking.

In New Zealand any fine effusion of a fine mind stands out like a pretty deed in a dark world, an outward and audible sign of an inner and cultural grace. The schools fall residuary legatees by default of the traditional guardians and exemplars of good speech; the Law and Church set themselves no formal standards of diction; the mass media of communication are more vulgarian than cultural influences; and in politics good manners in speaking are rare. One suspects that in deference to the gospel of commonalty, politicians who could speak well choose to speak badly as a sort of protective coloration, so that they might not be thought to set themselves above their natural equals. If public education is to provide any corrective to this national deficiency it will require to formulate programs of speech education consonant with its own needs and taught progressively throughout the schools, teachers' colleges, and universities. That such a proposal may well seem to most New Zealanders to be derisory is the measure of backwardness in a community where the average vocabulary is fewer than five thousand words, triteness is the linguistic vice, and lip-lazy lockjawed speech is normal even among those whose profession is education.

To the traditional basics of literacy and numeracy, New Zealand has yet to add fluency as a *sine qua non* of an indigenous culture.

BIBLIOGRAPHY

Beaglehole, J. C. *The University of New Zealand.* Wellington, 1937.
Condliffe, J. B. *The Welfare State in New Zealand.* Wellington, 1959.
Ewing, J. L. *Origins of the Primary School Curriculum.* Wellington, 1960.
Melvin, Kenneth. *New Zealand: The Small Utopia.* Wellington, 1962.
Murdoch, J. H. *The High Schools of New Zealand.* Wellington, 1943.
Nichol, J. *The Technical Schools of New Zealand.* Wellington, 1940.
Parkyn, G. W., ed. *The Administration of Education in New Zealand.* Wellington, 1954.
Thompson, A. B. *Adult Education in New Zealand.* Wellington, 1945.
UNESCO. *Compulsory Education in New Zealand.* Paris, 1952.
——. *Secondary Education in New Zealand.* Paris, 1962.
Watson, John. *Intermediate Schooling in New Zealand.* Wellington, 1964.
Webb, Leicester. *The Control of Education in New Zealand.* Wellington, 1937.

SCIENCE

R. D. BATT

IN the fourteenth century the Maori came to New Zealand to settle, and some of their skills of that time could now be included in descriptions of the sciences of navigation, agriculture, and medicine. Not one, but several, canoes made the long voyages across the Pacific from embarkation points which seem likely to have been at least twelve hundred miles from New Zealand. The guiding of the canoes by the priests has been described as purposive navigation, but no details of their navigating methods have survived in the traditional narratives of the Maori. Elsdon Best has claimed that the achievements of the Maori as deep-sea voyagers, explorers, and colonizers formed a remarkable and unique feature of their history, and Sir Peter Buck has reminded us that the "Coming of the Fleet" took place approximately 150 years before Columbus, using a compass, crossed the Atlantic to the West Indies.

The Maori were agriculturalists; their settlements in New Zealand flourished largely because the colonizers introduced food plants, including the kumara (sweet potato), the taro, and the yam. Much of their time was taken up with planting, weeding, and storing their crops, and Keith Sinclair has noted that they were able to grow their crops below the forty-fourth parallel, which was nearer to the South Pole than any other cultivation in pre-Columbian times. An important food was the berry of the karaka tree (*Corynocarpus laevigata*), which was said to have been brought to New Zealand by the chief Turi in the canoe *Aotea* about A.D. 1350. Before the berries could be used as food, a poison (β-nitropropionic acid) had to be removed. One can only speculate as to how the Maori began the practice of leaching the poison from the berries by storing them in flax baskets suspended in water.

It is claimed by Elsdon Best that the Maori had no knowledge of medical treatments, because the natives believed that sickness and disease were caused by evil spirits, but in a recent article on New Zealand medicinal plants, Brooker and Cooper state that Captain Cook and other early European visitors to New Zealand observed the use of plants for medicinal purposes by the Maori. Over 120 New Zealand plants have been described as effective for conditions ranging from headaches to "boils, burns, cuts, and pains in general."

Although New Zealand was discovered in 1642 by Abel Tasman, European interest in the country dates from the voyages of Captain Cook, who first sighted the new land in 1769. Europeans were first left in New Zealand, as members of a sealing party, in 1792, and although a mission was established as early as 1814, the first body of immigrants with a definite scheme of colonization did not arrive in Port Nicholson until 1840, to found the town of Wellington.

The interest of European scientists in the country began with the visit of the noted botanist Sir Joseph Banks, who accompanied Captain Cook on his first voyage. During 1769, Captain Cook spent six months exploring the New Zealand coastline, allowing ample opportunities for Sir Joseph Banks and a fellow scientist, Daniel Solander, to collect specimens of New Zealand plants. Banks considered that the flora lacked variety, but the unique nature of the plants compensated the scientists, and very few of the large collection of species described by Banks had been reported elsewhere. The material taken back to England by the scientists would have formed the basis of a valuable description of the New Zealand flora, but it was left to later visitors to publish details of the plant life in the colony. Over a century later, Sir Joseph Hooker undertook to edit Sir Joseph Banks's journal of Captain Cook's first voyage around the world. Working from a transcript of the journal in the British Museum, Hooker published it in 1896.

Sir Joseph Hooker had himself visited New Zealand in 1841 with an expedition on the way to Antarctica. During a three-month stay at the Bay of Islands in the northernmost part of the country, he made many excursions into the countryside with William Colenso, a missionary-printer, who for sixty-five years studiously pursued his interests in zoology, botany, and ethnology in New Zealand. After Hooker's return to England, Colenso continued to send him botanical material which eventually formed the basis of his *Handbook of New Zealand Flora* (1864–1867), a comprehensive dictionary of New Zealand plants. Hooker retained a remarkable interest in the colony and subsequently had a considerable influence on its scientific developments. It has been suggested that in later years he became a sort of oracle to men like Haast, Hector, and Hutton: when they were in trouble or despondent because the Government would not build a museum or threatened to reduce the grant to the New Zealand Institute, he could always be relied upon to cheer them up with good advice and occasionally his influence would help to make things a little more satisfactory.

After his return to England, he became assistant director at Kew Gardens, and in 1865 succeeded his father, Sir William Hooker, as director, a position he held for twenty years. He was a close friend of Darwin, who had also visited New Zealand briefly in 1835 during the voyage of the *Beagle*.

The first professional scientist to work in New Zealand was Dr. Ernst Dieffenbach, who had been selected by the directors of the New Zealand Company in 1836 as surgeon and naturalist of the *Tory* expedition. He had a broad scientific background, and his *Travels in New Zealand*, published in 1843, may be considered rightly as the first scientific description of New Zealand. The book included his experiences as a scientist and explorer in a country where there had been very little European influence on the Polynesian community. After Dieffenbach's departure in 1841, practically no scientific activity occurred in the colony for the next twenty years. I. D. Dick, in *Science in New Zealand,* has stated that "if the prospects of wealth from gold and coal had not become so entrancing towards the end of the fifties and in the early sixties, it is quite likely that New Zealand would have been spared the expense of employing scientists until the turn of the century."

Gold was discovered in 1842 at Massacre Bay, Nelson, by an exploring party under Captain Wakefield, but the find attracted little attention at the time. In 1852 gold was found at Coromandel and in Otago, and later finds were made elsewhere. However, it was not until large alluvial deposits of gold were discovered in the South Island in 1861 that gold-mining led to a tremendous influx of population and a subsequent alteration in the economic structure of the country. Although the sheep population had been increasing rapidly during the 1850's, wool was displaced by gold as the most valuable export during the 1860's. The phase during which gold production was the colony's major industry lasted for approximately ten years, and it is not surprising that New Zealand science during this period centered on geology.

In 1858 Dr. Ferdinand Hochstetter arrived in Auckland as geologist on the Austrian frigate *Novara,* and the commodore acceded to a request by the Auckland Provincial Government that Dr. Hochstetter might undertake geological surveys of the country, especially in the Auckland province. In all, Hochstetter remained in the colony for nine months, and with a newly acquired friend, Julius Haast, he surveyed the thermal regions, Lake Taupo, and parts of the Waikato. He also examined the Nelson area, in the South Island, the work in this island being considerably extended by Haast in later years. In 1867, Hochstetter, then a professor in Vienna, published the results of his work in *New Zealand: Its Physical Geography, Geology, and Natural History.*

Hochstetter's work laid the foundations for subsequent extensive studies by Haast, Hector, and Hutton, three geologists who dominated the scientific scene in New Zealand during the latter part of the nineteenth century. In 1860, Haast was appointed geologist to the provincial government in Canterbury. Hector was appointed in 1861 to a similar position in Otago, where he remained until he became director of the newly established New Zealand Geological Survey in 1865. Hutton was appointed geologist to the Otago Provincial Government in 1873. The work and achievements of these remarkable men have been described by Jenkinson, who considered it a "miracle" that three such outstanding scientists were available in the new colony at the time that the provincial and central governments recognized the necessity for instituting scientific exploration and survey. All three scientists were elected fellows of the Royal Society, and knighthoods were conferred on Haast and Hector.

The period of provincial government in New Zealand ended in 1875. By this date there were an impressive number of national scientific institutions, including the Geological Survey, Colonial (later Dominion) Museum, Colonial (Dominion) Laboratory, Colonial (Dominion) Observatory, the New Zealand Institute (later the Royal Society of New Zealand), and the University of New Zealand, with its two constituent colleges in Canterbury and Otago. Each of the four metropolitan centers already had a museum.

The establishment of the Geological Survey in Wellington, under the direction of Hector, led to a concentration of scientific work in the capital city. The potential extent and value of the natural resources of New Zealand had been demonstrated at the New Zealand Exhibition of 1864–1865. Following the recommendation of the commissioners of the exhibition that a full survey of the colony's resources should be undertaken, the government established the Colonial Museum and Colonial Laboratory in Wellington. In addition to supervising the work of the Geological Survey, Hector took over the direction of these new institutions and later accepted responsibility for the Meteorological Office. When the New Zealand Institute was established in 1867, Hector added the office of manager to his list of duties and remained editor of the *Transactions* of the Institute for the succeeding thirty-five years.

In 1885 he was elected chancellor of the University of New Zealand.

In the early years the work of the Dominion Laboratory was virtually the work of one man, William Skey, an analytical chemist who moved from Dunedin to Wellington with Hector in 1865. Until 1896, Skey was the only full-time chemist employed by the New Zealand government. Even fifty years after the establishment of the laboratory, despite a rapid increase in scientific interest in the colony, its total staff was only fourteen.

Many of the industries now established in New Zealand were first considered by the laboratory staff in the latter part of the last century. For instance, in the laboratory records for 1868 is the following note: "Inquiries have been addressed to the Department as to the most favourable localities for the construction of salt works; among other information obtained in reply was the composition of the water adjacent to New Zealand as compared with the sea in the Northern Hemisphere." The salt industry, based on evaporation by dry winds, was established eventually in 1948, and by 1965 it was producing approximately 50 per cent of the country's annual salt requirement.

In 1870 the Colonial Laboratory reported analyses of cast iron produced from iron sand in Taranaki. During later years many attempts were made to utilize the iron sands profitably for iron and steel production, and investigations were directed particularly towards problems associated with the comparatively high titanium content of the sands. Within the last few years, the establishment of an economically feasible steel industry has moved a step nearer realization, and it is now likely that this will become an important New Zealand industry within the next decade.

During the latter part of the nineteenth century, while scientific effort centered on geological surveys and the possible exploitation of the country's natural resources, the economy of the country was becoming increasingly dependent on primary production. Since the decline of gold production in the early 1870's, the major exports from New Zealand have been pastoral products, and the expansion of the sciences has been regulated by the demand for servicing and research in the primary industries. B. L. Evans, who has written a history of farming in New Zealand, has divided the growth of the pastoral industries into four well-defined periods. The first is from the start of colonization until the introduction of refrigeration in 1882; the second from the start of refrigeration until 1914; the third from 1914 until 1936; and the fourth from 1936 to the present. Each period has been characterized by some feature new to farming or by some change in agricultural organization. During the 1840's and 1850's farming was carried out only to meet home requirements, but wool and grain were exported from 1860 and remained the main farm exports until the introduction of refrigeration.

The first shipment of a refrigerated cargo left New Zealand in the *Dunedin* in 1882, and so began the rapid growth of the frozen-meat industry. Cereal cropping remained important during this period, and with the increase in the number of dairy cattle there was a steady development of the dairy industry. Sinclair has stated that "between 1896 and 1914 butter production went up nearly 500 per cent and the output of cheese by over 1000 per cent." During this period, too, the foundations were laid of the present system of grassland farming, until according to Evans, "grass had become New Zealand's most important crop." In 1880, Lincoln College was opened to train agriculturalists and in 1892 the government established the Department of Agriculture.

The period from 1914 to 1936 was characterized by two major economic depressions and a brief intervening period of prosperity, during which the rate of land settlement decreased. By 1925 the total area of farmed land in New Zealand was about 43,000,000 acres; in 1960 the total farmland area was estimated at 44,000,000 acres. During the 1914–1936 period, the dairy industry grew, with the Jersey cow as the predominant breed, until dairy products ranked with meat and wool as major exports. Cereal cropping decreased to the point where New Zealand changed from an exporter to an importer of grain.

Problems were arising in agriculture for which answers had not yet been found overseas, and this period marked the introduction and rapid development of scientific servicing and research facilities in New Zealand. The dairy industry was the first to recognize the requirement for New Zealand–based research. This led to the establishment in 1927 of the Dairy Research Institute, which concerned itself with scientific and technical problems encountered in the industry, with investigations into methods for the manufacture of new types of dairy products, and with attempts to find new outlets for these. In the Department of Agriculture, the extension service was developed to make scientific information about farming more readily available, Massey Agricultural College was founded, and the Department of Scientific and Industrial Research was established by the dominion government.

A major problem in the mid-1920's came from the pressure to farm poorer lands, since by this time most of the better land had been occupied. There was an additional problem in the deterioration of pastures and the need developed for scientific research. New institutes, which were established to extend investigations into agricultural problems, included the Soil Bureau and the Grasslands Division, both of the Department of Scientific and Industrial Research. A seed certification scheme for the improvement of pasture plants was introduced, and extensive use of top-dressing of pastures became a feature of New Zealand farming.

The period from 1936 to the present time has been characterized by a continuing and remarkable increase in production. Referring to this, Sinclair has made the following comments:

Since the war (1939–45) there has been an agrarian revolution. Greater mechanisation, better pastures and pasture management, new methods of developing poor land and especially the use of aerial top-dressing on a scale employed nowhere else, have led to a remarkable increase in production. Despite the fact that the farm labour force fell by a sixth during the war—and never recovered—farm production rose thirty-six per cent in the years 1938–1955, a sixty per cent gain in productivity per worker.

In 1951, W. M. Hamilton (later the director-general of the Department of Scientific and Industrial Research) published an excellent article on "Farming in the New Zealand Economy and the Role of Research." This paper referred to the very high productivity per labor-unit in farming in New Zealand, where "the average farm worker produced 50 per cent more than his opposite number in Australia, twice that in Argentina, five times as much as in Britain, and twenty times as much as in Japan." In commenting on this

139

remarkable variation in productivity, Hamilton emphasized that Australia and New Zealand are unique in being the only two countries in the world where farming shows a higher productivity per head than secondary industry. Comparative figures for several countries have been included in Table 1.

Table 1. Comparative productivity in selected countries
for selected years *

Country	Net productivity per head engaged in		
	Primary industry	Secondary industry	Tertiary industry
New Zealand (1934–1935)	2,444	1,490	840
Australia (1925–1934)	1,524	905	800
United States (1937)	661	1,852	2,765
Great Britain (1936)	475	815	1,775
Canada (1925–1934)	618	1,855	1,578
Japan (1934)	120	550	795

* Adapted from Colin Clark, The Conditions of Economic Progress (2d ed.; London, 1956).

These figures are, of course, now approximately thirty years old, but in the interim the level of productivity per head in New Zealand has continued to rise. It may well be asked how New Zealand farmers have become so efficient in production. An explanation, in part, is that the country is endowed with a climate exceptionally favorable to grass growth. In addition, it has been possible to adopt a system of farming which makes the smallest possible demands on labor while achieving a high production level per acre.

Assessing the part science has played in this very high level of production is a difficult task. Although government-sponsored research may be regarded as an investment, it is virtually impossible in most cases to calculate a research dividend. That science has made valuable contributions in New Zealand would not be contested, and the most striking illustrations would undoubtedly be in the fields of trace-element chemistry and biology and in plant breeding.

SCIENCE

New Zealand soils are known to be deficient in a variety of elements, including boron, cobalt, copper, fluorine, iodine, molybdenum, and selenium. The demonstration of cobalt-deficient soils in certain areas of the country led to the development of large areas for highly productive farming. The ruminant disease known as bush-sickness had been studied from the beginning of the century by Bernard Aston, who began this work shortly after his appointment, in 1899, as chemist in the newly established Chemistry Division of the Department of Agriculture. Bush-sickness and similar conditions had been recognized by agriculturalists in isolated areas in various parts of the world, and in particular in Australia, Europe, North America, Africa, and New Zealand. These areas were unsatisfactory for raising sheep and cattle in spite of the growth of ample pasture of satisfactory quality. Ruminants in these areas showed a loss of appetite, emaciation, debility, and progressive anaemia, leading ultimately to death. By contrast, non-ruminants in the same areas remained in good condition. The anaemia suggested an iron deficiency, and in fact, it was shown that plants in these areas were often low in iron content: some iron licks were found to be effective in treating the condition. During the late 1920's and early 1930's, while bush-sickness was being studied in New Zealand, the similar condition of coast-sickness was under investigation in Australia. Almost simultaneously and independently it was shown that cobalt was the missing trace element in the diet. In Australia the work was carried out by Marston and his co-workers and by Filmer and Underwood. In New Zealand the names of Aston, Rigg, Grange, Taylor, Dixon, Askew, and Miss Kidson were prominent in unravelling the cobalt story. The importance of this research work to New Zealand has been stressed on many occasions. Until the late 1930's ruminants did not flourish in the pumice-shower areas of the Rotorua-Taupo district, but after the treatment of the soils in this region with cobalt, the same land in 1963 carried 146,000 beef cattle, 77,000 dairy cattle, and 1,000,000 sheep. The annual export value of stock from this area is now approximately $10,000,000. This spectacular effect of cobalt addition is cited for a severely deficient area of about one million acres. It has now been shown that of the total twenty-one million acres under cultivation in New Zealand, some five million acres would exhibit some level of cobalt deficiency.

Cobalt was first applied as a top-dressing in 1936, and now the condition of bush-sickness is prevented by the use of cobaltized-superphosphate. Before the discovery of cobalt deficiency in the volcanic-ash areas of the central plateau of the North Island, large areas were planted in exotic forests which now form the basis of New Zealand's most recent major industry, timber.

The work on cobalt-deficient soils directed attention to other trace-element deficiencies. Of special significance was the work of Dr. I. Cunningham, director of the Wallaceville Research Station and subsequently the first dean of the Faculty of Veterinary Science established at Massey University in 1963. From a study of unthriftiness in calves raised on reclaimed soils, he found a copper deficiency which could be remedied by top-dressing with bluestone. An extension of this work showed that the ratio of copper to molybdenum in soils influenced plant growth and animal health. Some soils contain a comparatively high level of molybdenum, sufficient to have a toxic effect on stock; in others a shortage of molybdenum results in poor pasture growth. The recognized requirement for a correct balance of these two trace elements has been an important scientific development for the country's agriculture, and the economic consequences of these discoveries are considerable.

Current studies of trace-element deficiencies have shown that extremely small doses of selenium can prevent general ill-thrift of young sheep, lamb deaths, and low fertility in ewes. The selenium-deficiency diseases have been shown to occur in areas where the pastures contain less than one part of the element in fifty million parts of pasture dry matter.

Trace-element studies have been prominent not only in the agricultural and veterinary sciences, but also in medicine and dentistry. In the well-leached soils of New Zealand, iodine occurs in very low concentrations in many areas, particularly in the central plateau of the North Island (approximately the same area as that shown to be low in cobalt), and in the Taranaki and Canterbury provinces. In an early study, W. N. Benson, F.R.S., Sir Charles

Hercus, and C. L. Carter described low levels of iodine in soils; where the iodine content of soils was lowest, the incidence of endemic goiter was highest. In 1925 the incidence figures for goiter in school children were: Auckland, 26 per cent; Wellington, 21 per cent; Canterbury, 56 per cent; and Otago, 27 per cent. At the end of 1924 a law was passed which provided for the addition of one part of iodine to 250,000 parts of table salt. However, by 1934 only 30 per cent of the average daily consumption of salt was iodized, and it was clear that the amount of added iodide was too low to have any appreciable effect on the prevalence of goiter. An increase, recommended in 1939, was made legal, and since 1943 one part of potassium iodide has been added to 20,000 parts of salt. Goiter has now almost completely disappeared in all parts of the Dominion.

Goiter is a very common condition in animals in New Zealand. In addition to the cases due to iodine-deficient soils, it has been found that stock fed on chou moellier and kale, members of the cabbage family, also developed goiter due to the presence of goitrogenic substances in these plants. This work led to the discovery of the thiouracils as effective agents in controlling overactivity of the thyroid gland. The Endocrinology Department at the Otago Medical School has played a distinguished research role in this work and in the general field of thyroid metabolism and disease.

New Zealand soils are also deficient in fluoride. The community shows a high level of dental disease which had been related to this deficiency, and this has prompted recommendations that town water supplies should be fluoridated. Although some municipalities have implemented the recommendations, there are still large sections of the population which have an inadequate intake of fluoride in the diet.

Plant-breeding research in New Zealand has been directed mainly towards improving wheat and pasture plants for the country's conditions. The first significant attempt to produce improved wheat varieties in New Zealand dates back to the work of Dr. Frederick W. Hilgendorf at Lincoln Agricultural College in 1910. In 1928 the Wheat Research Institute was established with a wheat-breeding section at Lincoln College and a cereal laboratory in

Christchurch. Dr. Hilgendorf was the first director and Dr. O. H. Frankel (now Sir Otto Frankel, F.R.S., of the Commonwealth Scientific and Industrial Research Organization in Canberra, Australia) joined the Institute in 1929 as the first plant breeder and geneticist. Dr. Frankel made a major contribution to wheat breeding in New Zealand and in 1950 was appointed director of a reorganized Crop Research Division. He left New Zealand in 1952 after twenty-three years, during which time a large number of wheat varieties had been bred and tested.

One of the first wheat hybrids developed in New Zealand was released in 1921 as Cross 7. This strain was a replacement for Solid Straw Tuscan, and although the yields were similar, Cross 7 produced a flour that removed the need to blend local wheats with imported Canadian wheats. For many years Cross 7 made up about two-thirds of the wheat grown in New Zealand.

In 1957 the annual report of the Department of Scientific and Industrial Research described a new wheat species called Aotea, which had been released to the farmers of the Canterbury and Marlborough districts. This species, which had taken sixteen years to develop, showed an average increase in yield over Cross 7 of 27 per cent. By 1960, Aotea made up 86 per cent of the total wheat production and the change of species had increased the value of the harvest by about one million dollars. Presenting the development in terms of land economy, in 1942 some 8,700,000 bushels of wheat were harvested from 258,000 acres, while in 1960 a harvest of similar size required only 163,000 acres, a saving of 95,000 acres. In a single year, the increased wheat returns covered the total cost of wheat research in New Zealand for thirty years.

Research on wheat has continued. A new mildew-resistant strain named Hilgendorf 1961 was introduced in 1961, and in the 1963–1964 season this wheat accounted for 18 per cent of the national harvest. The annual consumption of wheat in New Zealand is approximately 16,000,000 bushels, of which 9,000,000 were produced locally in the 1963–1964 season.

The breeding of new strains of pasture plants has been a continuing and remarkably successful scientific program in New Zealand.

144

It is difficult to estimate accurately the contribution that improved strains of grasses and clovers have made to pasture production.

In the early years of settlement in the South Island, European grasses and clovers were sown after the land had been plowed. Fire, rather than plow, prepared the land for sowing in the North Island, and for many years hundreds of thousands of acres were burnt and sown year by year. For a time there was remarkable growth, followed after some years of stability by the deterioration of pasture composition. The decay posed a problem for both the farmer and the scientist. A partial solution was found in top-dressing with artificial fertilizer, a practice which increased considerably between the two world wars.

The other main development in the program to stabilize pastures centered on the pasture plants themselves. In a history of grassland research in New Zealand, B. L. Evans referred to Sir Bruce Levy's recognition of the great production potential that could result from plant improvement by breeding. Levy was director of the Plant Research Station of the D.S.I.R., and in 1935, Dr. L. Corkill was appointed to his staff to develop the breeding of pasture plants. In the following years, the plant-breeding work was built up until this became one of the Division's major functions.

In the early 1930's, although attention had been directed by plant breeders to improving both perennial and Italian ryegrass, it became apparent that some intermediate type of grass was required. The Grasslands Division undertook a major program to develop a type of ryegrass that, while having a degree of permanence greater than Italian, yet had a higher palatability than perennial ryegrass. A result of this work was an intermediate type to become known as short-rotation ryegrass. Although the grass was developed primarily for the short duration pastures of the South Island arable lands, its use has been extended, and now it is sown widely through New Zealand in both arable and dairying districts. The introduction of short-rotation ryegrass was an important milestone: it was the first valuable hybrid grass for New Zealand pastures. The *New Zealand Official Year Book* for 1965 shows that the annual export value of the seed alone is now worth about $500,000.

145

Another important advance in pasture development was the adoption of subterranean clover following the recognition that it would respond well to superphosphate and thrive on country that was too dry in summer for white clover. In 1910 subterranean clover was regarded as a rare plant occurring only in some areas of the Auckland Province. By the mid-thirties, following the widespread use of phosphatic fertilizers, the incorporation of subterranean clover into pastures had extended to almost all districts with soils which were moist in winter but dry in summer.

Evans noted that up to 1960 improved strains of perennial ryegrass, Italian ryegrass, short-rotation or H1 ryegrass, cocksfoot, timothy, white clover, and broad red clover, or cowgrass, had been bred in New Zealand and released to the farmer through the seed-certification scheme.

The group of scientists who have contributed to the remarkable development of New Zealand pastures includes Dr. Leonard Cockayne, F.R.S., his son A. H. Cockayne (who became the director-general of the Department of Agriculture in 1936); Sir Bruce Levy, the director of Grasslands Division, D.S.I.R., from 1936 to 1952; J. W. Hadfield, the architect of the seed certification scheme; Dr. L. Corkill, the present director of the Grasslands Division of D.S.I.R.; and the late Dr. P. D. Sears, the previous director of the Division.

Two overseas developments in agriculture which have been extended to a unique degree in New Zealand are artificial insemination and aerial top-dressing. Research over the past twenty-five years has established and consolidated the practice of artificial breeding of dairy cows. Artificial breeding is not a New Zealand discovery, but the extent and rapidity with which the technique has been adopted is certainly a feature in New Zealand. The program uses semen from selected sires proved capable of lifting production in their daughters. In the 1963–1964 season, surveys by the Herd Improvement Department of the New Zealand Dairy Production and Marketing Board showed that there were 352,000 artificially bred dairy cows in milk in New Zealand (17.2 per cent of the national herd) and that the average butterfat production of these cows was 20 pounds higher than that of the rest of the na-

146

tional herd. The additional production will amount to approximately 4,500 tons of butter in the 1966–1967 season. Continuing research, and the resulting technical improvements, have raised the average number of inseminations per bull from 4,376 in 1960 and 7,505 in 1963 to 10,440 in 1965. The inseminating dose has been reduced from 10 x 10^6 spermatozoa to 7.5 x 10^6 so that inseminations per bull reached 14,000 in the 1966–1967 season. No country has introduced artificial breeding into the dairy industry on a scale comparable to that operating in New Zealand, and so far there have been no indications that the technique will lead to any deleterious effects on the industry.

Since over 50 per cent of the land in New Zealand is more than one thousand feet above sea level, the aerial application of fertilizer was a logical development. The very rugged contour of much of the country has been a challenge to the farmer and a handicap to production. The rapid expansion of aerial top-dressing has been one of the most notable developments in agriculture in the postwar years. In 1964 more than half the fertilizer used in the country was applied from the air, the amount distributed in this way being 746,795 tons over an area of 6,588,998 acres.

The present extensive use of fertilizers dates back to the work of B. C. Aston in trials between 1908 and 1916. The discovery by Sir Albert Ellis of the extensive Nauru phosphate desposits has had a profound effect on New Zealand agricultural developments. The chief fertilizer used is superphosphate, which is manufactured in New Zealand from imported phosphate and sulphuric acid made locally from imported sulphur. This industry can be said to be the only large-scale basic chemical industry in the country. The content of sulphur in fertilizer is particularly important for some farming areas of New Zealand which have sulphur-deficient soils.

The nature of New Zealand's mountains, lakes, and rivers makes it admirable country for the development of hydroelectric power schemes. Full advantage is being taken of the power potential, and an extensive system of hydro-dams has been built since the first large station was opened at Lake Coleridge in 1915. Through experience with such schemes, New Zealand engineers have gained a notable expertise with large-scale dam construction and the resul-

147

tant power generation. The potential generating capacity which might eventually be developed from the water resources of New Zealand has been estimated at about 1,500,000 kilowatts for the North Island and 5,000,000 for the South Island. Recently a system for power transmission from the South to North Islands was put into operation using a cable connecting the two islands across Cook Strait.

Some power is being generated in the North Island from thermal stations, and about 14 per cent of the North Island total comes from the geothermal station operating at Wairakei in the Lake Taupo area. Within a region of one hundred by thirty miles in the North Island volcanic area, there are many hydrothermal areas associated with Quaternary volcanism. Because of a shortage of power in the North Island, survey work started in 1950 to investigate the possibilities for large-scale hydrothermal power production in the Taupo area. Geologists, geophysicists, geochemists, and engineers worked jointly and their results paved the way for a 200,000-kilowatt power program. The first machine commenced generating in November, 1958, and by 1964 the Wairakei scheme was producing power at a capacity of approximately 190,000 kilowatts. The scheme now operates on geothermal steam from bores which are 4, 6, or 8 inches in diameter, drilled to depths from 570 to 4,000 feet. Well-head pressures may vary, with closed bores, from 50 to 500 pounds per square inch. Investigations are proceeding to examine the possibilities of developing other geothermal resources.

In the nuclear sciences, New Zealand has made little progress, which is somewhat ironic, for Lord Rutherford (1871-1937), the eminent atomic scientist and director of the Cavendish Laboratory at Cambridge, was born in New Zealand and received his early education here. (Yet it should be noted that his academic appointments were all overseas—first at McGill and then at Manchester.) The Institute of Nuclear Sciences, established as part of the Department of Scientific and Industrial Research, has some excellent equipment, but no research reactor. Planning has started for building nuclear power stations, and discussions have begun on the siting of the installations; it is thought that the first power generated from nuclear reactors could be fed into the national grid in the early 1970's. It can be claimed that the country is ill-prepared for nuclear power production: there are inadequate university training facilities in the nuclear sciences, minimal provisions for radiation biology training and research, and no previous experience of reactor research or operation.

In 1923 the territories of the Ross Dependency came under the jurisdiction of the New Zealand government. The area includes an estimated 160,000–170,000 square miles of land and 130,000 square miles of permanent ice shelf. In December, 1956, a New Zealand expedition under the leadership of Sir Edmund Hillary sailed for McMurdo Sound to participate in the Commonwealth Trans-Antarctic Expedition and also take part in the planned work of the International Geophysical Year. Sir Edmund Hillary and four other New Zealanders reached the South Pole on January 3, 1958, and the crossing of the continent was successfully achieved on March 20, 1958, when Sir Vivian Fuch's party reached Scott Base.

Since 1957 there has been a continuing program of scientific work at Scott Base, with special emphasis on seismology, geomagnetism, ionosphere, meteorology, aurora, and glaciology.

In the practice of medicine, New Zealand-trained doctors have a worldwide reputation, and a number have developed their skills to become leaders in their fields overseas. These distinguished practitioners include Sir Harold Gillies, Sir Arthur Porritt, Sir Robert McIntosh, Dr. Murray Falconer, Dr. J. A. Stallworthy, the late Sir Archibald McIndoe, and the late Dr. William Hawksworth.

Among the distinguished medical scientists who have been associated with New Zealand medicine are Professor Denny Brown (Harvard University), Sir John Eccles, Nobel laureate, who for six years (1944–1950) acted as a stimulus to medical research while professor of physiology at the Otago Medical School, and the late Dr. F. Bielschowsky, distinguished in the field of cancer research. Among the younger medical men, Dr. A. W. Liley, the innovator of the successful technique for transfusing blood to an unborn baby, and Dr. B. Barrett Boyes, the heart surgeon, are outstanding in their specialties.

New Zealand had a single medical school which graduated about one hundred doctors each year. A variety of research fields have been developed at the school, including investigations on hypertension under the direction of Sir Horace Smirk; endocrinology, with special reference to thyroid and pituitary function, under Dr. H. D. Purves; and hydatids research under Dr. M. A. Gemmell. In recent years the metropolitan hospitals have established their own research groups; those in Auckland will be associated with the second medical school recently established there.

The infant-mortality rate in New Zealand is among the lowest in the world. In part, this is due to the work of Sir Truby King, a doctor who, from his work in nutrition, rationalized the feeding of infants. Through the Plunket Society (The Royal Society for the Health of Women and Children, founded in 1907), he initiated a nationwide system of trained nurses and hospitals for the care of mothers and infants.

The training of scientists in New Zealand began with the foundation of the universities. The University of Otago was established in Dunedin in 1869 with power to grant degrees in arts, medicine, law, and music. Four chairs were established, and it has been claimed as unprecedented in the history of English or colonial universities up to that time that a chair of mathematics and natural science should be one of the foundation chairs. The first holder of the chair was Professor John Shand, a graduate of the University of Aberdeen, who came to Dunedin in 1871. He taught in the University until 1913—for forty-two years and until he was nearly eighty. In 1886 his department was divided, upon the establishment of another chair, his choice of subject at this time being physics. The first professor of chemistry in New Zealand was also a foundation-chair appointment to the University of Otago. In the early 1870's, Professor J. G. Black, a graduate of the University of Edinburgh, took up his appointment. He had a wide acquaintance with many branches of science and lectured at the University on chemistry, mineralogy, geology, and metallurgy.

The emphasis on science at the University of Otago was copied by the Canterbury University College at Christchurch when it proceeded with appointments to foundation chairs. The first professor of mathematics, appointed in 1875, was C. H. H. Cook, a highly respected scholar, to whom Lord Rutherford acknowledged the debt he owed for his thorough undergraduate training. As Rutherford's early studies were guided by a foundation professor at Canterbury, so also were the studies of J. W. Mellor, the distinguished chemist, stimulated by Professor J. G. Black, the foundation professor of chemistry at Otago.

Following the establishment of the University of Otago in Dunedin, a move was made to establish a colonial university, and all subsequent university foundations in the other centers became constituent colleges of the University of New Zealand until this went out of existence in 1961 and the colleges became autonomous universities, with Lincoln College as a constituent college of the University of Canterbury.

New Zealand now has five universities with science faculties: Otago, Canterbury, Victoria, Massey, and Auckland. Each university has some special school or professional science course: at Otago there are courses in medicine, dentistry, home science, and surveying; at Canterbury there are faculties of agriculture and engineering; Victoria University of Wellington has a close association with both the Institute of Nuclear Sciences and the applied mathematics section of the D.S.I.R.; Massey University has faculties of agricultural and horticultural science, veterinary science, food science, and biotechnology, and has recently introduced science teaching with emphasis on the functional biological sciences. The University of Auckland has an engineering school and will have the country's second medical school.

The establishment in Australia of a committee under the chairmanship of Sir Keith Murray in 1956 led to a detailed survey of the role and operation of the universities and the eventual establishment of the Australian Universities Commission. In 1959 a similar committee on New Zealand universities was set up under the chairmanship of Sir Hughes Parry. The report of this committee has led to important developments in university education in the country: the University Grants Committee was established in 1961 when the constituent colleges of the University of New Zealand became autonomous; an extensive university building program was introduced with striking improvements in the facilities for several

151

of the country's pure and applied science faculties; finance for university research work increased, and encouragement was given to the extension of graduate work in university departments by the provision of a large number of generous postgraduate scholarships tenable in New Zealand by candidates for doctorates. The first chairman of the Grants Committee was Dr. F. J. Llewellyn, formerly vice-chancellor of Canterbury College and previously professor of chemistry at the University of Auckland. Dr. Llewellyn recently returned to Great Britain to become vice-chancellor of the University of Exeter. His work has contributed greatly to the new tempo of education in New Zealand.

Many of the country's distinguished scientists have been trained through its own universities, and many have carried out their work as university teachers. The contributions of a number of the country's eminent scientists have been mentioned already: Sir Bruce Levy; L. Cockayne and his son, A. H. Cockayne; Sir Peter Buck, the distinguished Maori ethnologist; Sir Theodore Rigg; and N. H. Taylor. Not mentioned, but as distinguished, have been Sir William Benham in zoology, Sir Charles Cotton in geomorphology, Sir Thomas Easterfield and L. H. Briggs in chemistry, J. E. Holloway in botany, G. H. Cunningham in mycology, H. G. Forder in mathematics, D. B. Macleod in physics, W. N. Benson in geology, and Sir Ernest Marsden in physics and scientific administration.

An account of the country's science would not be complete without reference to the scientists who, although New Zealand born, worked and gained eminence overseas. Pre-eminent was Lord Rutherford, born in Nelson in 1871, the fourth son of James Rutherford, a flax miller and small farmer. He graduated from Canterbury College in 1895 with double first-class honors in mathematics and physical science and won a scholarship to Trinity College, Cambridge. The details of his remarkable career have been fully documented. Undoubtedly Rutherford is New Zealand's most distinguished son.

Other notable scientists with New Zealand associations include W. H. Pickering, a space scientist; A. C. Aitken, mathematician; K. E. Bullen, seismologist and applied mathematician; Peter Whittle, applied mathematician; Sir Frederick White, scientific administrator; F. J. Turner, geologist; and M. Wilkins, molecular biologist.

The future role for science in New Zealand will probably differ from that of the present and the past. New Zealand has been dependent on farming as the basis of its economy. In 1964 almost 93 per cent of the country's overseas earnings were from pastoral products. Of the total income of about $10,300,000,000, dairy produce accounted for 23 per cent, meat 27 per cent, wool 36 per cent, and other primary products 4 per cent. The nature of the country's industries has been reflected clearly in New Zealand science. Now a pointer to possible change has come with the moves by Britain to join the European Economic Community.

The Parry Report on New Zealand universities discussed various aspects of the country's scientific development and cited problems which may be anticipated at this stage of the country's economic growth. The report affirmed that the encouragement and development of science and technology in New Zealand will be vital to the economy and prosperity of the country. It was considered to be a fair assessment of the situation to say that the New Zealand community is not yet fully aware of the effect on material progress of neglecting science and technology. To quote the Parry Report:

The expansion of secondary industries in New Zealand and the further improvement of primary industries call for the development of human and material resources with scientific, engineering and technological skills and enterprise of the highest quality, and this not in a small number of very clever people, and not by imitation of overseas practice, but in a large number of highly qualified well-educated people who will invent, adapt and improve manufactures suitable and peculiar to the New Zealand environment. Most of these advances stem from university-educated persons; in short, from scientists, technologists, economists and administrators.

We feel that New Zealand is not fully aware that one of the main causes of its lack of progress in the development of secondary industries is its tardiness in developing technological education.

In the last decade or so research and development in New Zealand have been concentrated on the problems of the primary industries and have come mainly through the agricultural colleges and the Government research institutions of the Department of Agriculture and the Department of Scientific and Industrial Research under the stimulus to produce more wool, meat, dairy products and timber products. Secondary industry's contribution and participation in research and development have been small and sadly lacking in many fields. Industrialists are now awakening to the fact that more qualified personnel and more complex skills are essential to their progress. They have in the past put little pressure on the universities for professional engineers and scientists and even now seem to find it difficult to prescribe the sorts of educated persons and complex skills they need. The universities, too, have been slow to grasp the fact that it is a matter of concern for them, and as a consequence have been slow to develop teaching and research in the applied sciences and technologies.

Recognition of the need for better coordination of the country's scientific work led to the establishment of the National Research Advisory Council in 1963. The Council set up committees to analyze the scientific situation in the country and summarized reports of the committees were submitted to the Minister of Science in 1965. Of prime importance in future scientific planning will be the potential supply of scientists. It is expected that the future demand for scientists will be defined in the report of the Manpower Committee of the Advisory Council, which has delayed reporting until it had the opportunity to read the recommendations of the other committees.

The number of pure and applied science graduates from the New Zealand universities is shown in Table 2.

Extensions and adjustments to this pattern of scientific training could follow from the deliberations of the Advisory Council.

If the country is to diversify the economy to offset threats to traditional markets, an increased investment in science will be essential. The Parry Committee has commented on the present low level of investment, which is surprising in a country which has reaped such handsome rewards from the work of its scientists. Frequently, in recent years, grave concern has been expressed at the comparatively slow rate of scientific expansion in New Zealand. The 1961 report of the D.S.I.R. stated: "We would once again emphasize the need for more support for scientific investigation in New Zealand if we are to sustain or improve the standard of living of a population projected to reach three million in little over 10 years and four million in under 30 years." In the Department's 1963

Table 2. University graduates* in pure and applied science, 1950, 1956, and 1962 †

Year	Graduates from all faculties	Agriculture		Dentistry and medicine		Engineering		Home Science and Food Technology		Science	
		No.	% all faculties	No.	% all faculties	No.	% all faculties	No.	% all faculties	No.	% all faculties
1950	1,110	54	4.9	132	11.9	105	9.5	11	1.0	254	22.8
1956	1,030	22	2.1	138	13.4	75	7.3	7	0.7	179	17.4
1962	1,958	68	3.5	138	7.0	201	10.3	9	0.5	501	25.6

* Excluding doctorates.
† Based on the Department of Scientific Industrial Research publication, *Scientific Research in New Zealand: Expenditure and Manpower, 1953–1962.*

annual report, concern was again expressed: "Events of the last two years have served only to emphasize the urgency of the need for increasing our research effort; e.g., in improving productivity and efficiency in both agricultural and marketing industries and in adapting products to meet the needs of new markets." The figures in Table 3 were given, comparing expenditure on science in New Zealand with other countries.

Table 3. Expenditure on research and development

Country	Year	Expenditure	
		As percentage of gross national product	Per head of population £ (U.K.)
U.S.A.	1960–61	2.8	28.0
U.K.	1958–59	2.5	9.3
U.S.S.R.	1960	2.3(?)	13.0
Sweden	1959	1.8	8.7
Japan	1960–61	1.6	1.6
West Germany	1959	1.4	5.6
France	1961	1.3	5.4
Canada	1960	1.2	7.8
Norway	1960	0.7	3.7
Australia	1960–61	0.6	3.2
New Zealand	1961–62	0.3	1.9
Malaya	1959	0.26	0.33
Ghana	1960	0.2	0.14

The total scientific research expenditure for the whole country in 1963 was estimated at about 11.2 million dollars, of which government departments spend 9 millions, the universities 0.77 millions, and industry 1.25 millions. Approximately 36 per cent of the total research expenditure was spent on agricultural and fisheries research (4.4 million dollars).

Although concern is often expressed about the over-all rate of scientific expansion, account should be taken of the rapid growth that has already taken place in some fields. Of special significance to New Zealand science was the decision to distribute a part of the profits from the national lotteries for the support of medical and

SCIENCE

scientific research. Large items of equipment, such as electron microscopes, computers, nuclear magnetic resonance instruments, and mass-spectrometers have been made available to the country's scientists through the Golden Kiwi Lottery Board. A number of New Zealand laboratories would now approach international standards in equipment and general facilities.

A requirement for a rapid expansion of scientific effort in New Zealand may be imposed on the country by changing world markets. The complete and profitable adjustment of the country's science to its needs has been a feature of the past. It is reasonable to expect successful adaptations of its science and scientists to meet the changes of the future.

BIBLIOGRAPHY

Burton, P. *The New Zealand Geological Survey: 1865–1965*. Department of Scientific and Industrial Research Information Series, No. 52. Wellington, 1965.
Callaghan, F. R., ed. *Science in New Zealand*. Wellington, 1957.
Department of Agriculture. Annual reports.
Department of Scientific and Industrial Research. Annual reports.
Evans, B. L. *Agricultural and Pastoral Statistics in New Zealand: 1861–1954*. Wellington, 1956.
——. "Grassland Research in New Zealand." *New Zealand Official Yearbook*. Wellington, 1960.
Jenkinson, S. H. *New Zealanders and Science*. Wellington, 1940.
Jones, D. W. Carmalt. *Annals of the University of Otago Medical School: 1875–1939*. Wellington, 1945.
One Hundred Years of Chemical Research. Department of Scientific and Industrial Research Information Series, No. 46. Wellington, 1965.
Sinclair, K. *A History of New Zealand*. Harmondsworth, 1959.

RELIGION

J. J. MOL

ALTHOUGH organized settlement did not begin in New Zealand until 1840, there were by that time a number of Maori who professed the Christian faith.

The religious revival in Britain during the last part of the eighteenth century gave rise to the founding of the Church Missionary Society in 1799 by lay and clerical evangelical members of the Church of England, and one of its early activities was the sending of two tradesmen-missionaries (a carpenter and a ropemaker) to help the Reverend Samuel Marsden, chaplain of the New South Wales settlement, to teach the Maori the simpler crafts and to prepare them for the Christian gospel.

In 1814, Marsden and a small band of missionaries and their families set out from Sydney for the Bay of Islands, where they landed on December 13. Marsden purchased land from the Maori chiefs, converted some and interested others, and with tremendous energy and boundless enthusiasm directed the work of his followers, some of whom labored in translating the New Testament into Maori to assist in the dissemination of Christianity. Marsden soon returned to Sydney, where he established a seminary for the instruction of Maori chiefs and their children, but on his numerous sojourns in New Zealand he managed to record Maori legends and genealogies, spread the Christian doctrine, carry out meaningful exploration, and advance the study of Maori ethnology. His great shortcoming, however, seems to have been his inability to appreciate Maori culture, and he was especially severe on such aspects as seemed to be inimical to evangelical middle-class British Christian thought.

Unfortunately for the early missionaries, traders and whalers had about as much contact with the Maori as the missionaries themselves, and the Maori, who were frequently engaged in wars with neighboring tribes, showed a clear preference for the guns of the traders and whalers to the crafts and creeds of the Christians. Since the missionaries required a complete understanding of the catechism and a general profession of Christian faith, conversions were understandably slow, and it was not until 1825 that real progress in baptisms was made. Thereafter conversion became more widespread, and among the salutary effects of the proselytizing were the emancipation of tribal slaves and the abandonment of cannibalism.

Between 1830 and 1860 the influence of the Church Missionary Society's numerous activities in New Zealand expanded, as did the influence of the Methodist missions; the Roman Catholic mission, established in 1838 under French sponsorship, at first claimed large numbers of conversions, but these statistics were later revised, and the Catholic missionary influence was relatively modest. Through schools, hospitals, and chapels, the Maori were presented with middle-class morals and manners and the cultural expressions of European society, but they were largely eschewed, so that after about 1860 the influence of the missionaries upon Maori and hence on New Zealand culture in general diminished.

Yet the missionaries had prepared the Maori for British annexation of New Zealand, and so their political role should not be entirely overlooked.

PATTERN OF NEW ZEALAND CULTURE

The first settlement in New Zealand intended to colonize the islands was established at Port Nicholson (Wellington) in 1840, and by 1848 a group of Presbyterians had decided to found their own settlement at Otago; then in 1850 a number of Anglicans established themselves at Canterbury. By so doing, these early settlers, whose actions were reminiscent of events in the United States, established regions of religious influence that have been maintained to the present and introduced forms of worship that have been virtually unchanged.

When André Siegfried visited New Zealand in 1904, he found that "no tradition remained so strong as the religious one." This was not necessarily a compliment. It could mean—in fact, it did—that although New Zealand was acquiring an identity of its own, in religious affairs it remained true to the Old World. "The religious buildings are in the same style as those in the mother-country; and the ministers preach on the same lines," he wrote.

Of course, this was to be expected. Any culture pattern which relates to the sacred is by definition more stable and more resistant to change. This is as true for the primitive tribe as it was for the European immigrants in the United States, and for the British immigrants in New Zealand in the last century. Of all the adjustments which migrants have traditionally made in a new environment, the religious ones have required most effort and time.

The denominational figures of the various censuses accurately reflect the influx and comparative strength of regional migrations. The absence of large-scale migration from continental Europe is visible in the numerical insignificance of Lutheranism. However, the prominence of migration from England is shown by the fact that throughout the history of New Zealand the Anglican and Methodist denominations constituted almost without exception the majority of the population.

Sometimes the original patterns of migration are still visible in the proportional distribution of denominations. The 1961 census figures show that close to half the population of Otago and Southland are Presbyterian, although not even a quarter of the total New Zealand population belongs to that denomination. This reflects the concentration of the Scots in these southern parts of the South

Island ever since 1848 when the first ship arrived. Apparently the Scots developed a fondness for New Zealand: there have always been relatively more Presbyterians here than in other countries with a predominant Anglo-Saxon pattern of migration, such as Canada, and particularly Australia and the United States.

A similar overrepresentation of Catholics on the west coast of the South Island also orginated in the attraction of the mining fields for the Irish, many of whom came to these areas from Australia. However, with only 15.1 per cent in the total New Zealand population, Catholics are relatively less numerous in New Zealand than in other countries of large-scale immigration.

On the other hand, migration patterns are not always responsible for overrepresentation of denominations in certain geographical areas. The Church of England has 48 per cent of the population of the east coast (North Island) statistical area, although only 34.6 per cent of the whole of New Zealand. So has Methodism 11.8 per cent of the Taranaki area (west coast of the North Island), but only 7.2 per cent of the whole of New Zealand. This is also partly explained by an arrangement between Anglicans and Methodists in 1837 whereby the former would concentrate their Maori mission work on the east and the latter on the west coast.

Throughout New Zealand history the relative denominational proportions have not varied a great deal. The slow decline of Anglican, Presbyterian, and Methodist denominational proportions and the slow increase of Catholic proportions in the non-Maori population over the last forty years are most likely due to the different fertility ratios of these four main denominations. There does not seem to have been a disproportional influx of Catholic migrants from overseas apart from approximately ten thousand Dutch Catholics who have entered the country since the Second World War. However, this amounts to only 8 per cent of the total Catholic increase from 1945–1961, and a closer look at the Catholic birth rate is therefore warranted. The 1961 census clearly demonstrated that the ratio of children of 0-4 years old to women aged 15–40 was much higher for Catholics than for the total population, as Table 4 shows. One can therefore expect this trend of Catholic increase to continue.

161

Table 4. Fertility ratios (number of children 0–4 years old, per 100 women aged 15–40) for selected denominations of the total New Zealand population

Denomination	1921	1936	1945	1961
Church of England	52.16	37.55	48.61	69.31
Presbyterian	52.45	39.35	49.79	69.97
Methodist	49.94	37.68	52.03	68.52
Catholic	53.22	42.10	52.60	88.74
Total population	52.46	39.36	50.88	74.34

The Catholic position on birth control is one important reason for the higher Catholic fertility. However, there are other factors: Table 4 shows clearly that the economic depression of the 1930's had quite an impact on the fertility rates of all denominations (including Catholics). The fact that Catholics tend to be overrepresented in the lower classes in New Zealand, which traditionally have a higher fertility rate, may also contribute to an understanding of the difference. On the other hand, Catholics tend to be slightly more urbanized and have a higher percentage in the "never-married" class, and these factors in turn would lower the ratio.

With the higher fertility of Catholics, one would also expect lower divorce rates in this denomination. The Catholic Church strongly opposes divorce, and the divorce rates of Catholics in the United States are lower than those of Protestant and interfaith marriages, and are far lower than those of marriages in which neither partner has a religious affiliation. This is not what the New Zealand divorce statistics show. In a pioneering study of the field, A. J. Nixon found that there was no striking disproportion between Catholics and non-Catholics among divorced females at the 1945 census, and that this was not due to the avoidance of remarriage by divorced Catholics.

Nixon calculated (presumably also from the 1945 census figures) that the proportion of divorced women to the total number of married women in the same religious groups was 2.41 per cent for Anglicans, 1.55 per cent for Catholics, 1.27 per cent for Methodists and 1.20 per cent for Presbyterians. We can bring this information up to date by calculating the 1961 ratios: 2.01 per cent for Anglicans, 1.50 per cent for Catholics, 1.46 per cent for Methodists, and 1.34 per cent for Presbyterians. Although the percentage range for denominational differences has become considerably smaller since 1945, the rank order between the denominations has remained the same. It is interesting that these ratios of divorced to married women per denomination are rather similar in Australia: 2.17 per cent for Anglicans, 1.46 per cent for Catholics, 1.42 per cent for Methodists, and 1.53 per cent for Presbyterians. The reasons for the discrepancies between the American and New Zealand findings can be manifold. Nixon found that there was in New Zealand "a fairly marked inverse relation between the ranks of divorce frequency and social status," and Catholics in New Zealand are over-represented in the lower classes.

Another important explanation not mentioned in the Nixon study may be the high proportion of interfaith marriages. Church records in New Zealand show that approximately one-half of the marriages celebrated in Catholic churches are mixed marriages. It is very likely that the female Catholic divorced-married ratio in New Zealand would be much smaller than 1.5 per cent if the mixed marriages could be excluded. Similarly, it could be reasoned as Nixon does that "if one were to make a division between devout and non-devout members of whatever church, it is likely that significant differences in divorce frequency would be found." This factor of devoutness, or "interiorized faith," is crucial for religious research, but there is no New Zealand project as yet which measures this factor and relates it to other social phenomena. The high Anglican divorce rate is probably related to the fact that the Church of England more than any other denomination has a very high percentage of nominal members, for whom the strict divorce regulations are not urgent and for whom religion is not meaningful as a uniting tie in marriage.

The importance of the hold of a denomination on its membership is obvious when the relation of Catholicism to delinquency in New Zealand is considered. O'Neill analyzed a survey of all New Zealand delinquency cases (aged seven to seventeen inclusive) during 1949–1951 which showed that 19.8 per cent of the delinquents were Catholics, although the proportion of Catholics in the total New Zealand population according to the 1945 census was only 13.45 per cent. Even after age was controlled (the proportion of Catholics in the age group of five to fifteen years in 1945 was 15.72 per cent) Catholics were still overrepresented. However, if we accept attendance at Catholic schools as a measure of the hold of the church on the membership (to send their children to Catholic schools is a matter of serious obligation for Catholic parents in New Zealand), then the majority of families from which these delinquents came can be classified as marginal members. "The 64% of the Catholic children at Catholic schools provided only 33.6% of the Catholic delinquents, while the 36% of the State schools provided 66.4% of the delinquents," O'Neill reports.

By speaking about "the hold" that a denomination has on its membership we are already discussing its vitality and power. The important role which the churches played in the initial settlement of the country (such influential centers as Christchurch and Dunedin were originally Anglican and Presbyterian settlements) does not necessarily guarantee a religious vitality. The very requirement that the early immigrants in these church settlements produce a clergyman's certificate "attesting him as sober, industrious, and honest and stating that he and his family were among the most respectable of their class in the parish" would favor moral decency, but not necessarily vital faith. How are we to measure the vitality of the New Zealand churches? Looking at the scene in a historical context, one can note the initiative of the laity in organizing churches and in sending for clergy. "New Zealand Christianity, too, had sufficient vitality to undertake foreign missions. These were chiefly in the islands of the Pacific, but several were in Asia." [1]

The New Zealand churches also had an effect on the values of the new country. As Keith Sinclair has written in his *A History of New Zealand* (1949), "The moral attitudes of society were moulded, perhaps more decisively than in Australia or the United States, by puritanical forms of Christianity and by the evangelism

[1] K. S. Latourette, *The Great Century*, "History of the Expansion of Christianity," V (London, 1949), 194.

which permeated most Christian churches last century." Still, this effect is rather ambiguous, as Dr. Sinclair readily admits when in the same breath he characterizes the prevailing New Zealand religion as "a simple materialism."

The effect of the New Zealand religious institutions on politics has been similarly ambiguous. On the one hand, there is no historical evidence that any of the churches, as organizations, were responsible for the specific measures of advanced social legislation. On the other hand, there were several clergymen, both Catholic and Nonconformists, who were very prominent in political radicalism. The Factory Acts of 1890 and 1894, which limited sweated labor, were largely the result of humanitarian crusading by ministers. More intangible, of course, was the influence of Christian laymen on the political climate of opinion.

A more tangible, but also inadequate, way of measuring the vitality of the New Zealand churches is to observe church attendance. It is an inadequate measurement, for the actual beliefs and the vitality of the faith are not expressed by merely sitting in a pew on a Sunday morning. Still, it is at least an indication of the degree to which the membership meets the expectations of a particular denomination. One can safely say that the influence of a church on the beliefs and attitudes of those who never participate in church activities is small indeed.

From 1874 to 1926 statistics were collected on the number of people in church districts who attended services. This information was furnished by church officials on a special form, "Census of Places of Worship." By totaling the number of people who attended services in each of the four main denominations, and by dividing them by the number of those who according to the census of that year stated that they belonged to each of these churches, one can arrive at some rough estimate of church attendance. Table 5 shows the results.

Although there is a rough consistency of church attendance for each denomination, the data should be treated with caution. Not all clergymen might return the form. They might tend to be too optimistic in their estimates. They might include or exclude the

165

Table 5. Number of persons attending church services in New Zealand expressed as a percentage of denominational membership according to the census of that year

Year of census	Church of England	Presbyterian	Methodist	Roman Catholic
1874	15.66	25.58	59.52	27.17
1878	16.41	26.91	60.24	22.96
1881	15.89	25.86	51.29	28.12
1886	17.38	30.41	52.69	32.17
1891	14.70	28.83	54.63	34.98
1896	17.01	30.48	56.03	36.52
1906	17.66	25.56	46.53	32.69
1911	12.94	23.55	48.61	34.26
1921	23.32	35.88	59.14	56.37
1926	25.30	34.72	50.76	52.95

occasional churchgoers and children. They might just add up the attendance of the various church services on a Sunday without deducting those who frequented more than one service.

To obviate this last possibility, the church officials were also asked in 1916, 1921, and 1926 to indicate the number of persons usually present at the largest-attended service of the day. Table 6 shows that the figures obtained from this question substantially decrease the percentage of church attenders in the total denominational membership. Of course these figures probably underestimate the active proportion in each church, as those who worship only once on Sunday, but at a different service, are not now counted.

Table 6. Number of persons usually present at largest-attended service of the day expressed as a percentage of denominational membership according to the census of that year

Year of census	Church of England	Presbyterian	Methodist	Roman Catholic
1916	11.97	23.32	39.58	35.56
1921	11.18	20.14	35.88	35.86
1926	10.60	19.52	28.32	31.87

More recent and more accurate surveys of church attendance confirm that the Church of England suffers most from merely nominal adherence. A survey by the *New Zealand Herald* of church attendance on Sunday, July 17, 1949, in Auckland city showed that approximately 4 per cent of the Anglicans, 32 per cent of the Presbyterians, 26 per cent of the Methodists, and 75 per cent of the Catholics worshipped that day. A Christchurch survey in 1962 found that in a sample of 988 randomly chosen inhabitants, 11 per cent of the Anglicans, 18 per cent of the Presbyterians, 25 per cent of the Methodists, and 68 per cent of the Catholics had been to church on the previous Sunday. Even allowing for a considerable margin of error in all these figures, the low Catholic percentages in Tables 5 and 6 remains very puzzling. We know from similar statistics in Australia and the United States that Catholic attendance is presently hardly ever below 60 per cent. Comparing the different surveys and opinon polls regarding weekly church attendance in other Anglo-Saxon countries, it is generally true that in all these countries Catholic attendance is uniformly high (60–70 per cent), but that with the exception of the United States, where one in three attend church, at the most one in five Protestants in Australia, England, and New Zealand worship weekly.

New Zealand is also part of the general Anglo-Saxon pattern with respect to sex ratios in religious affairs. At the 1961 census the ratio ranged from 160 women to every 100 men in Christian Science, to only 30 women to every 100 men returned as atheist, with the Methodist 108, Presbyterian and Church of England 103, and Catholic 102 females for each 100 males.

However, the differences between the sexes are more pronounced when we look at frequency of worship. In the Christchurch survey the attendance ratio of females over age twenty per 100 males over age twenty was 133 for Anglicans, 142 for Presbyterians, 125 for Methodist, and 105 for Catholics. In the same survey single people over age twenty proved to be about twice as active in Church as married people. It was also found that after the age of fourteen in the non-Catholic denominations, church activity declined rapidly until the middle twenties when the percentage of churchgoers in the total population remained at a constantly low level. This is a rather important finding, because it indicates that in Protestantism children are expected to attend church and Sunday school, but that religious activities and adult behavior are dissociated. This religious passivity of parents determines the New Zealand child's values and aspirations much more than the values communicated in sermons and Sunday school lessons.

How is the religious pattern related to the class structure in New Zealand? The first comprehensive stratification study of New Zealand society has yet to appear, but there are indications that the main New Zealand denominations are not randomly distributed over the population. William Pember Reeves, writing in *The Long White Cloud* (1924), had an interesting observation on this point:

> In proportion to their numbers, the Scots are more prominent than other races in politics, commerce, finance, sheep farming and the work of education. Among the eighty European members of the New Zealand House of Representatives there has seldom been more than one Smith, Brown or Jones and hardly ever a single Robinson; but the number of McKenzies has often been three. The Irish do not crowd into the towns, or attempt to capture the municipal machinery, as in America, nor are they a source of political unrest or corruption. Their Church's antagonism to the National Education system has excluded many able Catholics from public life. Some 2,400 Jews live in the towns, and seem more numerous and prominent in the north than in the south. They belong to the middle class; many are wealthy. These are often charitable and public spirited, and active in municipal rather than in parliamentary life.

The different occupational distribution of Catholics in New Zealand has also been noted by Nixon, who attempted to find evidence for his thesis that Catholics are more prone to divorce because they are overrepresented in the lower classes:

> Catholics, being 13.5% of the community, comprised only 10.9% of the farming population, 11.1% of those in medical and hygienic services, 12.4% of those in education, religion, arts and sciences, 10.2% of those in finance, banking and insurance. On the other hand, they comprised 18.1% of those in the liquor trade, 20.1% of those in hotel work, 17.3% of those in fishing and trapping, 16.5% of those in forestry, 15.1% of those not adequately describing their occupations, 15% of those in sport and entertainment. . . .

The Christchurch survey found similar disproportions. In this study the category "professions" was rather broad, as it included

168

not only lawyers, architects, and executives, but also teachers, big farmers, and so forth. Of the 403 Anglicans of the sample, 19 per cent belonged to this category; of the 241 Presbyterians, 22 per cent; of the 105 Methodist 16 per cent; and of the 143 Catholics 6 per cent. It is likely that the heavy underrepresentation of Catholics and the slighter underrepresentation of Methodists in the New Zealand professions would apply to the entire population. The Christchurch data are generally in line with both observations and findings in Australia, Great Britain, and the United States with the exception that in the United States the Methodist and the national percentage of professionals are about the same.

What rationale lies behind these denominational discrepancies? At least in New Zealand it does not appear that the Irish Catholics had less access to positions of honor, wealth, and status. The New Zealand figures could be at least partially explained in terms of the relative absence amongst Catholics of certain values which are functional from the institutional religious point of view, but disfunctional from the point of view of the secular society. Gerhard Lenski, who did a large-scale research project on religion in Detroit, found that there were important value differences between the Catholic, Protestant, and Jewish interviewees. On the basis of his data he distinguishes between intellectual heteronomy (obedience to the dictates of others) and intellectual autonomy (thinking for oneself). He says, in his book *The Religious Factor:* "Upper-middle-class Detroiters are far more likely than lower-working-class Detroiters to value intellectual autonomy above heteronomy, and within all of the class levels, Jews and white Protestants are more likely than Catholics to do this."

However, the above paragraph should not be interpreted to mean that the access to desirable positions was not occasionally hindered by interfaith rivalry. The open antagonism in the early days of the colony to the Catholic Bishop Pompallier is a case in point. Another later example was the virulent Protestant Political Association, which was formed towards the close of the reign of the Catholic prime minister, Sir Joseph Ward, "to discredit Sir Joseph and his Government on religious grounds." On the other hand, compared with the American anxiety regarding the religion of their presidents, New Zealanders seem to have generally shown less undue concern. As Leslie Lipson comments in *The Politics of Equality*, "The prime ministers accurately depict the relative strength of New Zealand's sectarian divisions. Nine of the eleven were Protestants; two (Ward and Savage) were Catholics. Vogel, who belongs to the older period, is the only Jew ever to have been premier." One of the present leaders of the Labour party in New Zealand was Nordmeyer, a Presbyterian minister.

The religious institutions in New Zealand are generally held in high respect by the entire population. Even the large numbers of those who keep away from the churches still vaguely assume their special sacred position in society. Those who are not involved in the life of the churches are often apologetic about their lack of religious concern and hardly ever antagonistic. This is reflected in the esteem with which the clergy is held. In a large sample of people who were asked to grade thirty occupations socially, the Nonconformist minister was ranked fifth behind doctors, country lawyers, company directors, and business managers. Significantly, the semiskilled and unskilled classes gave the Nonconformist minister a lower rating than the higher classes. He also received a higher rating from females than from males.

In other studies conducted in Australia, a distinction was made between "Clergyman with university degree," "Clergyman with some university training," and "Clergyman with no university training." As in Australia, a university degree increases the status of a minister in New Zealand. Whether he has a university education or not largely depends on the requirements of his denomination. In a study of all active parish ministers (ninety) of the Anglican, Baptist, Church of Christ, Congregational, Methodist, and Presbyterian churches in the Christchurch area, Richard Thompson discovered that degrees were held by 75 per cent of the Presbyterian, 67 per cent of the Congregational, 49 per cent of the Anglican, 44 per cent of the Methodist, and 10 per cent of the Baptist ministers. Thompson also went into the home background of these ministers, and he noticed that "an unusually large number of Methodist ministers came from the homes of skilled workers (40%), Presbyterians from farms (29%), Baptists from professional homes (30%), and Anglicans from vicarages (23%)." Some of these findings, such as the ones regarding the university degrees of ministers, are likely to be approximately true for the whole of New Zealand; on the other hand, it is rather likely that the professional home background of Baptist ministers is the exception rather than the rule.

The appraisal of the vitality and function of religion in New Zealand has so far been based on the few available accounts and studies. Do they also provide a sufficient basis for the appraisal of the future for religious institutions in New Zealand, or are we to rely soley on impressionistic speculation? Although sociology is hardly ready for predictions of the future, there are a number of concrete indications in the present which will inevitably have a bearing on that future.

We started out by mentioning the tenacity of religious patterns. This means that we can expect slight rather than drastic changes. We can also expect that the historical capacity for self-vitalization in Christianity may make a fool of any prophet of doom, and there have been a considerable number both inside and outside the churches in the last few centuries. This is particularly true in New Zealand, where the religious situation does not seem to have changed much. There appears to be in every generation a core of church members who will perpetuate and consolidate the religious function of interpreting life from the point of view of a specific undiluted Christianity. This does not mean that there are no acute danger signals in some of the New Zealand religious institutions or indeed in the entire Western world of which it is so much a part.

One of these danger signals from the point of view of traditional Christianity is that the actual religion of the New Zealanders (the areas in life which are sacred, in which one has a large emotional investment, and for which one is an unwitting missionary) has increasingly less to do with the professed religion of the churches. The framework of meaning that motivates even the average churchgoer seems to be informed by the secular values of scientific humanism or materialism rather than Christian salvation. The alienation from historic Christianity runs parallel to the erosion of functions of the traditional religious institutions. The more specialized and diversified societies become, the more religious tasks (such as

171

science, medicine, philanthropy, psychological care, and even ethics) are taken over by non-religious organizations. Many church-goers continue their churchgoing habits because they feel under obligation, or because religion in some vague way decorates life for them.

Another danger signal is not only the erosion of the traditional Christian belief-system, but also the lack of loyalty of Protestants to their churches. The percentage of the New Zealand population who state that they have no religion, or object to stating their religion, has increased from 2.94 per cent in 1901 to 9.15 per cent in 1961.

Although our Table 5 seems to indicate an increase in church attendance, the more reliable recent investigations seem to show that at the most one-fifth of the adult Protestant population goes to church regularly. The younger generation in the major Protestant churches is intent upon making their religion more relevant to daily life. The question is whether increased social relevance will also increase membership loyalty. The actual problem of the New Zealand major Protestant denominations (and for that matter, their overseas counterparts) is their amorphous social structure; the membership does not feel bound by the norms, and this dilemma cannot be solved by programs of social action only. This problem is, of course, much less acute in Catholicism and the small sects, and one can therefore expect a very slow increase in both numbers and influence of these religious organizations at the expense of the middle-class churches in the years to come.

At the same time, however, this lack of cohesion in the major Protestant denominations is also an indication of the essential Protestant tone of New Zealand society. The alliance of the culture and the religious institutions can indeed be regarded as a position of strength: the churches are socially thoroughly respectable, and their pronouncements on national ethics are taken seriously, although not necessarily implemented and not necessarily well informed. However, the alliance has other weaknesses, which are a consequence of amorphous and secularizing tendencies: the churches will generally be in the rear guard rather than the vanguard of social change. This is not necessarily because of ecclesiastical conservatism, but because an independent controversial and progressive policy may weaken the tenuous hold on the membership even more. The option of decreasing one's involvement in a religious institution is more easily taken when there are no sanctions against such a move. Where such social sanctions and/or individual guilt feelings regarding apostasy exist, the church can follow a more independent, perhaps even vanguard, line of action. This is rather evident in the area of race relations in New Zealand. The hold of the major Protestant denominations on both *pakeha* and Maori members as expressed in church attendance figures is rather weak. When the Maori do not feel at home in the more formal *pakeha* worship services, they tend to frequent (if they go to church at all) the Maori services.

Three denominations (Ratana, Mormon, and Ringatu) account for almost a quarter of the Maoris, but have only 0.30 per cent of the non-Maori figures. The Ratana Church began with the charismatic Maori leader Ratana, who in 1918 saw a vision that commanded him to heal his Maori people physically and spiritually and win them back to Jehovah. It has many sectarian characteristics such as informality in service and self-supporting clergy. Its doctrines are predominantly Christian: belief in the Trinity, in Christ as Savior, and the Bible as God's revelation. In the 1930's the Ratana movement became heavily engaged in social and political matters. From 1943 to 1963, Labour candidates drawn from Ratana held all four Maori seats. The main social function of Ratana has been to provide supratribal unity in the Christian faith and act as a significant rallying point for Maori renaissance.

The Ringatu Church is much older than Ratana. It also combines Christian and Maori traditions and emphasizes faith healing. It was started in the 1860's by Te Kooti, amongst others, and he is still revered as saint and prophet. One of the distinctive features of this religion, which gave it its name, is the upraised hand, *te ringa tu*, which takes the place of the Amen of the Christians. There is no written liturgy, but the text is wholly memorized and transmitted from generation to generation. All members take part in the liturgy, and each can conduct the service if called upon.

In contrast to Ratana and Ringatu, the Church of Jesus Christ of

Latter Day Saints has not emerged from the Maori themselves. Its predominance cannot be explained as with the others by the specific functions it fulfilled for Maori society. Although the Mormons pay the appropriate attention in their church clubs to Maori history, genealogy, arts and crafts, and although they encourage such lively Maori activities as singing and dancing (which the older Christian missionaries frowned upon), its strength lies particularly in its non-Maori mode of social organization and the dedication of its unpaid American missionaries.

Any integration policy of the major Protestant denominations (and there is much pressure toward such a policy) inevitably flounders because the membership does not want integration and gets away with not wanting it. However, the Catholic and particularly the Mormon hold on membership is such that these denominations can much more successfully overcome the initial antagonisms. They can do this mainly because a decrease in religious involvement has inevitable repercussions (through conscience or through the opinion of those fellow church members for whom one cares) which the membership will want to avoid. And so both races learn naturally to worship together and get used to it. One can therefore expect in the future a continuation of successful integration policies by the more cohesive churches, such as the Roman Catholic and the sects, and a lesser success by the amorphous churches until integration in the other social areas becomes an accomplished fact.

This present and different position of the New Zealand churches on an amorphous-cohesive scale also affects their capacity to break through the inevitable embeddedness of class and culture. The amorphous churches generally will have to accept the *status quo* as it has developed through the like-seek-like motivation in the local congregations. This segregation is then automatically reinforced because those who are "unlike" feel free to drop out. However, the cohesive churches will be more capable of breaking through this crustlike mundane pattern by the capacity to make the religious norm more central. In spite of the centrality of a more purely religious norm, Catholicism and the sects have their own problems. The satisfaction of the mere performance (churchgoing) in Catholicism, or the ritualized good-fellowship as a substitute for Christian love in the sects, also constitute danger signals. They only differ in kind from the ones of the less cohesive churches.

However true all this may be on the level of institutional posture and relations, the future influence of Christianity in New Zealand also heavily depends on the very intimate encounter of persons at work, at recreation, or in the home. Churchgoers are judged by their fellow citizens on whether their Christian commitment makes a consistent difference. If it actually does, the churchgoer does not preach "at" them and does not appear better than they are: this is all the better for the esteem in which the churches are held. Even so, the translation of this esteem into active church participation is the exception rather than the rule in a secular society where a substantial number of males tend to associate religion with sissyness.

BIBLIOGRAPHY

Elder, J. R. *The History of the Presbyterian Church in New Zealand: 1840–1940*. Christchurch, 1940.
Lee, John A. *Socialism in New Zealand*. London, 1938.
McLintock, A. H. *The History of Otago*. Otago, 1949.
Mol, J. J. *Church Attendance in Christchurch, New Zealand*. Christchurch, 1962.
——. *Churches and Immigrants*. The Hague, 1961.
——. *Religion and Race in New Zealand*. Christchurch, 1966.
Moran, F. P. *A History of the Catholic Church in Australasia*. Sydney, 1894.
Nixon, A. J. *Divorce in New Zealand*. Auckland, 1954.
O'Neill, D. P. *Catholics and Delinquency*. Wellington, 1951.
Purchase, H. T. *History of the English Church in New Zealand*. Christchurch, 1914.
Sinclair, Keith. *A History of New Zealand*. Harmondsworth, 1959.
Thompson, R. H. T. *Training for the Ministry*. Christchurch, 1957.

ART

P. A. TOMORY

LIKE Gaul, the history of art in New Zealand can be divided into three parts. The topographical period, the transitional period, and the modern period—a rather similar pattern to that which obtains in the United States, and a pattern which is to be found in almost all ex-colonial countries. In painting or stylistic terms, the topographical period has little or no significance in relation to the modern period. In recent years, the art of some of the more creative topographers has been admired for its grasp of form or its rendering of the effects of Pacific light, but this admiration has only generated the comfort of a tradition in the creative attitude. For the modern artist has declared anathema the superficial representation of his country's "scenic attractions." This declaration is made all the more positive by the existence of an annual art competiton (the Kelliher Art Prize) which calls for this banal treatment of the New Zealand landscape. Fundamentally this is a reaction against the topographical instinct and is surely no more

176

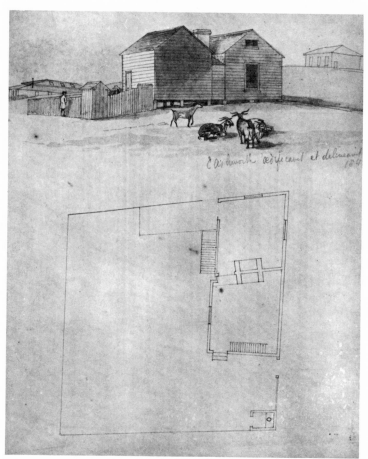

I. Pen and graywash sketch (1843), by Edward Ashworth, of a house designed and built by the artist. 10⅝ x 8. (Auckland City Art Gallery.)

II. "Milford Sound" (1863), watercolor by John Buchanan. 8⅛ x 19¾. (The Hocken Library, University of Otago.)

III. "Waiwera Hotel" (1877), watercolor by John Kinder. 8¼ x 14⅛. (Auckland City Art Gallery.)

IV. An academic building (1890), Victoria University of Wellington, in the old-style Neo-Gothic architecture favored during the nineteenth century.

V. "Otira Gorge" (1913), oil by Petrus Van Der Velden. 68 x 49¼. (Auckland City Art Gallery.)

VI. A group of houses in Auckland in the popular style of the 1920's. This style, derived from Art Nouveau, is known as "California bungalow." The repetition of similar but rarely identical elements makes for a pleasant street composition. (Photograph by R. N. Carrie.)

VII. "Phar Lap Winning the Melbourne Cup" (1936), totara carving by Chappie Hall. 10 x 35. (Otaga Museum.)

VIII. "Portrait of Mrs. Betty Curnow" (1942), oil by
Rita Angus. 30½ x 20½. (Auckland City Art Gallery.)

IX. "Entombment—after Titian" (1947), oil by Colin McCahon. 20½ x
25½. (Auckland City Art Gallery.)

X. An academic building (1950), Victoria University of Wellington, in the new functional style of the second half of the twentieth century.

XI. House of Miss Cater, Auckland (1955), Vernon Brown architect.

XII. "Figure" (1959), by Molly Macalister. Colored concrete, 40 inches.
(Auckland City Art Gallery.)

XIII. "Modulator" (1960), by W. R.
Allen. Concrete, 56½ inches. (Auckland City Art Gallery.)

XIV. "Arum Lily Pot" (1960), by Barry Brickell. Stoneware, 20 inches. (Auckland City Art Gallery.)

XV. A Maori woodcarver, clad in traditional dress, wielding the historic Stone Age implements of his craft—a greenstone (nephrite or jade) chisel, struck with a wooden mallet. Greenstone adzes may be observed in the foreground; these were the principal artifacts of the ancient Maori.

reprehensible than the modern Greek painter shaking his fist at the Parthenon. Perhaps in a generation or two, this reaction will have been weakened by a more widespread acceptance of modern art, but today this rejection of the topographical past and its contemporary equivalent plays no small part in conditioning creative attitudes in the visual arts.

A historical review of painting in New Zealand from 1770 to 1870 can only be relevant, within the terms of the present study, in the context of its influence on the modern spectator. This hundred-year period was given over to identifying and familiarizing the monumental and typical aspects of New Zealand landscape, principally for the purpose of survey, army strategy, and the encouragement of immigrants, and secondarily for the private pleasure of the practitioners and their immediate circle. There was and could be little direct contact with the New Zealand public, since the first Art Society was not founded until 1870, in Auckland, though some New Zealand watercolors were exhibited in Dunedin in 1860.

Nevertheless, this period is remarkably rich in the number of accomplished artists. The best would include Charles Heaphy (1822–1881), John Buchanan (1819–1898), William Fox (1812–1893), John Kinder (1819–1903), J. C. Richmond (1822–1898), George O'Brien (1822–1888), and Samuel Brees (1810–1865). Only Heaphy and Buchanan showed revolt against the topographical iconography, though their respective deviations, Buchanan's "Milford Sound" (Hocken Library) and Heaphy's "Mount Egmont" (Turnbull Library) may represent only their early and untutored attempts at topography, since their other work has the assured accuracy of the experienced topographer. There is so little of Buchanan's work extant that "Milford Sound" does appear as an eccentricity, whereas there are perhaps half a dozen works of Heaphy's in the same vein, which might indicate a personal as opposed to an official style. All these artists belong to the Romantic school. The process of discovery hardly leads to a classicizing attitude. But one could say of Richmond and Kinder that they were concerned with the underlying formal structure of the landscape rather more than with its dramatic elements. Richmond was, after all, a civil engineer and Kinder a classical scholar, and neither was

177

employed as draftsman: both were independent amateurs. The same could be said of Fox, who has emerged of late as almost the equal of Heaphy in his tonal control. These artists, at second hand, conveyed to the New Zealand public a pictorial account of their country's natural phenomena, and so established a visual identity of New Zealand. At this stage, however, this was a purely physical identity, for it is only rarely that one is stirred by any expression of feeling in these watercolors. The general absence of this quality is the reason one cannot relate this period to those that followed. Even if we consider transitional artists like J. C. Hoyte (1835–1913) and John Gully (1819–1888), who enjoyed both public demand and esteem, any element of feeling in their work is largely superficial. It is only perhaps when one looks at the work of Alfred Sharpe, of the same period, that one senses an attitude of self-identification: for instance, in his "Environs of Auckland," now in the Auckland Art Gallery.

New Zealand at this time harbored many itinerant artists, of whom little is known except their names, and they also contributed to the era "our imaginative pre-history," as Charles Brasch has called it.

It would be difficult to establish a time when a more feeling conception became general. The year 1890, when Van der Velden, Nairn, and Nerli, mature professional artists, arrived, has usually been accepted, but this year, although convenient, disregards the work of artists like David Con Hutton (1843–1910), John Gibb (1831–1909), and Alfred Walsh (1859–1916), who were all painters of feeling active between 1875 and 1890. (Walsh may be claimed as the first serious New Zealand artist, since he was professionally trained at the Dunedin School of Art by Con Hutton.) Not one of these three reveals any element of the topographical instinct that is so obvious in the work of both Gully and Hoyte. In the eighties artists were somewhat arbitrarily assigned to two groups, the "popular" and the "serious," but because the period is so little documented, it is difficult to discover how these serious artists fared in their relationship with the public. The Dunedin circle around W. M. Hodgkins appears to have been small, insulated, and amateur in its outlook, as witnessed by Frances Hodgkins' youthful excitement at Nairn's introduction of the nude life class. Painting in New Zealand in 1890 was still a polite art.

Petrus Van der Velden (1837–1913) was, as the *Lyttelton Times* recorded in its obituary of him, "a Bohemian of the best type." Allowing for the naïveté of the expression, it nicely describes the man, whom Van Gogh likened to George Eliot's Felix Holt, the radical. Van der Velden betrays almost the same symptoms as Gauguin. He threw up his partnership in a successful printing firm to take up painting at the age of thirty-one. Leaving a growing reputation, he sailed for New Zealand in 1890. The reason for his emigration was probably his lifelong fear of persecution. His letters reveal abrupt changes of mood and decision. In his last years he resorted to the consolation of alcohol and painted little. He exhibits the tragedy of the serious artist brought to his knees, not by antagonism, but by the sheer indifference of society. If he wished for respect, sales of his pictures, and the solidarity of a serious circle of painters, he arrived seventy years too early. Yet his great series of paintings devoted to the Otira Gorge resolve the New Zealand landscape, for the first time, into a symbol of anger and hope. New Zealand is proud of Frances Hodgkins, but she contributed little to New Zealand culture compared to Van der Velden; besides his paintings, he passed on through his pupils an example of uncompromising integrity. The preservation of this integrity in the soft-center conformity of New Zealand society has made its creative artists as unwanted as a reinforcing rod in Pavlova cake. Van der Velden would have found his own brand of contentment only during the past five years.

James Nairn (1859–1904) was not dissimilar in character. He was a product of the Scottish impressionist school and came to New Zealand for his health's sake. He was, it seems, as extroverted as Van der Velden was introverted. One imagines him a true Bohemian: not only did he redecorate his cabin on the ship he arrived in, but he used the walls of his Wellington house as canvases. He did, however, gain a place in artistic society, not only as a teacher at the Wellington School of Design, but as a council member of the Academy of Fine Arts; but this did not create any great demand for his pictures. Both he and Van der Velden were dependent on their friends, admirers, and former pupils for patronage, a pattern that persisted for the serious artist during the next fifty years. Through these two artists both expressionism and impressionism were introduced to this country at the professional level, but this was less important than the establishment of a nucleus of serious young New Zealand artists. Girolami Nerli (1863–1926), for instance, set Frances Hodgkins firmly on her career. Nerli came to New Zealand from Australia, where he had arrived in 1885 and where he had already gained a reputation in Sydney. One pictures him flitting from one tragicomic imbroglio to another, a kind of artistic remittance man, constantly on the move until his return to Italy about 1914. He belonged in style to the Italian realist group headed by Fattori. Slightly sentimental in its conception, his work was more acceptable than that of Van der Velden and Nairn. He was mainly concerned with figure subjects, which were an antidote to the regimen of landscape painting, and the early Hodgkins watercolors reflect his influence. Mention should also be made of Edward Fristrom (c. 1860–c. 1942), active as a teacher and painter in Auckland from 1903 to 1915, since his influence was as strong as the others in founding the modern movement in this country, particularly in Auckland, which was then a stronghold of photographic realist painters like Lindauer, Goldie, and Steele.

The outbreak of war in 1914 severely affected the young movement. Many of the artists had already gone to Europe: Owen Merton in 1904, Grace Joel in 1906, Raymond McIntyre in 1909, Mina Arndt in 1911, Frances Hodgkins in 1913, and Francis McCracken in 1914. Few came back, and so by 1918 almost all progress had stopped. Survivors like John Weekes (1881–1965), T. A. McCormack (b. 1883) were unable to do much but hold the fort, for none of the better artists between 1918 and 1930 was forceful enough in style or temperament to open up new avenues.

By 1930 light began to break on this desolate scene. In addition to the undercurrent stream of emergent nationalism, which got its strength from the generation of the twenties, there were two major stimulators of new directions in painting, R. N. Field, of the art department of the Dunedin Technical College, and Christopher

Perkins, who worked almost exclusively in Wellington. Field had developed a style that was a compound of Fauve and German expressionism, and Perkins was a follower of Paul Nash, the English neo-Romantic: both found a sympathetic following. There had been a more direct link with German expressionism since Mina Arndt had studied in Berlin under the influence of Corinth, and Flora Scales (who was to help Toss Woollaston) had worked with Hans Hofmann in Munich. It was hardly the color that New Zealand artists used, but the subjective and plastic treatment of the forms that was new. This was a percipient borrowing, since there was nothing better to render both the naturalistic appearance of the volcanic, eruptive landscape and to infuse it with symbolic content. After a long break, therefore, a conceptual link was made with Van der Velden. Perkins' influence, which may be detected at its best in the early work of Rita Angus gave rise to what is known, perhaps frivolously, as the Dead Tree and Old Colonial House School; its effective period ran from about 1938 to the early fifties. Largely illustrative and literary in concept, it did attempt to create a popular symbology of New Zealandisms, but it was too laden with the topographical instinct to be anything more than a picturesque cul-de-sac and offered no viable avenue for the progressive artist.

There seems no doubt now in looking back at the thirties that, *pace* the New Zealand tenderness for the overseas expert, the real regeneration of painting came from Field's group of artists in Dunedin. For, besides others, Woollaston studied with him in 1932 and Colin McCahon from 1937 to 1939. Also in Dunedin were Charles Brasch and Rodney Kennedy, the pioneer collectors of serious painting in this country.

Christchurch can also claim importance at this time with a similar group of artists, of which Rita Angus was one. It is possible to see in the work of Woollaston and Rita Angus the two trends that largely direct New Zealand today. Woollaston, international in style, drew mainly on European expressionism and Cézanne, while Rita Angus presented a regional style which, although analogous to kindred conceptions elsewhere, maintains its individuality. In this respect, one might quote the artist herself: "For me, New Zealand

181

is, in essence, medieval." Similarly, Grant Wood painted his "American Gothic" in the thirties after seeing fifteenth-century German painting on a visit to Germany. Stanley Spencer at the same time was influenced by the Italian primitives. This selection of unsophisticated influence would come naturally to the painter concerned with an ex-colonial regionalism, particularly as it was supported by the nonconformist antipathy to the urbanized "aristocratic" art of Wood's Middle West and Angus' New Zealand. Both Angus and Woollaston not only subscribed to the interpretation of landscape in oil and watercolor, but also to the identification of the New Zealander through the portrait. Woollaston's portraits of his wife (1936 and 1939) and Angus' well-known "Betty Curnow" (1942)—all now in the Auckland City Art Gallery—show their individual perception besides illustrating the matriarchal bias of New Zealand society.

From the late twenties the modern movement had its own platform in the Group, a loosely knit association which has continued to hold annual exhibitions in Christchurch. In those years it was the only evidence of serious contemporary painting presented to the public. The artistic center had now moved to Christchurch, where there was a small galaxy of artists, writers, and poets. There was in the late thirties apparently a greater homogeneity in the arts than there is today. Perhaps one other locality should be mentioned in discussing this period, for almost by coincidence it has had a long connection with painting. This was the Mapua-Motueka district, south of Nelson. James Nairn died at Motueka in 1904; Mina Arndt lived and died there; Woollaston lived at Mapua from 1931 to 1949, with only brief absences, and he still returns there and to the Upper Moutere Valley to paint; Colin McCahon spent periods in Mapua from 1939 to 1947. In its way, this area played as important a part in New Zealand painting as Pont Aven had done in France, for without the continuum it provided for painting and discussion from 1939 to 1948, it is doubtful whether painting in this country would be where it is today.

There is no New Zealand painter who has so consistently retained his original "motif" as Woollaston has with this Nelson landscape. It was there also that he had some brief tuition from

182

Flora Scales, the source of his expressionist form and brushwork. This period until 1950, when he moved to Greymouth, is marked by a sustained quality in Woollaston's work. Since then, and probably through the enforced isolation he has experienced on the West Coast, there have been considerable fluctuations in output and quality. In contrast, Rita Angus has moved about more, but her painting has remained remarkably constant in quality. Her earlier work, both in the handling and color, was akin to embroidery, an applied art which she has practiced. Lately the color has become stronger, more intense, and more broadly applied. But the late medieval vision has remained.

Complementary to the work of both these artists has been that of Colin McCahon (b. 1919), who first emerged as a painter in 1938–1939. It is complementary in the sense that both regionalism and international styles are brought together to make the same formal analysis of the landscape as Woollaston, but McCahon has invested this analysis with a symbolic content that stems from an intense regional vision, like that of Angus. Intense is the key word, for the intensity of his conception has a touch of the messianic about it, equally matched by strong dynamic forms and color. These thundering passages have been interspersed with calm lyrical periods, for instance the religious works of 1947 to 1950, which were followed by the Kauri and French Bay paintings of 1950–1953. Complementary, too, has been his welding of the Cézanne-Cubist-Mondrian direction to the stylized landscape forms of the Italian quattrocento, forming an individual style which he has sustained throughout the many facets of his insight. McCahon's insight does not lead him to ex cathedra utterances of doom, for if there is despair in the dark hollows of his hills there is also a corona of hope in the light of his horizons. In his later, more abstracted work, white splits or fragments the black. McCahon is the most profound artist that New Zealand has produced and also one of the best painters, for his control of tone in an almost monochromatic range is masterly.

Since the early fifties artists have proliferated, and the over-all quality of work has risen to the extent that painting in this country is now a major force in cultural development. It has, at the same time, become more diverse in direction and style. The postwar decades have been marked by the emigration and immigration of many artists. Thus, as in other countries, it becomes more difficult to present a coherent account. The three artists mentioned above have indigenously developed styles, for none of them has spent more than a year out of New Zealand. Although the same can be said of a few of our contemporary painters, they have experienced wholly different pressures and influences. Urbanization, the maturing of the national identity, swifter means of communication, the growth of patronage, and the increasing professionalism of the schools have combined to change the traditional pattern. Any opinion on current art must be hedged about with reservations. If some continuity of conception and attitude can be detected, then it is in the most general way, and perhaps not occasioned by familial ties, but through coincidence or accident. One might say, therefore, that Milan Mrkusich (b. 1925) and Don Binney (b. 1940) exhibit, in the former's emblematic paintings and in the latter's bird and landscape pictures, the same medievalism that inspired Rita Angus. It is worth noting that both artists have established their own styles entirely within the New Zealand context. As opposites, one could name Robert Ellis (b. 1929) and Pat Hanly (b. 1932) as representatives of urbanized and more sophisticated trends: Ellis with his series of aerial images of towns, and Hanly with his Figures in Light paintings. Ellis has worked in New Zealand for eight years; Hanly painted in London for five.

Similar remarks could be made about the remainder of the established artists, but no greater coherence would be achieved. One thing is certain: the painting becomes better year by year, and more artists demand notice, necessitating a fluid critical attitude. It would, however, not be foolhardy to take an optimistic view of the future.

Such optimism has been partly inspired by the visits to these islands by Nikolaus Pevsner and Sir Herbert Read, who pointed out several painters of merit. In the last three years, with the support of the Arts Council and the Department of External Affairs, exhibitions of contemporary New Zealand art have been sent overseas, to Japan, Malaysia, and India, to London, Brussels,

184

Paris, and Australia. This official recognition has helped to bring about a greater acceptance of the contemporary artist by the New Zealand public.

The first European-style houses to be built in New Zealand were imported from Sydney in prefabricated sections. One of these is still occupied on the beachfront in Russell, Bay of Islands. The plan was two rooms divided by a central corridor, with a lean-to at the rear. This accretive architecture is still practiced, since the main materials, wood and iron, can so easily be adapted and manipulated. These small colonial units were never intended for permanent dwelling, but many have survived. Their prototype was the English cottage, and therefore working-class in status. For the middle classes the Indian bungalow type with the surrounding veranda was adopted (a parallel source was probably the United States), and the Kemp house at Keri Keri, Bay of Islands, is claimed to be the first of the type. It was considered an eminently sensible design for the northern New Zealand climate, with its brilliant, burning sun (high actinic value) and tropical rainstorms. Aesthetically, the corrugated roof or kauri wood shingles and the weatherboard (clapboard) walls presented a corruscated surface for the brilliant light to play on, while the deep veranda provided a spatial façade for the house block. The roof was usually broken at the inside edge of the veranda. Occasionally, dormers were let in to give light to the attic space, as in the Mission House at Waimate North, Bay of Islands.

Slightly later in the century, the L-plan homestead was developed from a similar Indian bungalow type, this dividing living from sleeping quarters. A veranda was run round the inside of the L. These designs were introduced by the missionaries and the army, the vanguard of British colonization. The army introduced a further type in the narrow-façaded, two-storied dwelling with steep roof but with no veranda, which can be seen in the Tinakori Road area in Wellington. These fundamental plans still shape a great deal of New Zealand architecture in both private houses and schools.

The accretive tradition has dealt heavily with the veranda, for by filling it in with wood or glass, euphemisms like "sunporch" and "spare bedroom" were added. The function of the veranda has now been taken over ineffectively by the ubiquitous venetian blind, a higher status symbol than the holland blind. The veranda solution for light and heat in the North Island has never been satisfactorily replaced. Instead, the intrusive picture window has created fresh difficulties, since for privacy and the prevention of fading they have to remain shuttered. In the South, the colder winters have necessitated smaller window areas.

Until the beginning of the First World War, most architecture was imported. This not only applied to styles, but also to material elements such as stucco ceilings and iron frettings. It is interesting to observe, however, that at the end of the nineteenth century a fairly high degree of standardization had been achieved in joinery elements despite the small population and consequent demand of the time. There is a town-hall-clock type, for instance, which stretches across the Antipodes from Perth to Auckland. This was the period which created the myth that anything that came from overseas must be better than the indigenous article. The myth, which still continues, embraces ideas and people. New Zealand nursed its isolation as though it were an idiot child, fiercely resenting criticism of its condition, but accepting with a stupefying humility the superiority of progeny born elsewhere. Apart from its sociological influence, this myth has blunted and retarded the arts in this country and no more so than in architecture.

There was hardly a change from this position until the beginning of the Second World War, certainly none in larger buildings. One may admire, for instance, the warehouses in various towns, with their simple and restrained proportions and early Victorian shallow-arched windows. Constructed in wood, they are repetitions of the fine brick warehouses of England. One suspects that there was little New Zealand participation in the planning of these. There was also respectable architectural design to be found amongst commercial buildings, particularly banks. Their restrained neoclassicism is often to be preferred to recent contemporary work in the same field. One also may claim some element of pioneering in the use of new materials, for instance, in the reinforced concrete of Grafton Bridge in Auckland (1902), but again it bears no characteristics of a native genius. In the large structure, no Louis Sullivan arose to

186

give New Zealand a place in the architectural hierarchy. There was simply no demand in a country so seriously undercapitalized. An agrarian economy requires no architectural monuments other than the wool shed and the warehouse.

To find signs of individual architectural expression, one must examine the domestic range of housing. If the period to 1914 was largely English colonial in character, there was a change in orientation after this. Where the Australian travels to Europe via the Suez canal, the New Zealander goes by way of Panama.

It is thus that California offers a home from home for the New Zealander, in climate, flora, and in architecture. Before 1920 the Californian bungalow was firmly established as the popular house unit. These units were also successfully arranged into street façades, as in the Ponsonby and Epsom areas in Auckland. It was an importation of genius that has hardly been matched since; with its recessed short porch with veranda and its extended eaves, it was ideally suited to the climate. Nevertheless, the ties of empire proved stronger. New Zealand architects gained their diplomas in England, and even when the first school of architecture was established in 1917, its largely English-trained staff reoriented architectural thinking to Europe and Britain, and the American contact was all but broken. The stagnation of the depression years did nothing to help progress. Two monuments of municipal European neoclassicism arose between the wars in the shape of the Auckland Museum and the Dominion Museum in Wellington. Ponderously situated on the tops of their respective hills, they serve as symbols of insensitive importation, significant only in their bulk as they straddle the landscape. On the domestic scale, New Zealand's principal towns in the thirties acquired, with no great benefit, debased versions of the Maxwell Fry–Bauhaus derivative of the curved-bay-front house or single-story flat block. Almost invariably the solid balustrade hid the poverty of a sloped corrugated-iron roof. In the larger apartment buildings, one finds variants of Queen Anne mansions. It would be wrong, however, to suggest that there were no houses of merit in this period, but they were too rare to make any impression on the general pattern.

Like the other arts, the new architecture had its genesis in the last year of the Second World War. As in other countries, the returning servicemen were impatient with apathy and anxious to step firmly into the twentieth century. The arrested immigration of the depression and manpower losses through emigration and war had done much to rob New Zealand of both practical and intellectual competiton. (Visitors to these shores still complain of a Victorian atmosphere.) One could say, if somewhat cruelly, that New Zealand was controlled and directed by old men. They dominated the architectural firms. However, the first two postwar issues of qualified architects from the school in Auckland have materially altered the face of New Zealand architecture. Mention should also be made of the Architectural Center in Wellington, which created a public awareness of architecture and town planning through exhibitions and discussion. Unfortunately, there also has been an epidemic of dull to hideous building by housing firms and group housing schemes. The government, through its architectural division, played an equivocal part in postwar housing: excellent apartment buildings on the one hand, and depressing single-unit planning on the other. In the last six years, however, private capital has enabled the nongovernment architects to compete with large buildings, where formerly the government had a monopoly. In most cases, however, these large buildings are inevitably variants of the international style of curtain-wall multistory block, but at the moment they offer a certain glamor to the urban scene of New Zealand, which is largely low-storied because of the earthquake risk.

An ever-recurring architectural argument is that of regional idiom versus the international styles. The growth of a national identity has sharpened the attack on the unadapted import, person, or thing. At the same time, the goal of a regional style becomes distorted, caused by the overconscious effort to reach it. Nevertheless, this search for a regional expression is very real, whatever the opinions of United States or European pundits. The very statement that art is international is rejected here as patronizing, as well it may be in Tanzania or Ceylon, since it implies that the indigenous creative artist should give up the struggle and join the trifid-like international conglomerate. Recently, the government's engagement of Sir

Basil Spence to design a new Parliament House created an architectural storm of protest, for a national competition would have provided a considerable and necessary stimulus to local architects. So far, therefore, and by necessity, regional expression has come through the domestic house and small building. Much is owed in this direction to the late V. A. Brown, who lectured at the Auckland School of Architecture from the early forties to 1964. Because of his emphasis on relating space, design, and materials to a local scale of human activity and perception, two generations of architects have been intensely concerned with the domestic house. There were, too, other pioneers in the late forties and early fifties: the architectural firms Pascoe and Hall in Christchurch, Plishke and Firth in Wellington, Gordon Wilson, the government architect, Tibor Donner, the Auckland City Council architect, and R. H. Toy.

In recent years, other names have appeared, such as John Scott in Hawkes Bay, E. J. McCoy in Dunedin, Peter Bevan and F. M. Warren in Christchurch. In Auckland, Bill Wilson, Ivan Juriss, Peter Middleton, James Hackshaw, and others have all contributed to giving a regional significance to the domestic unit. However, it is worth noting, and with some satisfaction, that the article and plates which appeared in the Commonwealth number of the *Architectural Review* (October, 1959) are already out of date, because of the increase of private capital and confidence. Private architectural firms are now handling almost as much of the large-scale building as the government architectural division. Whether or not criticism can be leveled at many of these buildings, this dissemination of architectural patronage has led to greater diversity of approach and the growth of healthy competition. One factor, nevertheless, is still missing, and that is criticism. The profession's own journal and *Home and Building* are the only publications dealing with architecture. Neither can be said to offer anything on the level of the English *Architectural Review*. In a way, the architects are themselves to blame for a situation which many of them deplore. Their aspirations to the high professional status of law and medicine make them resentful of anything but the most reserved professional comment. In two recent architectural conferences, however, critical discussions have been held at which several delegates expressed

189

their astonishment that they found them stimulating and helpful. The most recent emanation of this changed attitude is the formation in Auckland by professional architects and senior architectural students of a group to foster an informed critical approach to modern architecture. This is a hopeful sign in a country which so often views criticism as either personal attack or favoritism.

In conclusion, one might take an optimistic view of the architectural scene. The spate of large buildings has given a much-needed monumental nucleus to the principal cities, and the progressive atttitude to the smaller unit, provides an imaginative continuity of regional architecture, despite the rash of builders' speculation housing in the suburbs.

As in the other visual arts, sculpture in New Zealand has a short history, even though its practice goes back to the turn of the century. It is, perhaps, here that one would look for some connection with the art of the Maori, but there is none; long ago the Maori carver was rigorously restrained from any deviation from the traditional norm. There is certain evidence to show that one or two carvers were prepared to marry the two cultures, introducing European motifs into the curvilinear style. One of these, in the Otago Museum, "Phar Lap Winning the Melbourne Cup," although of no great aesthetic merit, certainly sustains the belief that there were possibilities for a genuine folk art which Maori and *pakeha* could share together. But the insistence, on both sides, that the Maori should preserve his traditional arts at all costs killed this development. Only a few years ago, indeed, Walter Nash, then prime minister, made the same impassioned plea for preservation. Thus, the paradox has arisen that while social commentators and authorities seek an equal place for the Maori in contemporary New Zealand, sentimentality and *tourismo* wish to thrust him back two centuries. Consequently, those Maori who have adopted the European styles have done so in painting rather than in sculpture.

What sculpture was done before the Second World War ranked in mediocrity with that of many other countries. New Zealand has its small crop of public monuments, many devoted to memorials of the First World War and if, in time, they gain the patina of indifferent respect, they have done nothing to allow public patronage of the sculptor to make headway until very recently. For it is generally accepted that public and private commissions are essential to the life of sculpture. There were other factors that slowed sculpture's regeneration, principally that of media, for there is an absence of good stone in New Zealand, and bronze casting was almost unknown and certainly not generally feasible. This resulted in the painted plaster cast or cast cement for large works, unless funds permitted metal casting in Australia or England. Large-scale wood carving was not practiced except in isolated cases, and so sculpture almost reverted to the art of the miniature. New Zealand art has often taken a leap forward due to the stimulus of a single individual; so it was with sculpture when Alan Ingham (b. 1921) returned home from working with Henry Moore. Setting up a small foundry in Auckland, Ingham almost at once was responsible for renewed interest, particularly when he was able to cast occasional small pieces. Auckland can claim the best sculptors in the country: among them should be mentioned Molly Macalister, Alison Duff, Jim Allan, Anne Severs, and Greer Twiss. But they are not unchallenged by Russell Clark (d. 1966) and Tom Taylor in Christchurch. For all of them the last few years have been years of hope, since commissions from public and private sources have materialized and provided competitive stimulus.

All these sculptors work, in the main, in representational forms, although Jim Allan (b. 1922) has worked from time to time at geometric abstractions: one work now in the Auckland Art Gallery suggests his considerable potential in this direction, but recently he has returned to figure groups. His works reveal the influence of his British training. Technically he is many-sided, producing works in marble, cement, welded steel, and cast bronze. His main commissions have been a Stations of the Cross series for the Futana Chapel in Wellington (architect, John Scott) and a Maori figure for Whakatane, commissioned by a public-spirited citizen of that town. Recently he won a competition for a public work at Pakuranga, a suburb of Auckland. He has shown few works in exhibitions and seldom works on a domestic scale.

His opposite is Alison Duff (b. 1914), who was trained at the School of Fine Arts, University of Canterbury, and then spent ten

191

years in Australia. She owes little to external influences, for her style is almost entirely directed by her imagination, so that the tidy critical mind would find it difficult to reconcile her series of Heads of Hillary—solid, rocklike variations on one of the conquerors of Everest in cast cement—and her delicate welded-steel-rod figurations of New Zealand birds. Recently she received a commission from the Queen Elizabeth II Arts Council for a bust of the New Zealand writer Frank Sargeson. This was an apt choice, since Alison Duff, of all the sculptors, has a regional perception.

On the other hand, the sculptor with whom she is usually linked, Molly Macalister (b. 1920), has drawn mostly from the contemporary Italian movement, creating figures which are innately monumental and possess a timeless quality. Her "Seated Maori Youth" (Victoria University of Wellington) might well illustrate Gauguin's dictum: "Let everything about you breathe the calm and peace of the soul. Also avoid motion in a pose. Each of your figures ought to be in a static position. . . ." She recently completed for the Auckland City Council an over-life-size Maori figure which is in bronze, but previously she has used mainly cast cement and, in her early works, wood.

Molly Macalister's interest in the Italians may have been inspired by the arrival from England some years ago of Anne Severs (b. 1931), who had worked with Marini in Milan. Rather similar in style, and yet carrying a more refined and sophisticated presence, the works of Anne Severs explore the same humanist subjects, although there is a greater feeling of tension about them. Her drawings are particularly distinguished.

The youngest member of this group, Greer Twiss (b. 1937), has probably created the greatest interest of late. In two exhibitions he has shown a series of athletes and a series of marchers. Partly inspired by newspaper action-photographs, he created single figures or groups of athletes jumping or running. He made a real sculptural use of the distortions effected by speed and physical exertion. Thus, in these groups he creates a majestic and sometimes frightening façade of strained and dynamic human machinery. The prowess, of late, of New Zealand athletes in world competitions rendered these figures timely and symbolic. The marcher groups explored similar sculptural ideas, but with flags and banners acting as foils to the figures below. All these works are in bronze, cast in his own foundry.

The foundation, a few years ago, of a Society of Sculptors, under the aegis of Professor Paul Beadle, has given the sculptors a professional unity which is already bearing fruit in the shape of commissions.

In the South, Russell Clark sculpted for many years, but he tended to be very eclectic in style, ranging from the abstract ear on the Timaru Telephone Exchange through the Mooresque "Family Group" in Hay's Supermarket in Christchurch, to a naturalistic head of an old Maori in Takaka marble. He is probably the most experienced in commissioned work, for he recently won a closed competition arranged by the Queen Elizabeth II Arts Council with an impressive non-figurative group to be sited in front of the Little Theatre in Lower Hutt. Tom Taylor has also made a lead relief for the Qantas office in Christchurch.

From this review it is not difficult to see that the main sculptural trend is representational and humanistic, and in this way coincident with New Zealand painting; this is what might be expected at this stage. Urbanization has not yet reached that point where man takes an antipathetic view of his fellow men, his sentiment blunted and antagonized by overcrowding. New Zealand's small population in a large landscape will ensure for some time that the figurative subject, whatever its form, will be the main concern of its sculptors.

The studio potter and the studio jeweler have perhaps suffered the most from the vagaries of import control. For the first decades of this century, New Zealand subsisted on imported ceramics and jewelry. If there was any studio activity it was amateur and certainly spasmodic. Towards the end of the Second World War, however, the dearth of imported wares gave rise to the practice of these two crafts, to which could be added weaving and book-binding. But this was a short-lived renaissance, since the freeing of imports in the late 1940's once more filled the shops, and the studio craftsman had to give up the struggle. In relation to this renaissance, mention should be made of Helen Hitchings' Gallery in Wellington. She was the pioneer dealer in New Zealand, and her enthusiasm for all the arts is warmly remembered. In 1949–50 she was sponsoring potters like William Newland and Kenneth Clark, both of whom are now well known in England, and Len Castle, who will be mentioned further. There was good turned woodwork by Roger Sullivan and jewelry by Edith Morris, as well as occasional furniture designed by E. A. Plishke, the architect. How well one can say in New Zealand, as perhaps in other developing countries, "Too soon!" Various enterprises have come to grief through a misfortune in timing, while later efforts have succeeded.

The turning point for the studio potter was created partly by the Labour government of 1957, which banned all semiluxury imports, and the return of Len Castle from the Leach pottery at St. Ives. Another important factor was the annual Art and Design Summer School, arranged by the University of Auckland Extra-Mural Department. In its early years it offered for painters, sculptors, and potters a companionable workshop. The position today is quite astonishing, not only for the numbers of able potters, but for the quality of the work produced. Even with relaxed import conditions, there are now at least six potters working full time. No small part has been played by Helen Mason, who, besides being an artist of note, generated a National Association and edits its lively *Quarterly* in Wellington. Geographically, potters are well distributed. There is, of course, no indigenous tradition in the craft, so that considerable adaptations have been made of overseas styles, principally English and Japanese. The robust shapes and freedom from sophistication of medieval English form have appealed rather more than contemporary English studio pottery. The Japanese influence has been exceptionally strong, implemented in no small way by the visits to this country of John Chappell, an English potter working in Japan, Takaichi Kawai, and Shoji Hamada himself. Visits to Japan by Helen Mason, Doreen Blumhardt, and Terry Barrow have strengthened this bond. Bernard Leach has also made an extensive tour of the country. Local clay and glaze sources, fired in locally designed kilns, have also contributed to a feeling of independence and confidence.

Discussion of individual potters must be reserved for the few who combine a technical proficiency and a creative spirit. Len Castle has had probably the longest career, although he took up the craft full time only a few years ago. Like most of the professionals, he has to fire a regular quota of domestic ware: mugs, bowls, plates, herb pots, and the like. His more individual works are large pots and molded dishes. Glazes range from dark to light, and the surfaces usually carry relief or reverse-relief patterns, which creates an intentional texture apart from that made by the glazes in firing. All Castle's pots have a refinement about them that lifts them away from their English or Japanese prototypes, while still retaining their essential robustness of form.

On the other hand, Barry Brickell comes nearest to being innately a New Zealand potter. Living in virtual isolation at Coromandel, he has devoted himself entirely to potting for the last six or seven years. All his work is informed by a philosophy that might have stemmed from William Morris, simplicity, honesty of purpose in all things, form created by the "feeling" hand and eye, sensing the potential of the material directly, rather than through existing exemplars. Brickell describes a good pot as being "animated," gaining spirit from an organic form and texture. Quasimedieval in content, this philosophy, though by no means unique today, is an invocation of the early colonial attitude to European sophistication in all things. Somewhat irrationally, sophistication has been equated with materialism, which demands the uniform, insensitive object of conveyor-belt production. Brickell sells his pots in order to combat this demand, to restore a feeling for the "honest" and the "animated." Hence his impatience with bread-and-butter lines, which he still has to produce. Even so, each coffee mug, for instance, preserves its individuality. There is no doubt that medieval English pottery has had its influence on him, but each fresh departure is directed by his genuinely creative mind.

Of the Japanese influence, Helen Mason is perhaps the best example. Since her visit to Japan, her work has taken a more assured line, both in slab and wheel forms; she is also moving towards larger forms. This tendency may be the result of a growing connoisseur demand for the individual pot, and if all our galleries and museums would start an active policy in this direction, a further incentive would be added. Rather like the sculptor, the studio potter requires this demand to truly fulfill himself.

For the public there is no lack of sources from which they can acquire studio pottery. Dealer galleries in Wellington, Auckland, Christchurch, and Dunedin carry most potters' work and temporary exhibitions fill any gaps. The work of New Zealand potters has been exhibited in a major show in Australia, and large pots by each of the three major potters discussed here were included with a touring exhibition sent to Japan, Malaysia, and India in 1964–1965. How long the present boom will last is difficult to predict, but with the right kind of encouragement our major ceramic artists should continue, as they are now, making a very serious contribution to our culture.

It is perhaps a universal phenomenon that good typography usually emerges from the publication of poetry. New Zealand typography is no exception, for we associate the two best-known names, Denis Glover, himself a poet, and Robert Lowry, with the early editions of New Zealand poets. As early as 1932, Lowry was showing his work in *Phoenix*, in which appeared the poems of R. A. K. Mason, Charles Brasch, A. R. D. Fairburn, and Allen Curnow.

In 1934, Lowry established the Unicorn Press in Auckland, where he was joined by Ronald Holloway with his Griffin Press. After the war Lowry, with two partners, created the Pelorus Press, and a little later, as a side venture, the Pilgrim Press. Until his death in 1963, Lowry worked at the Wakefield Press. Glover had started printing in 1933, and in 1937 he founded the Caxton Press, which he re-established after the war. A few years later he moved to Wellington and joined H. H. Tombs at the Wingfield Press. Recently he has worked as a free-lance printer and typographer. Glover is a classicist, with a sure sense of balance and form in letterpress and space. His selection of face and paper is usually in impeccable taste. Lowry, on the other hand, took greater risks, and when successful his layouts have a vitality often lacking in Glover. A romantic, Lowry moved his medium about like a baroque architect, so that there is a sense of movement; oppositions of masses and sudden voids of space created exciting passages of print, but his taste was not unerring.

The foundations laid in the late thirties and the forties have now borne fruit to such an extent that it is almost invidious to mention names. The presses mentioned are still working and producing, on the whole, books of high quality. However, the good printer must have a good client, and here should be mentioned the outstanding publications of the Schools Publications Department, aided since the late forties by the Government Printer. In a smaller way the Auckland Art Gallery has a deserved reputation for its catalogues, which have been printed mainly by the Pelorus and Wakefield presses. Commercial printing has improved out of all recognition in the last five or six years, and in the field of advertizing, the main agencies have been instrumental in creating work comparable to the syndicated advertisements of overseas firms. Here the proliferation of industrial firms and the opening of new trade avenues in the past few years has allowed greater expenditure on advertising. Economic diversity often leads to other benefits than just an improvement in the balance of payments.

In comparison, the graphic arts are the most neglected media in the country. In fact, there has never been a time when these media have been prominent: consequently, indigenous printmakers of any quality are very rare. Closely related to typography was the work of Mervyn Taylor (1906–1964), a wood engraver of considerable merit. His illustrations and end-blocks decorate the pages of many publications. In the mid-thirties, the cartoonist Trevor Lloyd (d. 1937) made a considerable number of etchings that have recently won wide approval, straightforward and unassuming studies of the New Zealand bush. The best impressions are comparable to similar work elsewhere in the same period. In the last few years a few painters have turned to printmaking, like Robert Ellis (woodcuts) and Pat Hanly (monotypes), with some success. Regular print-makers like Roy Cowan and Juliet Peter in Wellington and Kees Hos and Louise Henderson in Auckland produce decorative work often of a high technical order, but most of their work lacks solid content. An encouraging sign is the recent development of silk-screen printing.

PATTERN OF NEW ZEALAND CULTURE

The resurgence of printmaking in Europe and the United States has, surprisingly, created no echo in New Zealand, even though regular exhibitions of prints have been toured throughout the country. It may be that the New Zealand artist is still primarily concerned with "the major statement" in painting or sculpture, and that the print demands a connoisseur audience that does not yet exist in this country in sufficient numbers.

New Zealand was by no means backward in establishing, quite early, machinery for the education of its artists. There are, however, many reservations to be made about the quality of the end product. The first school of art to be founded was in Dunedin in 1870. At this time Dunedin was the artistic center, mainly through the activities of William Mathew Hodgkins, the father of Frances Hodgkins. This art school, now an appendage to the Dunedin Technical College, remained a force until the 1930's. Teachers like Hutton, Nerli, O'Keefe, and R. N. Field were responsible for the training of many good artists in their respective periods. But until the turn of the century artists tended to work and learn from individuals, like Van der Velden in Christchurch and James Nairn in Wellington. By 1900 the two major schools of today, the Canterbury School of Art and the Auckland School of Fine Arts, were established—although not in their present form. Both schools now are university departments, but initially they were privately endowed. Between them they provide secondary-school art teachers for the Education Board. The careers of both schools have been uneven, and each has passed through the doldrums of rigid academicism, thereby creating, as in other countries, a generation of serious artists with no formal training. The position is now much changed. From their inception the art schools tended to recruit staffs from England; the belief in the "overseas expert" was a fundamental tenet of New Zealand philosophy until the last decade. While there were several exceptions, many of the teachers lacked two essentials, imagination and liberalism. Consequently, style and technique were imposed from above to such an extent that as recently as ten years ago the Auckland school could mount an annual students' exhibition that looked like a one-man show. The notion of appointing New Zealand staff with established artistic reputations was slow in gaining acceptance. It is true that Alfred Walsh (1859–1916), who was trained in Dunedin, was appointed to the school in Christchurch in 1886, but it was not until the late 1940's that New Zealanders in any number were engaged.

Both schools were incorporated with their respective universities at about the same time, and since then, and largely within the last five years, they have re-established their reputations. From exhibition catalogues one can draw the evidence that most artists of twenty-five and under are the products of either school. At first only the major arts were taught, but now there are two flourishing departments of design. As yet they have had little influence on the industrial field, except through the private work of their staffs, but eventually they will supply trained designers, for the school at Auckland is already planning a full industrial design course. (Departments of design already exist in Wellington and at the Seddon Technical College in Auckland, although the latter is primarily concerned with apprentice training.)

Art teaching in the schools has also improved in recent years; it is particularly effective where the art specialist has a sympathetic headmaster. Teaching methods are similar to those in use overseas, but there is still a shortage of trained personnel, while many teachers of the older generations are using outworn methods. What is completely absent is the teaching of art appreciation and art history. Although some schools make use of their local galleries, this is entirely dependent on the enthusiasm of the individual teacher, so there is nothing like the programs in operation in the United States. However, because of changes in the entrance examinations of the art schools, secondary schools will have to provide short courses in art history and theory. This subject is taught at university level only at Auckland, and at present to first stage only, although there are good prospects of second- and third-stage courses, so that in time New Zealand will be able to supply its own art historians, both in the education field and for art gallery professional staffs.

Not so very long ago, to profess an interest in the visual arts in New Zealand was to be labeled a "beardie" or a "weirdie," and the arts were generally reserved as a woman's domain. Here again attitudes have changed remarkably quickly; in 1965, for the first time, equal numbers of male and female students studied at the School of Fine Arts in Auckland. This is yet another sign of maturity, and a mature attitude to the arts surely presages maturity in other directions. One may presume, if this maturity is evident at the student level, that there is promise of an informed and perceptive society for the visual artist in the future.

From 1928 until 1946 the visual arts in New Zealand were served by the journal *Art in New Zealand*; from 1945 to 1951, by the *Arts Year Book*. For the last fourteen years there has been no publication devoting itself entirely to the arts. This is paradoxical, since it is during the last decade that the greatest developments have occurred. Both of the journals mentioned maintained a precarious balance on their respective fence lines. Forward-looking editorials prefaced backward-looking illustrations. Criticism was proffered with a supine equivocation ("fair-mindedness" in local terminology), so that the reader now has no means of determining contemporary attitudes. Both publications are valuable, however, for the illustrations. For a picture of the immediate postwar years, the *Arts Year Book* provides a broad canvas of illustration, but little textual matter of value. *Art in New Zealand* had few illustrations, although its color plates were usually of excellent quality. Useful to a point are the articles devoted to single artists, and these are generally well illustrated, but the researcher now would exchange the studio chitchat for a few established facts. For all their faults, both journals lent some cohesion to the artistic milieu. The regular reports from the main centers that appeared in *Art in New Zealand* gave readers an over-all cover of various activities. Today this is wholly lacking, and information must be gathered by correspondence or by personal visits. Since there is no national daily paper, our newspapers are provincial in their coverage; the only other sources of any serious comment are the New Zealand *Listener* and the quarterly *Landfall*, but neither of these gives more than a sporadic look at the visual arts. National information has to be gathered from the annual touring exhibitions arranged by the Auckland City Art Gallery.

Turning to criticism in the daily press, one has to distinguish between the news cover, which is ample, and the art-criticism column, which in most cases has poor space allowance. Without doubt the *Christchurch Press* has offered not only the most space but the best criticism over the last ten years. In Wellington the *Evening Post*, while giving as much space to criticism, deserves little praise for its content; until recently, it followed the provincial newspaper policy of having a journalist rather than an art critic write on the visual arts. Even the *New Zealand Herald* in Auckland has resorted to employing a free-lance journalist. The *Auckland Star* has a better record, for it now uses three informed critics and runs a regular column on the visual arts. If serious commentary is now more available, it is still at the mercy of subeditorial scissors, which play havoc with coverage at times.

There can be little complaint on art-news coverage. Two controversies which made the international press, the sculpture of Henry Moore (1956) and the proposed purchase of a work by Barbara Hepworth for the Auckland City Art Gallery (1963), both rated more column-inches than probably any other news item in recent years. In general, the handling was reasonably fair, and both papers in Auckland editorially took the liberal view, the *Star* consistently and the *Herald* belatedly. Over the past decade, then, the New Zealand press has contributed to a more liberal public attitude to art, mainly through its news coverage. It should be emphasized, however, that within the last fifteen years one paper editorially accused an artist of contributing to juvenile delinquency and another opined that abstract art was the result of socialist and communist subversion. Even though these remarks were expressed in small provincial papers, they indicate a stratum of often violent opinion against the arts.

Further examples of this gross and often hysterical illiberalism towards art and artist can be found in letters to editors. If this is in evidence in other countries, it is by no means so damaging as it can be in a country of only fewer than three million people. The creative New Zealander now settled overseas could point his finger at this general attitude as the reason for his emigration. If this atmosphere is now dissipating, one might suggest that the purgation effected by these controversies has cleared the system of much of its gall. Praise is due to the mass media for the part they have played; press, radio, and television have contributed to the more general understanding and acceptance of contemporary artistic methods.

One of the most viable means of strengthening and deepening cultural roots is the museum, and New Zealand is comparatively rich in this kind of institution. Our general museums have enviable collections of Pacific art, and although Maori culture predominates, northern Pacific cultures are well represented; and it has been said that great art in New Zealand is best found in the ethnological collections rather than in art galleries. However, this remark is not so true as it was. New Zealand museums, in general, have not adopted the more closed policies of other countries and have collected widely, perhaps too widely, in all fields. Thus, Otago Museum has an excellent collection of ceramics, representing past and present. It also holds the only collection of Greek and Roman works in the country. Although diminutive by most overseas standards, this collection of small statuary and vases is of good quality.

Probably the best-displayed collection is that at the Canterbury Museum. Here there is a superb hall of oriental art and an excellent reconstruction of a street of the colonial period, with shops and displays of furniture and everyday objects. Attention to the colonial past is now arresting the once almost willful destruction of the past. Most other museums are concerned with this field, but none as yet can compete with the Canterbury display.

The Canterbury Museum has also contributed to the preservation of the French collection at Akaroa, where a small museum and period house have been stocked and furnished. The National Historic Places Trust has taken responsibility for the preservation of sites and buildings; for instance, the large-scale restoration of the mission house at Waimate North, Bay of Islands. Concern for a tangible past is further evidence of a developing maturity and a sense of national identity. Outwardly the New Zealander may still scoff at tradition as an inhibitor of progress, but now there has been sufficient progress to permit and even make necessary a lifeline back to the past. Further evidence of this desire is afforded by the intention of Auckland's Museum of Transport and Technology to establish a colonial village. In recent years the Art Galleries and Museums Association has publicized the possibility of a colonial museum area in the Bay of Islands—the earliest European settlement in New Zealand—an area fortunately far enough away from any of the major towns to generate those provincial jealousies that have rendered sterile many another proposal. These and other efforts have done a great deal to establish an ethnic tradition for the European in New Zealand. There has always been a concern for preservation of the Maori tradition in its multitudinous forms, both in making collections and in field work.

The museums at Wellington and Auckland have for some time had a policy of collecting furniture and artifacts, both English and those that can be ascribed to New Zealand manufacture. Thus, in the field of three-dimensional applied arts the museums have done something to provide exemplars. Much more could be done; each new generation of New Zealanders stands a better chance of affecting his material environment with improved taste.

Unfortunately, the contribution of the art galleries has been slighter. Little money and few bequests hardly allow for the existence of rich collections, but on the other hand lack or rather the nonappointment of professional staff has preserved many of the country's galleries as unwitting museums of their nineteenth-century prototypes. Contemporary attitudes to the visual arts are today almost entirely conditioned by temporary exhibitions and commercial galleries. Until the 1950's neither of these sources was available in any effective way. New Zealanders traditionally have been the most avid buyers of art books in the world; the painters (with few exceptions) were completely insensitive to the texture of their medium. Their painting was flat, like color reproductions. In the last ten years this aspect has been rectified, and Aucklanders, at least, have seen more exhibitions than their counterparts in any Australian city. The Auckland City Art Gallery implemented a policy of introducing overseas exhibitions of all kinds. This effort, assisted by the British Council and cultural organizations in other countries, has ensured a regular flow of exhibitions around New Zealand. The outcome has been rewarding: public awareness and demand, resulting in the establishment of dealer galleries and thereby serious recognition for the New Zealand artist.

Linked to the interest in the colonial past is the widespread concern with the topographical art of the nineteenth century. The best two collections of this period were originally the result of the enthusiasm of individuals, Dr. Hocken in Dunedin and Alexander Turnbull in Wellington. Besides other benefactions, they presented to the libraries named after them comprehensive collections of the nineteenth-century watercolorists, many of whom are now also represented in the provincial galleries. Several exhibitions have been devoted to them in recent years, resulting in a more coherent account both of the chronology and the quality of these artists and incidentally in soaring prices on the art market. As an instance, a good watercolor by J. C. Hoyte ten years ago would fetch from $25 to $40; today prices have reached $300.

Of the galleries in the four main cities, only those in Dunedin, Wellington (the National Gallery), and Auckland merit discussion, for the McDougall Gallery in Christchurch has the poorest collection in both senses of the word. Dunedin has had the benefit of donations of quality, and in its purchasing the aid of overseas advice. It is particularly strong in the English School, both oils and watercolors, and gained from the collection numbering in hundreds donated by Archdeacon Smythe some years ago. Paintings by Constable, Turner, Wilson, Gainsborough, Reynolds, Raeburn, and others are held. Continental schools are represented sparsely, although there are several good examples. Its policy toward New Zealand painting has not been so informed: its holding of earlier artists is inadequate, and its attitude to contemporary artists has been timid. Timidity has been the keynote in this respect of all the galleries except that in Auckland, which is the only one where painting of the last twenty years has been collected seriously.

The National Gallery in Wellington was founded only in 1936. Although it took over a small collection from the New Zealand Academy of Fine Arts, its collection can hardly be termed a national one. Inadequately staffed and financed by successive governments, its activity is barely measurable, though it has acquired a reasonable collection of contemporary English painting and some

Continental works, among them an early Derain and a very good Marquet. There is also a good collection of English eighteenth-and nineteenth-century watercolors. It has the best old master print collection of all the galleries, due to two gifts from Bishop Monrad, a Danish political exile, and Sir John Ilott, so that both Dürer and Rembrandt are well represented. It also houses a national portrait gallery, which is hardly distinguished artistically, except for a portrait of Captain James Cook by John Webber and one of Katherine Mansfield by Estelle Rice. Its New Zealand collection is strong in the early watercolors and the work of some of the foundation members of the modern movement. Otherwise, it has given no support to the contemporary artist.

The gallery at Auckland is the oldest in the country, having been founded in 1886, largely through the generosity of Sir George Grey and J. T. Mackelvie. The latter left a collection and an endowment which has enabled the gallery to purchase several notable works. Its collections range over the earlier European schools, particularly of seventeenth-century Italian painting and twentieth-century art. Its group of sculpture (mostly 1900–1920) is the best in Australasia. Its print collection includes a large group of French nineteenth-and twentieth-century works, and also a fine collection of works of the German expressionist period. The New Zealand collections have grown in the last twelve years so that they now offer the only comprehensive coverage in the country. Important also is its collection of the works of Frances Hodgkins, the only New Zealand-born artist to achieve an overseas reputation. Although none of her important work was done in New Zealand, she, like Katherine Mansfield, has been a symbol of hope and aspiration for the serious artist.

Art societies abound, but in general character they do not differ from those elsewhere. Often their obscurantist views have impeded progress. At the time of their foundation, the art societies provided the venue for exhibitions and an artistic nuclei. Their most important period was from 1870 to 1900, when the presence in the country of overseas contemporary painters and the natural effect of the European revolutionary movements caused splinter groups to be formed, for instance, the Sketch Club of Wellington under the leadership of James Nairn. Inevitably the gap widened and the societies lost their professional stiffening. In one or two towns, such as Nelson, Hamilton, and Gisborne, the art society manages the local public gallery with some success. Only the galleries at Auckland, Wanganui, and Christchurch are a direct charge on the taxpayer. Dunedin's gallery is managed by a gallery society with assistance from the City Council. In fact, local body support is quite inadequate, and recently the Art Galleries and Museums Association decided to take the matter up with the Municipal Association. In contrast, all the larger museums are a charge on their respective provincial local bodies and are administered by trusts. The Auckland City Council subscribes $50,000 annually to its gallery and $20,000 to the museum, but such a contribution is unequaled by any other authority. However, the wind of change has been blowing gently through the woods of indifference of late, and the next few years should see a marked improvement in public support for the arts.

Apart from the benefactions to the galleries already mentioned and the collecting of a few private individuals, one could say that until six years ago there was no outstanding patronage of the visual arts in New Zealand. In 1895, the painter Van der Velden complained in bitter terms that he never sold any pictures. For the serious progressive artist this remained the situation until very recently. The selection of works for exhibitions of the earlier painters has revealed that they also were dependent on a few enthusiastic collectors or family friends. Acquisition of popular painting, the local euphemism for it being "traditional art," has always been considered *de rigueur* by the well-to-do. Artists of this caliber can earn up to $8,000 a year once they receive the accolade, generally bestowed by the press publicity of their sales. What a thing is worth is often the yardstick of evaluation in New Zealand: recently, an American scientist interviewed on the radio was asked the cost of his equipment rather than the aim of his research. Large sums are being spent nowadays throughout the country on such furniture pictures.

Auckland ten years ago was notorious as a city with no picture buyers, but the situation is now much changed since the advent of dealer galleries. The pioneer gallery in this city, if we except a slightly earlier and largely abortive effort, was the Ikon, now unhappily defunct. But in its brief existence of four or five years it brought the serious artist and the public together properly for the first time. The change in the Auckland buying pattern was due largely to its efforts and to the support it had from artists. Auckland may now boast of half a dozen enterprises which deal in serious contemporary art. Dealers have been major patrons of the contemporary artist in Europe and the United States, and they have also been so here.

By far the most decisive act of public patronage was the foundation of the Arts Advisory Council in 1961. This body has now been superseded by the Queen Elizabeth II Arts Council, which has preserved the policies of its predecessor while it has acquired autonomy and a larger financial grant. It works in much the same way as the Arts Council of Great Britain and the Canada Council. There are specialist committees for the major arts, and an elected council determines policy. For the visual arts, it makes travel grants for artists, art teachers, and museum staffs; grants funds for major overseas exhibitions; sponsors New Zealand exhibitions abroad; purchases for its own collection of contemporary New Zealand art; assists galleries to purchase major works of art; commissions works of art for public places; and subsidizes nonprofit organizations such as the Federation of Art Societies.

The formation of the original Council was the result of much work by individuals and societies in pressing the government for greater assistance for the arts. For many years the Department of Internal Affairs had made subsidies of a like nature, but on such a small scale as to be inadequate. The present Council has worked well, despite criticisms from several quarters. For instance, while opera, music, and drama were well served, it took time to persuade the Council that an exhibition of any quality requires almost as much financial backing as other enterprises. However, this situation is improving, for subsidies totalling $12,000 for major exhibitions were being made in 1965 compared to $3,000 earlier. There is no doubt that the Council, in the years to come, will prove the major force in maintaining a high *professional* standard in the arts

207

in a country that, for decades, has worshiped at the shrine of amateurism.

While the state has made its contribution, industrial patronage has lagged. For the last nine years, Sir Henry Kelliher has provided generous prizes in a national competition, but its conditions are so restrictive—it demands virtually photographic realism—that no serious artist has been attracted to it. Inevitably the prizewinners have been the successful commercial painters. It is doubtful if any art competition contributes much to the general progress. Of a better kind is the competition sponsored by Hay's Ltd., of Christchurch, and it has attracted more serious attention. In the decoration of buildings, the Colonial Sugar Refining Company, Shell Oil Company, Imperial Chemical Industries, and Caltex have been active in engaging serious artists. At this stage, however, there is still reluctance on the part of industry to rely on professional advice from both architects and others, so that many projects are aborted through lack of confidence.

Considering the position of the visual arts in New Zealand culture in the past, and the place now being created, one can only be sanguine about the future, so great has been the change wrought in a matter of one or two generations. Artists and their arts are alike becoming a discernible part of the national cultural fabric.

BIBLIOGRAPHY

Firth, Cedric. *State Housing in New Zealand.* Wellington, 1949.
McCormick, E. H. *Letters and Art in New Zealand.* London, 1940.
——. *The Works of Frances Hodgkins in New Zealand.* Auckland, 1954.
Sinclair, Keith, ed. *Distance Looks Our Way: The Visual Arts.* Auckland, 1961.
Smith, Bernard. *European Vision and the South Pacific.* London, 1960.
Toombs, H. H., ed. *A Century of Art in Otago.* Dunedin, 1948.

MUSIC

JOHN A. RITCHIE [1]

THE New Zealander is a musically reticent being. He does not sing at Rugby matches in community fashion like the Welshman, nor does he give way to unrestrained enthusiasm as a listener. He likes music, but he is not prepared to defend what he likes as though it were his home team. He is not a sophisticated concert-goer. On the other hand, he does go to concerts. He is able to show unmistakably his approbation of an unusually fine performance. To have a New Zealander on the receiving end of one's music is to have a quietly responsive, if undemonstrative, listener, a genuine auditor, a man of the *via media*.

Those of us who make music also lack the intensity of artistic utterance that characterizes the Jew, the Italian, or the Russian. We have learned our art in the refined English manner, and while sometimes we try to break the bonds of politeness and decorum, we

---

[1] Mr. B. W. Pritchard kindly provided considerable assistance in many aspects of this chapter.

nevertheless, on average, contrive to preserve calm rather than convey passion. But we possess certain positive qualities that surprise even ourselves. Our national trait of being able to improvise in everyday things carries over to our musical performance. Not that we make up the music as we go; but there are occasions when, in the face of extraordinary adversity, we accomplish what no one has any right to expect with our present resources.

In summary, we are a nation of accompanists rather than soloists. Our orchestras respond to the visiting maestro; our pianists excel when accompanying virtuoso singers and violinists; but we lack that spark of immediate and violent personal inspiration that the music itself elicits from the musician whose roots are embedded in the Old World. It is not a fault: it is an inevitability. Time will force us to reckon with the realism and immediacy of art.

Our musicians receive their training from a variety of sources, unsystematic and uncoordinated. At the age of six, the fortunate child will be taught by an infant-school teacher who can play accompaniments to a few imaginatively chosen songs. But the following year chance determines whether his next teacher will have any inkling of, or liking for, music. At thirteen, the post-primary school he attends may be the one in ten that offers tuition in instrumental music, or the one in twenty that follows a curriculum leading to the School Certificate music examination. As a piano student, learning privately, he will be advised to abandon music for a year or two in order to concentrate on more academic subjects. In such circumstances it is no wonder that the musical profession is under-supplied with new recruits.

Compared to older countries, New Zealand takes a superficial interest in music. For years we ran an Art Union—a regular form of lottery—the proceeds of which did not go to art. In an out-of-doors country, sport rightly takes precedence; social security follows closely; but, very wrongly, music is not promoted with the vigor and prodigality it deserves because, so far, we are not ready with the political and social attitudes, let alone the dedicated understanding, which impel musicians in their endeavors. No New Zealand prime minister could yet dare, as did the late President

Kennedy, "to look forward to the time when my country rewards its artists as well as it does its businessmen."

To put it simply, music in a young country is secondary in importance to the necessities of life, and politicians are not unwilling to remind us of this. Above all, in New Zealand, art depends on the individual. So often, over the last century, there has been in the right place at the right time a man who has exploited the circumstances and created something of artistic importance. Far from being an evolution, the history of New Zealand's music is the story of great men wrestling successfully with frustration and apathy. From their efforts emerged trends that have led to our present state. It is clear that each line of development can be traced back to an England that, although our forebears left it, possessed a cultural climate of tangible strength in music.

The present choral emphasis, the late development and later appreciation of instrumental music, and the popularity of the band movement are to a greater or lesser degree the legacies of the English ancestry of musical developments in New Zealand. Dominating the English musical scene at the time the first shiploads of settlers left for these antipodean islands was the awakening interest in choral music. Throughout Britain, choral societies were established in even the smallest urban centers, while festivals of various descriptions became important annual fixtures.

With such a background it is not surprising that amateur choral societies, outside of church choirs, were the first organized musical groups in the new colony. Only eighteen months after the founding of the Canterbury Settlement in 1850, a choral society and singing class was established in Lyttelton. However, the honor of having the first choral society in New Zealand must be Auckland's, for there in 1842, after a lecture on music delivered by Thomas Outhwaite, registrar of the Supreme Court, a musical society was formed, which that same gentleman conducted and assisted with his ample store of manuscript and printed music. By 1855 another choral society had been founded, with Joseph Brown as conductor, and this was joined by the Auckland Philharmonic Society under a

211

Mr. Beale, in 1858. In the southern extreme of the colony the Dunedin Harmonic Society was active in 1858, while in Nelson and Wellington harmonic societies were founded by 1860.

An educative aim was stressed by these early musical groups. Some had actually been formed from singing classes, as had the Christchurch Harmonic Society in 1858, while others had singing classes attached to them, a measure that provided a supply of reasonably competent new members. Above all, these groups were community ventures. They were to be a means of providing a "togetherness" in the new settlements. The pattern was particularly clear in Christchurch, where the Lyttelton Choral Society was founded by the Lyttelton Colonists' Society for the benefit of the settlers; the Christchurch Philharmonic Society was formed at a public meeting called for that express purpose. Rarely were early musical groups founded by individuals. Indeed, musicians capable of, or experienced in, establishing such activities were few in number, and those having that ability were prepared to pool their knowledge for the benefit of the community.

After about two decades, this pattern of organization changed, for the professional musicians who arrived with increasing frequency from the late 1860's began to organize their own musical groups. F. Weber, who founded his Philharmonic Society in Christchurch in 1869, was one of the first to exemplify this new organizational pattern, and in 1870, his efforts were followed by Robert Parker and his Mendelssohn Society. From then on the pattern of formation was set, and individual organization has remained the dominant trend to the present.

Early societies were usually short-lived; divisions and cliques in the ranks were frequently experienced, while unpredictable public support gave little encouragement to continual effort. The Lyttelton Choral Society, which existed until 1857, had one of the longest lives of societies established in the pioneering decades. Usually, choral societies in all centers lasted for only two or three years. The conception of a musical society as a group in which individual talents and aspirations were subordinated to the interests of the group as a whole was but faintly perceived. Rather, the earliest societies could be considered as "groups of soloists." To be sure, the vocal forces were concerted for part songs and choruses, but it is equally certain that each member, whether as vocalist or instrumentalist, expected a share of the public's approval for his efforts as soloist during the concerts. Those who considered themselves unjustly treated left the society, and internal jealousy and dissension were rife. As the *Lyttelton Times* commented on May 26, 1865:

All societies of this kind are conducted under great difficulty. There are so many motives producing differences and dissension that as a general rule they break up in a very few years. The main difficulty is the selection of those members who should take the solo parts. It is found that societies get broken up into parties and cliques, so that the defalcation of a disappointed syren is the signal for the desertion of an appreciable section of the whole.

But short-lived choral societies were not the only form of musical activity in the colony. A more far-reaching effect on the population, despite the educational aims of the choral groups, was achieved by the band movement, which grew from the influx of English military regiments and the development of the Volunteer Movement during the Maori Wars in the North Island. Regular open-air concerts were often provided by these regimental bands. In Auckland, for example, the band of the 58th Regiment frequently gave public concerts in the grounds of the old Government House.

The local volunteer forces soon demanded musical accompaniment, and in 1859 the Taranaki Militia and Rifles was formed, closely followed by the Wanganui Volunteer Band. Although the South Island was not beset with conflict between Maori and *pakeha*, the volunteer movement swept throughout New Zealand, and in 1860 a band was established in connection with the Dunedin Volunteers. Five years later the Port Chalmers Naval Volunteer Band was formed. The Christchurch Volunteer Brass Band was organized in 1863, the following year a Drum and Fife Band, and in 1868 the band of the Canterbury Yeomanry Cavalry.

The sixties clearly mark the sowing of seeds in a new field of musical enterprise, and despite the departure of Imperial troops in 1870, the band movement continued to grow in popularity until even the smaller towns had reason to boast of their assemblage of brass instrumentalists. The first bands on the West Coast appeared at Westport in 1869, and at Greymouth the following year. By 1874 bands, either volunteer or civilian, had been organized at Oamaru, Clyde, Timaru, Nelson, and Gisborne, and the movement was eclipsing choralism as the most popular and extensive type of musical activity in the colony.

Bands of a different description were those arranged for special social occasions. These were impromptu groups and included any settlers of any instrumental capability. A piano, a harmonium, a concertina, and one or two violins was usually the total assemblage, but the entertainment provided by these bands did much, in town and country settlement alike, to enliven the hard life of the early colonists. Typical is the evening's entertainment presented in the schoolroom at Rangiora, a small North Canterbury rural center, during the sixties:

George Hewlings on the harmonium; Horniblow on the dulcimer; Merton and two friends in a violin, 'cello and concertina trio; an orchestra of brass, fifes and drums with a few stringed instruments and a choir singing part-songs and madrigals. This was supplemented by songs, recitations, charades or dramatic readings.

These homemade amusements were always welcome, for visits of touring musicians were few and far between. New Zealand was not a profitable field of endeavor; settlements were isolated, and travel was at best precarious and slow. Although Miss Redmayne, an intrepid Dunedin personality, had by 1858 organized tours to the Canterbury and Nelson districts as well as to Invercargill, her example was not followed. Even in the larger communities the number of professional musicians was negligible, for colonial life could offer few opportunities for the specialist teacher. Full-time music teaching was rarely possible: the jack-of-all-musical-trades was most likely to succeed. The man who played Mozart one evening, who taught pupils during the day, who played the organ and led choral services on Sunday, was just as likely to provide music for the local dance and to arrive next day to tune the piano.

On the other hand, trade in sheet music and musical instruments was early established in the major towns. By 1854, Dunedin firms were importing instruments, and in 1861 the first firm dealing solely in instruments and music was established. By 1865, Charles Begg, using native timber, had constructed the first four pianos to be made in New Zealand.

While the pioneering decades of New Zealand settlement had witnessed the establishment and growth of choral societies and the band movement, as well as the beginnings of teaching and commercial musical undertakings, it was not until the 1870's that concerted instrumental music made its first tentative appearances. Occasionally an assemblage of miscellaneous instruments (with the ubiquitous harmonium to "fill-in the missing parts") had accompanied the efforts of local choral groups, but in Christchurch in 1871 a society was established "for the improvement of orchestral performance" and aimed at "uniting the instrumentalists of the city into an orchestra for the regular weekly practices of classical music." This was the Christchurch Orchestral Society; its conductor and founder was Alex Lean. Among the original members were four violins, one viola, two celli, two cornets, and one each of oboe, bassoon, trombone, and tympani. Included in its library were overtures and symphonies. In its first concert, given in May, 1872, Haydn's Symphony No. 17 was presented. This was the first occasion on which a symphony was performed in its entirety in Christchurch, even though a ballad was inserted between the first and second movements to help sweeten such "intellectual entertainment."

To Lean, the symphony was the *raison d'être* of the orchestral society, but the public failed to share his enthusiasm. Musically, he was a man ahead of his time, for he lived in the English atmosphere which regarded choral music as the greatest form of artistic expression, and at a time when a group of singers, competent or otherwise, was easier to assemble than an orchestral or chamber group. Choral singing was deemed much more respectable.

Although many first performances of Haydn and Mozart symphonies in Christchurch, and possibly in New Zealand, were given by the Society in the following years, its concerts were poorly patronized. However, Lean held resolutely to his "symphonic ideals" and refused to compromise with popular taste. In fact, it was his uncompromising artistic policy that forced New Zealand's

215

first orchestral society into recess in 1878. This was, of course, a bitter decision for Lean. His experience had taught him that in every audience there would be a small proportion of people who relish classical music, some who desire to learn, and others who attend as a matter of fashion. As he wrote, the public "do not go to concerts for music—as a mass they know nothing about it—how could they when all the teaching they get is that the pianoforte is the summum bonum of music, all beyond, eccentricity?"

The Orchestral Society was succeeded in 1879 by the Amateur Orchestral Society, which until 1891 provided instrumental music in Christchurch. Its success, if its struggling existence can be so termed, did not lie in improved performances or in an increased public appreciation of orchestral music, but was bought at the cost of a much more popular style of program. Lean's symphonic school receded apace and programs consisted of selections and solos.

In other centers orchestral music was away to a similarly late start. Wellington had an orchestral society in 1879, while one in Dunedin appeared about 1880 and another was established there in 1886. This last society from 1889 to 1930 was under the baton of James Coombs, a professional violinist. However, like its northern counterparts, this group failed to gain public support for instrumental music, although it was not forced into recess. As with the later Christchurch group, it attempted to overcome its difficulties by placing popular items on its programs, and often gave "request" programs comprising items selected by audiences at earlier concerts.

The turning point in the history of instrumental music in New Zealand came at the close of the nineteenth century. At the New Zealand and South Seas Exhibition held in Dunedin in 1890, a special orchestra, comprising forty-five players and including instrumentalists not only from Dunedin but from other New Zealand towns and Australia, performed before enthusiastic audiences much music not previously heard in New Zealand. Even more important, Signor Squarise, conductor of the Exhibition Orchestra, straightaway settled in Dunedin and with Herr Berrmeyer founded the Otago Conservatory of Music. This period marks the beginning of

216

the influx of foreign or European-trained musicians into New Zealand, musicians who were to become the dominant instrumental teachers and who were to occupy leading positions in nearly every major center. Choral developments were a legacy of England, but orchestral music was virtually commenced by, and for many years remained the domain of, musicians of Continental birth, or artists who had studied at European conservatories, especially Leipzig.

This produced a considerable increase in the number of instrumental players in the community. In Dunedin, Squarise was the recognized leader of orchestral work until his retirement in 1933, and the Philharmonic Orchestra that he established in 1904 at times numbered eighty players, the majority of whom were his pupils.

In Christchurch, F. M. Wallace, a pupil of the violinist Ferdinand David, was appointed conductor of the Amateur Orchestral Society in 1891, and from the time this group amalgamated with the Musical Society in 1894 to form the Christchurch Musical Union, he conducted the combined choral and orchestral forces until 1905. In those years the instrumentalists particularly reached an unprecedented peak of attainment, and the results of Wallace's teaching were seen in the increased number of musicians available for orchestral work.

These local efforts for the development and appreciation of orchestral music were consolidated by the performances of the fifty-six-member orchestra assembled for the Christchurch Exhibition in 1906–1907. Once again members came from various New Zealand towns and from Australia, and at the close of the Exhibition the orchestra, under Alfred Hill, toured New Zealand. During its regular afternoon and evening concerts immense quantities of orchestral music were performed. Mendelssohn, Mozart, Wagner, Beethoven, and Schubert "afternoons" or "evenings" were frequent. Never before had so much orchestral music been heard by so many. The orchestra had come of age in New Zealand.

But while orchestral music did not make its full impact until the turn of the century, the bands, from 1870, had been going from strength to strength. This was the people's music par excellence. Nearly every town supported at least one brass band, and in smaller centers the band often provided the only opportunities for the public to hear music of any merit. In large towns or small, the open-air band concerts in public parks were for many families the outing of the week. Thousands who in all probability had never entered a concert hall heard traditional airs, hymns, marches, and songs and made their first contacts with opera in the selections then so much a part of the standard band repertoire.

The 1880's also saw the growth of band contests. A feature of the annual review of troops held by the New Zealand Volunteer Forces was the regular competition between garrison bands. Gradually civilian bands took part, and by 1883 contests were held throughout the country. But since music was only part of the military pageant, there was no organizing body to ensure that the contests were properly conducted, and it was not until the Oamaru contest in 1886 that a standard test piece was introduced. A year later, at a Christchurch contest, the United Brass Bands Association of New Zealand was formed. Thereafter the arrangements continually improved and the standard of band-playing was so raised that by 1897 the Invercargill Band undertook a visit to contests in Australia; in 1903 the Hinemoa Band became the first New Zealand band to visit England, and in 1965 a national brass band toured the United States with some success.

Today, despite the growth in popularity of other forms of instrumental music, the band movement still remains an important force on the New Zealand musical scene. As "music for the people" it began, and in a country with egalitarian ideals, where choral and orchestral societies face some social prejudice, the "people's music" it will surely remain. While similar social patterns produced a comparable band movement in Australia, it is of interest to note that, inexplicably, today band music has now almost wholly disappeared in that country.

The growth of choral societies from 1870 was neither as spectacular as that of the bands nor as slow as the orchestral societies. Although many of the groups established in the preceding decades had passed into oblivion, choral singing was still a most respectable group activity and developed steadily.

This time saw the widening of choral activities and the beginning of specialized groups. The Christchurch Liedertafel was established with W. G. Rhind as president and Arthur Towsey as conductor in 1885, and a similar group was formed in Dunedin in the same year. This society became the Royal Dunedin Male Voice Choir in 1915. The year 1892 marked the beginning of a Liedertafel in Wellington, and a similar male voice group was established in Auckland in 1893. Choirs for ladies' voices began only a little later: a Liederkranzchen in Dunedin in 1890, and one in Christchurch in 1892. Groups which specialized in part songs and madrigals, rather than extended choral works, were also appearing and adding diversity to the musical life of the cities.

In contrast to the earliest choral groups, the later societies generally led a more stable existence. The concept of the choral society had crystallized; the difficulties and dissensions caused by choice of soloists had largely vanished and been replaced by discipline and a more mature outlook among members. By 1855 the *Lyttelton Times* was able to report:

Auckland has a choral society which excites the envy of all kindred societies in the colony. With the strongest orchestra in New Zealand, a roll of 248 performing members and 305 subscribing members, with its hall and library of music, this Society has achieved a position for which all others sigh. It keeps together a large body of singers, it performs good music worthily—it carries forward annually a respectable balance of profit. The great lesson that the Society has taught New Zealand musicians is that by combining and keeping together, obedient to discipline, tolerant of mannerisms and idiosyncrasies of conductors, and determined at all reasonable cost of time and trouble to do the duty they have undertaken, the musicians of the large centres of population can do great things as greatly as it is possible under all colonial circumstances.

Nor was this prosperity localized. In 1888 and 1889 the Christchurch Musical Society assembled over three hundred singers for performances of *Messiah*, and in succeeding years its contemporary, the Motet Society, gave massive performances of *Elijah, Judas Maccabaeus*, and *Messiah* with a similar-sized chorus. By 1905 the Christchurch Musical Union numbered some two hundred performing members and over five hundred subscribing members, and these golden years of prosperity lasted well into the new century.

Along with the changes in the performance of music in New

Zealand, the closing decades of the last century also witnessed considerable developments in its teaching. The pioneering decades attracted few professional musicians, and only by the seventies was their number significant. But from then on music teachers increased in number, particularly in the cities, and musical life was correspondingly enriched. Christchurch, for example, had only two or three teachers in early 1870; by 1886 their ranks had increased to nineteen, and by 1896 thirty-eight teachers advertised their services. The era of the full-time music specialist had begun.

The piano was the most favored instrument, and the Victorian attitude that some ability on the keyboard was the necessary accomplishment of all young ladies was much in vogue in the colony. Teaching, however, was often of a very high standard; many teachers had had continental training, and H. M. Lund, himself a pupil of Clara Schumann, was the pioneer of pianoforte tuition in Christchurch.

But other instrumental music was not neglected. In 1883 the Instrumental School of Music, with the principals of the Orchestral Society as instructors, was promoted in Christchurch for the teaching of all stringed and wind instruments. This was one of the first efforts to establish conservatory teaching in New Zealand, and its successors included the Otago Conservatory of Music and the Nelson School of Music, which was established by Herr Balling in 1893.

University interest in music was evident comparatively early in the history of New Zealand education. In 1883 the University of New Zealand made the decision to examine in its constituent colleges for a degree in music, although the first appointment of a lecturer in that subject was not made until 1889. In that year Herr Schmitt was appointed to the chair of music at Auckland University College and began his work of pioneering the first university school of music. Two years later G. F. Tendall was appointed lecturer in music at Canterbury College, and he was succeeded in 1902 by Dr. J. C. Bradshaw, who was appointed to the chair of music when it was established at Canterbury in 1938. Not until considerably later did music develop at the University of Otago in

Dunedin; in 1925, Dr. Victor Galway was appointed lecturer, and in 1939 he became that university's first professor of music.

Early university music courses were designed not only for degree candidates but also for music students or amateurs anxious to acquire some theoretical knowledge. Certificates were issued to these non-degree students, and the course was regarded as preliminary to study for a degree. However, it was on this elementary course that Canterbury College, at least, existed; forty-two candidates were successful at examinations held at the end of the first year, and in 1894, of the seventy-five students who passed the college examinations, only two were degree candidates. The universities at this time were providing courses and examinations similar to those now conducted by the London colleges of music.

As a supplement—indeed, often as an impetus—to local musical development, the tours of artists from overseas have had an important place in the history of New Zealand music. This country has been fortunate in both the quality and number of visiting artists who have performed in its theaters. To be sure, it was only New Zealand's proximity to Australia which induced many of these visitors to our shores. Australia had a considerable appeal to those artists left free to tour after the close of the English season, and although New Zealand meant extra revenue, it is clear that a tour of this country alone was scarcely profitable.

The earliest visitors were touring opera companies. In 1862 a group of four singers, styled "The English Opera Company," braved the difficulties of colonial life and enlivened the musical scene. Following them came Lyster's Royal English and Italian Opera Company, a company distinguished by its high prices and extremely varied operatic fare. Another Italian company arrived in 1872, and from that date there was an almost incessant flow of various companies and troupes. The Gilbert and Sullivan fever was caught early, and from 1882 on J. C. Williamson's presentation of these operas set an incomparable standard. Pride of place, however, must go to Fuller's Gonsalez Italian Grand Opera Company, which toured New Zealand in 1927 and again in 1928; with 150 members and a chorus of 60, it represented the peak of visiting operatic entertainment. Local opera was very much stimulated by the visits of these companies, and a multitude of usually short-lived amateur operatic societies mushroomed throughout New Zealand.

Visiting vocalists were led by Anna Bishop in 1869 and by Ilma de Murska, the "Hungarian Nightingale," who in 1876 in Christchurch drew audiences unprecedented for that city. But it was not until the 1890's that visits by singers were made with any frequency. Charles Santley, of English oratorio fame, appeared in 1890, and was followed by Trebelli, Ada Crossley, Albani, Clara Butt, John McCormack, Peter Dawson, Amelita Galli-Curci, Richard Crooks, and Lotte Lehmann, among many others.

On the other hand, visiting pianists in the nineteenth century were extremely rare. Arabella Goddard, who visited New Zealand in 1874, was supported on the program by vocalists and violinists. In Christchurch the one all-piano evening, presented by the Hungarian Henri Ketter, met with dismal failure. The visit of the youthful Australian pianist Percy Grainger, in 1903, began a steady stream of visitors that has continued to the present and includes such names as Paderewski, Friedenthal, Moiseiwitsch, Backhaus, Hambourg, Eileen Joyce, Solomon, Moura Lympany, and Rubinstein.

Neither did world-famous violinists neglect New Zealand. Mme Urso appeared before colonial audiences in 1880, and before the turn of the century Wilhelmj, Remenyi, and Ovide Musin had performed in this country, while since 1900, Kubelik, Heifetz, Kreisler, Menuhin, and Stern have undertaken comprehensive tours.

Although visits of chamber-music groups began with the American Mendelssohn Quintet in 1882 and continued with the Cherniavsky Trio in 1908, 1914, and 1924, and the Budapest String Quartet in 1937, this medium has until recently not figured largely, at least publicly, in New Zealand.

Tours by choirs and orchestras have been, of course, rather infrequent, but New Zealand has had its share of visits. Following the Fisk Jubilee Singers in 1887 came the Royal Welsh Choir in 1909, the Sistine Chapel Soloists in 1923, the Don Cossack Russian Male Voice Choir in 1926 and 1937, and the first of a series of visits by the Vienna Boys' Choir in 1935.

But perhaps most important of all in creating musical interest and influencing development in the respective musical spheres were the visits by the Besses o' th' Barn Band in 1907, the Sheffield Choir in 1910, and the New South Wales State Orchestra under Henri Verbrugghen in 1920.

The well-controlled singing of the touring English choir did much to refine the efforts of the choral societies which in small towns and large cities alike had become so much a part of musical activity in New Zealand. In each main center auxiliary choirs comprising members drawn from local societies combined with the visiting vocalists and benefited from this experience.

Thoughout New Zealand the broadening of choral activity, noticeable before the turn of the century, became intensified. Small specialized choirs and large mixed-voice societies appeared with increasing frequency. Between 1900 and 1930, seven new choral groups appeared in Christchurch alone in addition to the continued activities of the Musical Society and the Liedertafel. This city steadily established its position as New Zealand's choral city and in 1927 could count not only two mixed-voice choirs, each having over 150 voices, but also a long-established Liedertafel as well as the Male Voice Choir and the St. Cecilia Ladies' Voice Choir.

The New Zealand tour of the Christchurch Exhibition Orchestra in 1907 had not only served as an example to local amateur societies and given the public a new criterion by which to judge orchestral performances, but had also helped to create a widespread taste for orchestral music. In Christchurch this awakened enthusiasm was greater than the concerts of the orchestral section of the Musical Union could satisfy, and in 1908, under Herr Benno Scherek, the Christchurch Orchestral Society was established. Until about 1940, generally under the baton of A. J. Bunz and despite competition from theater orchestras of the twenties and the effects of the depression of the thirties, the Society was largely responsible for further orchestral development in Christchurch. Two shorter-lived orchestral groups were the Christchurch Symphony Orchestra (founded in 1919 under Alfred Worsley), which was comprised of male instrumentalists only, and the Laurian Club, a string orchestra established in 1932.

223

In Wellington the first municipal orchestra in New Zealand was formed in 1910, its establishment authorized by the City Council. In other New Zealand cities and towns various instrumental groups, consisting of enthusiastic amateur musicians, were being formed. At that time of expanding activity the visit of the New South Wales State Orchestra proved extremely valuable. Its disciplined playing stood as a fine example to many novice organizations, and undoubtedly its professional qualities gave new insight to many amateur instrumentalists.

Perhaps the most important aspect of the development of a true professional climate in music, outside teaching, is the orchestral situation. While it is true to say that in present-day New Zealand the position of an orchestral player is better than ever before, it is inferior to that prevailing in countries like Great Britain, the United States, and Australia. New Zealand lacks rates of pay competitive with those of overseas orchestras; hence the steady drain abroad of our best players. Our penchant is for sport rather than art, and consequently we lack a vocal body of opinion on matters musical. The story of the last thirty years explains the present complex scene and contains some hopeful signs.

When the cinema orchestras disappeared in the 1930's, pushed aside by talkies and mortally wounded by the depression, there seemed little hope of a professional life for a violinist or a flutist. Some ground was made up when, in the economic recovery which followed, a government-controlled national radio system was established. In each main city the radio stations recruited small orchestras, groups of about thirty players employed on a part-time basis, whose duty was to rehearse twice a week and play regular studio concerts. As a temporary expedient it was wise, but like so many temporary measures in a young country, this became the *status quo* for twenty years. Granted its continuity was broken on occasions by the temporary setting up of the Centennial Orchestra in 1940, by the manpower demands of a war, and by the eventual organization of a national orchestra in 1947, but the radio orchestras continued "stealing through the classics" week by week until 1960.

From the centennial celebrations and a very fine wartime air-force band grew the first full-time professional group, the New

Zealand National Orchestra. Controlled and administered by a government department (the Broadcasting Service), this seventy-member ensemble based in Wellington soon gained the support of the whole country and has weathered both political and artistic storms. Each conductor has contributed something at the right time. Andersen Tyrer, an Englishman stranded here during the war, gave it a promising start. Michael Bowles, an Irishman, and James Robertson and John Hopkins, both Englishmen, consolidated and enlivened it in turn. The present conductor is a Chilean, Juan Matteucci.

A tradition seems to have arisen that the conductor should be a foreigner. The only New Zealander to have any real tenure in the post was Warwick Braithwaite, for many years now popular as a conductor in Britain and Europe, who was conductor during an extended interregnum in the early 1950's. The concertmaster, however, (or leader, as he is called) has been a constant fixture, and in most New Zealanders' eyes Vincent Aspey is something of a national figure.

Besides following a regular concert schedule, the National Orchestra broadcasts regularly. Under John Hopkins, in particular, it has played many New Zealand compositions. It made possible a highly stimulating season of opera by an Italian company shortly after its formation, and it has since proved indispensable to the young opera and ballet companies that have sprung up indigenously. Above all, the National Orchestra has set standards in a country where the symphonic repertoire was not previously heard. It travels widely throughout a land that is geographically distended, and it frequently joins choirs in the provincial centers in presenting works for which the local orchestral resources are insufficient.

In 1947 the Boyd Neel Orchestra not only fired the imagination of audiences but also sowed seeds in the minds of the younger local musicians. The Alex Lindsay String Orchestra, formed shortly after, became the first of New Zealand's private enterprises in the artistic field. It has followed a distinguished career ever since, giving its support most conspicuously to local composers and producing a high standard of string playing that has attracted world-wide attention. Alex Lindsay (born in Invercargill in 1919), a fine violinist himself, also led the New Zealand String Quartet, which had a brief but splendid existence in more recent times. He is a true son of his country, and it is one of several recent musical tragedies that the lure of the London musical scene should have attracted him away in 1963.

The basing of the National Orchestra in Wellington denuded the rest of the country of many of the better players. It took a decade for comparatively large cities to recover, and even now it can be said that the teaching situation is not what it should be. In Christchurch the John Ritchie String Orchestra was formed in 1959. Its prototype was the eighteen-piece string ensemble with which Boyd Neel had enchanted all; but while modeled on the Lindsay Orchestra, it developed differently. Retaining its own identity, it became the nucleus of chamber and symphony orchestras in the city of its origin.

This Civic Orchestra Establishment, as it is now known, has had a distinct bearing on recent national developments. When the demands of opera and ballet became too great for the National Orchestra to meet them, the Broadcasting Service agreed to provide a small "pit" orchestra of between twenty and thirty players. This was erroneously called a concert orchestra. Its career was brief in abysmally primitive conditions: theatre pits in New Zealand have to be seen to be believed. The rates of pay were poor, the traveling demands excessive, and after two years the orchestra was disbanded. Clearly, one decision was wrong: either it was a mistake to set it up, or having set it up, it was a mistake to demolish it. Such things seem built into the ways of music in New Zealand. Makeshift methods and compromise solutions have frustrated musicians over a long period. This, allied with a gift for producing a scheme to which three or four controlling bodies contribute, leads to friction and disillusionment.

In any event, the solution to the latest crisis is an interesting one. Opera and ballet have been provided with a "core" of eleven principal players. These join the regional orchestras in Christchurch and Auckland for seasons in these cities and neighboring towns. This scheme poses many administrative and artistic prob-

226

lems; nevertheless, it presents the regional orchestras not only with a challenge, but also with money. The first problem to emerge is the difficulty of persuading non-musicians that all important decisions must be reached on artistic grounds. The first opera chosen was *Porgy and Bess*, stylistically and technically a challenging work by any standards. The inexperience involved in taking such a decision colors much of the country's effort in music. Opera and ballet administrators act as though highly experienced orchestras are available and show surprise when difficulties are pointed out. On the other hand, the choral societies have adopted a more realistic policy while exploring an interesting repertoire in the process.

One can report that *Porgy and Bess* has been a success; in fact, it is a landmark in the development of the New Zealand Opera Company. But those familiar with this opera will find it difficult to imagine an orchestra of twenty-eight players serving the composer's intention with fidelity.

The New Zealand Broadcasting Corporation, as it is now called, is the principal patron of the arts. It spends most on music. Overseas soloists regularly tour the country under its auspices. Through broadcasts it offers the local soloist most of his recital work. Orchestras from Boston, Czechoslovakia, and Poland have been brought for brief tours. A National Youth Orchestra, formed nine years ago and meeting once a year, has provided excellent stimulation for the younger generation.

But patronage of the arts is not one of New Zealand's strengths. Brewers help opera; all manner of firms advertise on programs; the occasional philanthropist offers a competition. By and large, however, we do not support music in the manner of other countries. The reasons for this are twofold: first, no income tax exemption is granted on monetary gifts; second, local bodies have no authority to set pay rates for the arts. Equally significant is the fact that the generation that can afford to be generous to music has precious little interest in it, because it grew up at a time when school music was either neglected or handled so unimaginatively as to repel rather than to enlist sympathy or interest.

In 1964 the six-year-old Arts Advisory Council was replaced by the Queen Elizabeth II Arts Council, whose policies are similar.

227

Financially, its resources are greater, but not prodigally so. Most of its money goes to sustaining opera and ballet; some aids the regional orchestra scheme, and the remainder is generally directed to gifted students for overseas study or to providing expert teaching within New Zealand in the form of master classes given by visiting artists. The Arts Council suffers from one of the political philosophies of a welfare state, which is that every asset should be shared by right and not by qualification. If it decides that a choir or a band is worthy of special assistance, it knows that a grant so given may result in dozens of similar applications, and until now it has proved reluctant to make embarrassing decisions. It is hoped that sooner or later merit will be fearlessly rewarded.

In some centers, notably Christchurch and Nelson, civic music councils exist. They are primarily coordinating bodies whose aim is to produce cooperation between musical societies, to promote and organize festivals, and to look after the welfare of their member bodies on a civic basis. Although hampered by lack of finance, it is surprising what these councils have achieved in the past. The Christchurch Civic Music Council has been in existence for more than twenty years and has done much to strengthen the city's cultural environment.

In a country where the professional musician is not highly regarded and in which labor is well organized, it is not surprising that so far the Musicians' Union has concerned itself largely with rates of pay and conditions of work. It has had a difficult struggle, because so many of its members are still part-time players and consequently not dependent on fees for their primary income. There is not the sense of urgency that might otherwise be the case.

Composers are loosely represented by APRA, the Australasian Performing Rights Association, which in addition to collecting performing fees, has also done a limited amount of promotion in the form of commissions and commercial recordings. Again, composers in New Zealand are necessarily part-time practitioners, but despite its small population, the country has produced quite a number worthy of mention. They follow no particular trend, although Vaughan Williams has clearly influenced many of them. No obvious symptoms of nationalism have emerged, but there is a healthy unselfconsciousness about much of their music which betrays worthy motives and little bombast. New Zealand composers might be described as a quiet lot; understatement could well be their chief fault. Certainly the majority know their craft well and appear prepared to let time produce a major figure in composition.

Most composers trace their beginnings to the universities. Of the older generation, two professor-composers, Professor Victor Galway at Otago University and Professor Vernon Griffiths at the University of Canterbury, influenced and encouraged many of their successors. Their followers, sometimes rebellious against the English traditions for which they stood, nevertheless are indebted to them in one way or another.

Of the middle generation, Douglas Lilburn (b. 1915) has had his work performed most. He has captured the attention of a wide section of the interested public. Three symphonies, a quartet, and much orchestral music of his are important; but equally significant and more approachable are the song cycle *Sings Harry* (to words by Denis Glover) and a work for string orchestra and narrator, *Landfall in Unknown Seas*, to a poem by Allen Curnow. Curnow and Glover are both New Zealanders, and shortly after the Second World War there was a time when it appeared likely and desirable that a wedding of New Zealand voice and verse might produce a whole corpus of significant indigenous work.

Like Lilburn, many of the postwar composers studied at home first and then in England. This pilgrimage was the expected thing. Larry Pruden, a singularly accomplished composer, returned with some Gallic flavor in his utterance. The others, Ronald Tremaine, J. V. Peters, David Sell, John Ritchie, Ashley Heenan, and David Farquhar, are now about forty and teaching in universities. The up-and-coming composers are their pupils, names which could well become important later. Venturesome and diverse, they include Anna Lockwood, Jenny McLeod, Kit Powell, and William Southgate, to name a few. One specially noteworthy composer is Anthony Watson, a violist in the New Zealand Broadcasting Corporation Symphony Orchestra, whose convincing handling of the quartet medium combines fluency in the twelve-tone technique with a real feeling for effect.

In addition to the individual efforts of men like Alex Lindsay, John Ritchie, and Owen Jensen (Jensen started the Auckland String Players in 1941), there is the notable pioneering work of Donald Munro, who formed the New Zealand Opera Company shortly after he returned from England in 1951. In its early years this company explored an interesting repertoire in the chamber opera genre. Menotti figured often, and there was a lively sense of adventure in the work undertaken. As it has grown and become big business, box-office considerations have loomed larger in its planning. Puccini and Verdi have predominated, but there have been some fine original offerings. Musically, the company has not always measured up to the standards set in production, but it receives growing public support.

The New Zealand Ballet Trust, too, has flourished. It is a smaller venture, somewhat reticent by comparison with its running mate, opera. From *Nutcracker* to potpourri programs it has offered a wide variety, breaking new ground in a fine *Petrouchka* in 1964, when a distinguished New Zealander, Alexander Grant, returned to inspire the company.

Undoubtedly, though some are ashamed to admit it, New Zealand's most notable musical groups are still its brass bands and its choirs. Six or seven bands are capable of the very highest technical standards, although their repertoire is often deplorable. Bands sent overseas have proved the equal of any met in competitions, and the band world thrives on organized competition.

Chorally, the situation may vary from place to place and year to year. The inheritance of the English choral tradition is nowhere better demonstrated than in Christchurch, a city of some 250,000 inhabitants. At the Anglican cathedral a choir of men and boys, lay clerks and children from the Cathedral Grammar School, sing daily services as is done in the English cathedrals. Two large choral societies, each possessing more than two hundred singers, are in existence. One, the Royal Christchurch Musical Society, conducted by E. R. Field-Dodgson, has traveled to Australia for the Adelaide Festival. The other, the Christchurch Harmonic Society, conducted by William Hawkey, traveled to London for the Commonwealth Arts Festival in September, 1965. Both have flown to all the main cities of New Zealand, performing works such as Walton's *Belshazzar's Feast* and Britten's *Requiem,* as well as many other standard works. Significantly, both conductors are young men. Most of the singers contribute a considerable portion of the fares on such travels, a testimony to their love of choral music and an exhibition of the true amateur spirit. Very high standards mark both choirs' work, and naturally there is a healthy competition between them.

There are other choirs in Christchurch. In addition to numerous church choirs, the Liederkranzchen for ladies, the Liedertafel for men, and the University Madrigal Singers, there are Women's Institute choirs, Townswomen's Guild choirs, and a variety of community choirs in stores and workshops. It is no wonder that the Christchurch Civic Music Council finds it an easy matter to oranize choir festivals.

Other cities may not equal the vitality of Christchurch choral activity, but there are in Auckland, Wellington, and Dunedin groups that from time to time sing excellently and explore exciting paths in the repertoire. The Dorian Singers in Auckland and the Dunedin Choral Society are now asserting themselves under young and imaginative English conductors. In Wellington for many years the Schola Cantorum held a pre-eminent position in New Zealand choralism. Its founder, a Canadian, Stanley Oliver, reached and maintained the highest of standards in a repertoire that ranged widely and adventurously. Very recently, Malcolm Rickard and his Hutt Valley Orpheus Choir has challenged the rest of the country with fine singing of more standard works.

Chamber music has a stronghold in this little country. Societies exist in many towns and cities, and they are federated under a national body which negotiates to bring the best offerings from overseas. Each year some eight thousand members hear six or more concerts. String quartets from France, Germany, Czechoslovakia, Russia, the United States, and Australia have been regular visitors since 1950. Chamber orchestras, octets, singers like Souzay, violinists like Ricci—on all these, members have been able to feast. The Chamber Music Federation of New Zealand has demonstrated what planned organization and the weight of numbers can achieve. Most visiting artists treat the antipodean tour as a plum worth picking. New Zealand artists have not fared so well in this sphere, a criticism which frequently finds its way to the Federation meetings. But the Federation has done much for the younger generation. Competitions have been promoted, and more important, advantage has been taken of the presence of visiting groups like the Berkshire Quartet and the Allegri Quartet to organize master classes for promising string players.

Generally, festivals are provincial in scope. Most of the larger towns have supported music festivals, but these have involved an abnormal concentration of concerts rather than programs of particular significance. Auckland is the exception to this. For several years the business community has been drawn into a three-weeks festival period during which national opera, orchestra, and ballet groups, and a number of local solosits and societies, have usually participated, while luster has been lent by distinguished overseas artists such as Julius Katchen, Gina Bachauer, and Alfredo Campoli. This is an annual event which appears very securely imbedded in the northern scene.

Expatriate New Zealanders return for such festivals or for national tours. Colin Horsley and the Maori Inia Te Wiata are two such artists. Others who at one time or another have returned are Alan Loveday and the late Richard Farrell. Few, however, have shown interest in returning to settle permanently in their native country. Some choose to stay in their homeland. The pianists Janetta McStay and Maurice Till have successfully wrought careers in the confined environment and frequently have shown themselves capable of equaling and surpassing standards set by internationally more famous musicians. Till, who accompanied Rita Streich, Elisabeth Schwarzkopf, Victoria de los Angeles, and many others, has demonstrated a comprehensive mastery in this specialized sphere. Both these artists and others, like Ken Smith, a trumpeter, and Mary Pratt, a magnificent contralto, could have succeeded in wider spheres.

A recent new venture was the Pan-Pacific Arts Festival held in Christchurch in February, 1965. Music and the fine arts were more evenly balanced than in Auckland, while some adventurous promotional steps were taken. From Victoria came the Melbourne Symphony Orchestra with Sir Malcolm Sargent; from the United States came principals, conductor, and producer for *Porgy and Bess*, as well as the Berkshire Quartet and a jazz band from Denver.

It is not easy to generalize about music in New Zealand schools. Some have no musical activity at all (although by legislation they are required to), while others have an organized and comprehensive scheme that would win admiration anywhere. Certain factors have a distinct bearing on each situation. The attitude of the headmaster and the musicality of the person in charge of music are paramount. The availability of any teacher at all with reasonable qualifications determines whether any attempt can be made to conform.

In 1933, Vernon Griffiths (b. 1894), a Cambridge graduate who had come to New Zealand as a teacher's college lecturer some years before, took up a position at the King Edward Technical College, a coeducational school in Dunedin. Quickly he introduced singing to every class. Through the use of part-time teachers he established a scheme whereby all pupils were given the opportunity to learn an orchestral instrument. Bearing in mind that the average stay of a pupil at this school was two years, it was something of a miracle that within three or four years the whole school of eight hundred children (aged thirteen to sixteen) was singing as a six-part choir and that an orchestra of some two hundred was playing. Broadly speaking, Dr. Griffiths, who later became professor of music at the University of Canterbury, based his philosophy of school music on certain principles: (1) a lesson a week and a daily supervised class practice for the instrumentalists; (2) a series of graded orchestras, the most elementary of which was used as bait to the beginner to sustain his interest; (3) choral singing closely allied to folk music until real skill opened the way to more taxing works.

Dr. Griffiths was a fine all-round musician, a gifted and resourceful composer and arranger, an excellent accompanist, and an imaginative teacher. As a trainer of children's voices he was expert. With the benign assistance of a headmaster who knew what music could do for a school, he was able to transform a humble technical college into a school that organized its classes not on I.Q., but according to voice classification. When he left the school in 1942, Frank Callaway (now professor of music at the University of Western Australia) took over and enhanced the work by improved organization and a more intensive instrumental program.

At the north of the South Island a similar situation developed in a boys' school, Nelson College. Ralph Lilly became music master in 1944 in this school, which had no assembly hall and seven hundred boys, most of whose voices had broken. It is said that the head-master appointed him in the hope that choral singing might help develop the corporate life of the school so lacking because of the absence of any sort of auditorium. Major rehearsals had to be held either out of doors or, on wet days, with the choir spread up the stairs and along the corridors. The triumphant rise of full-blooded vocalism under these conditions justified the faith placed in the power of music. An instrumental program also was embarked on, so that now Nelson College, an admirably equipped educational institution, boasts fine choral and orchestral work, provides the choir for the nearby cathedral, and has sent into the community many gifted musicians and enthusiastic music-makers. Similar descriptions could be given of music at the Hutt Valley Boys' School, the Christchurch Boys' High School, and a handful of others.

There is still no regularized training course for secondary-school music teachers. Such a course has been talked about, but little has been accomplished. Forty years ago four eminent musicians were brought to this country to strengthen primary-school music, a successful move which has not been followed up at the higher level. This state of affairs is all the more surprising when it is considered that New Zealand is one of the few countries in the world where music is a compulsory secondary-school subject of study. It is rightly called a core subject, but with the shortage of trained teachers its enforcement is unlikely to become a widespread reality. Music is as well catered for in examinations as any subject: school certificate, university entrance, and scholarship all boast their music examinations, but few candidates enter them.

For many schools the only contact with music beyond an occasional hymn or song at assembly is the concert given by touring players or local musicians. Schools' concerts can achieve some stimulation of interest. The Broadcasting Corporation Symphony Orchestra offers a few concerts in public halls to which several schools are invited. As a regular matter of policy the Christchurch Civic Orchestra Foundation sends its smaller orchestras into the high schools themselves on thirty or more occasions a year.

An advisor in school music to the Minister of Education was appointed some years ago and now regional advisors are working in many areas. Already there are signs of increased activity. The peripatetic specialist teacher of violin, cello, and woodwind instruments is now an accepted figure.

The teachers' colleges do not get a ready supply of musicians, and as a result they are often called on to deal with unpromising or even reluctant material. Progress is made, but it is slow, often being retarded by the national trait of indifference to artistic activity.

Over a long period the private teacher of music in New Zealand has sustained much of the country's prestige. It is impossible to assess what goes on in a studio, but it is fair to assert that most of the country's prominent musicians trace their achievement to this or that dedicated teacher, people like Ernest Empson in Christchurch, Ernest Drake in Dunedin. Catholic convents also have made their mark, not only in the larger areas of population but also in a number of less likely places: the "wild" West Coast, Hawke's Bay, and the like.

Private teachers, who are organized as a registered association, have occasionally viewed with concern the progress of large schemes based on class teaching. Both sides of the controversy often overlook the essential virtue of such moves: the involvement of great numbers in practical music. Provided that this quantitative aim accepts the desirability of future specialized individual teaching, it does little harm. Unfortunately, some of its protagonists have viewed it as an end in itself. Equally mistaken have been the studio teachers who fear such schemes will put them out of business.

In the last decade strong support has been given to the establishment of a central conservatorium. Its enthusiasts have overlooked the fundamental need for building from a wide foundation. They neglected the important starting place, the schools. Their arguments alienated not only the bulk of teachers and all the universities, but also those thinking people who deplore New Zealand's tendency in many things to nationalize and centralize. Most bodies concerned came out in favor of regional development based on the universities.

Four New Zealand universities have departments of music. Formerly, each offered the traditional bachelor of music course. Since the introduction of institutional autonomy in 1962, there has been a quite rapid diversification of curricula. Auckland had already established an executant diploma course; Wellington is now emphasizing performance certification; Canterbury offers diplomas in applied music and music education; Otago specializes in musicology. All these programs are additional to the Mus. B. and B.A. degrees. A doctorate in composition has long been in existence, although the degree has been awarded to only three persons: S. K. Phillips (Auckland), Vernon Griffiths (Otago) and J. V. Peters (Canterbury).

What is the status of New Zealand music at this time? Most people would agree that almost every avenue of training can be improved upon; there is a lack of continuity in our system of musical education and a lack of coordination on a national scale. These shortcomings give a clue to the likely future. It is to the schools that we must look first. The sooner we can be sure that every child will undergo a continuing graded course of study in the literature and materials of music, including regular choral singing and instrumental practice, the better it will be for the whole pattern of development. Only by this means can we be sure of a growing, interested audience. This should create also the environment in which, with some certainty, the hidden genius may be discovered at an early age and given the opportunity to realize fully his potential. A serious teacher-training program must be embarked on. To be even reasonably successful it will need to be the result of thinking big, because its policy must be directed towards a nationwide musical saturation.

Second, there will need to be a change of attitude to the economic structure of the arts. For too long New Zealand has capitalized on the generosity and enthusiasm of its musicians. There are many still who regard the concept of a performer being paid for his services as slightly repugnant. Even the churches often exploit their organists, though never their plumbers. But it is not only the general public who must become aware of professional realities. The government also has facts to face. In a country where the private patron has been legislated out of the scheme of things, the State must assume heavy responsibility. As the Chairman of the Queen Elizabeth II Arts Council, Mr. G. G. Watson, has written, paying tribute to the government for setting up the Council with a wide measure of autonomy, "I must also draw attention to the need for financial resources at a level that will enable it to function properly." It should be understood that, with its proclivity for bureaucratic control, New Zealand looks to its centralized grant-giving body, the Arts Council, for the necessary money with which to survive. Opera, ballet, orchestras, bands, and choirs are all, to varying degrees, dependent on it. Thus, a substantially increased contribution from the government can lead to security of existence for many organizations. This is the hope of the next decade. Expressed in more tangible terms, it could result in the establishment of full-time orchestras in Auckland, Christchurch, and Dunedin, a more even spread of choral and band activity throughout the nation, and the continued organic growth of ballet and opera.

It may be argued that the creative artist's future is not being taken into account. Mr. Watson, in his 1965 statement of policy, spoke of the need "to provide a stimulus to the composer, the playwright, the choreographer, and the artist to produce the best of which he is capable." This is right thinking. Composers will grow in stature and flourish when the means of playing their music are securely integrated into the permanent pattern of New Zealand's music-making.

Already, worthy tendencies are accepted in some spheres. A radio coverage exists in which one network devotes its entire time to serious music, drama, and the arts, much in the same manner as the B.B.C. Third Programme. Responsible positions, for long limited to overseas musicians, are now being offered to New Zealanders occasionally. The inroads of television have still to be experienced in full, but the signs indicate that music of a high standard holds its own. Given a period of tangible and steady progress, this small country could become a place of some importance in music. There is evidence that an advance is imminent, but it is frightening to know that the decisions of consequence are to be made by people many of whom are not noted for an intimate understanding of, or familiarity with, the art which so many distinguished New Zealanders have served.

BIBLIOGRAPHY

Campbell, M. *Music in Dunedin*. Dunedin, 1945.
Griffiths, Vernon. *An Experiment in School Music-Making*. Dunedin, 1941.
Hurst, M. *Music and the Stage in New Zealand*. Wellington, 1944.
Newcomb, S. P. *The Music of the People: The Band Movement in New Zealand, 1845–1963*. Wellington, 1963.
Pritchard, B. W. *Societies in Society: A Case Study in the Historical Sociology of Music*. Christchurch, 1964.
Watson, H. *Music in Christchurch*. Christchurch, 1948.

Recordings of Music by New Zealand Composers

Landfall in Unknown Seas. Kiwi Record LD-2.
Ring Round the Moon. Kiwi Record LD-3.

Kiwi Records are issued by A. H. and A. W. Reed, Wellington. These discs contain music by Douglas Lilburn, Ashley Heenan, Larry Pruden, David Farquhar and John Ritchie.

THEATRE

BRUCE MASON

SINCE 1929, when Al Jolson first sang "Sonny Boy" from a hitherto silent screen, the ancient rite of the living performer facing an audience, molding it to his purpose and being molded by it, has been a minority cult, a coterie enthusiasm, in the English-speaking world. Theatre was not thereby extinguished—its present vitality is higher than at any time in the century—but its status was limited and its area defined by the clamorous popular appeal of mass entertainment: radio, cinema, and all-pervasive television.

London and New York are the great cultural clearinghouses of the English language, and in both the living theatre still flourishes. Yet its audience, though vast, is still coterie, made up of a small core of genuine enthusiasts and the horde of visitors and tourists who pass through each city every day (an estimated 100,000 people in London), whose desire for a "light night out" is the fuel that keeps commercial theatre alive and makes possible, indirectly, such glittering shopwindows as the London National Theatre and the experimental off-Broadway circuit in New York.

PATTERN OF NEW ZEALAND CULTURE

In 1963 the present writer was New Zealand delegate to the International Drama Conference at Edinburgh; the subject of the second session was "The Playwright's Dilemma," defined by the chairman, Martin Esslin, as being "a choice between the morals and aesthetics of The Theatre of the Absurd and The Theatre of Commitment and Social Engagement." Arnold Wesker refused to consider this a dilemma and especially not his; "My dilemma is that of an artist in an indifferent society: nobody cares." Yet enough cared for his trilogy (*Chicken Soup with Barley, Roots,* and *I'm Talking about Jerusalem*) and *Chips with Everything*, both of which had lengthy London and New York seasons, for him to be a professional playwright now living comfortably on his royalties, one surmises. Were he living and working in New Zealand, he would write in lunch hours and at weekends, in the time he could snatch from teaching or from a Public Service desk.

A review of a new play by a New Zealand author some years ago began: "Last night we toiled up the hill to see what our budding Terence Rattigans were up to." Toil, note. It cannot be a pleasure. Aim? To rival Mr. Rattigan, whose current income had recently been publicly declared at £50,000 a year. No Rattigan, budding or in bloom, could ever earn enough by his craft alone to keep himself in New Zealand.

All artistic questions and evaluations in New Zealand reduce to one simple fact: fewer than three million people, thinly spread over an area somewhat larger than the British Isles. The standard of living is high, to be sure, but the country is not a rich one in the modern sense. It is still primarily a European farm, an economy of milk and honey rather than of nuts and bolts. There is no film industry, but two film units, one government, one private. The government film unit offers news and documentary, some of superior quality; the private company fulfills commercial assignments and made its first feature film in 1952, followed by a second in 1964. Television is in its infancy, with four regional channels, two in the North Island, two in the South. All of which suggests that the living theatre could be the main arena for public celebration of the national character and mores, its splendors and miseries, joys and sorrows. But it is not; there is plenty of theatrical activity, but

240

it is still fragmentary and fiercely parochial. After 125 years of organized European settlement, no national framework has yet been devised, no vessel fashioned, in which a viable and creative New Zealand drama can be held. It is the purpose of this essay to suggest why this should be so.

In a country so recently founded on a European image, twelve thousand miles from its roots, the theatre has had two public aspects, which I will call the Theatre of Public Phenomenon and the Theatre of Private Artifice. These terms could be relevant to the theatre in all English-speaking countries and to some others—France and Italy, say—but a commercial circuit can fuzz them or allow them sometimes to merge; New Zealand has never had a permanent indigenous commercial theatre and the categories have remained rigid and distinct.

Actors followed the wakes of the first ships very quickly after New Zealand was ceded to the British Crown by the Treaty of Waitangi in 1840; by 1844 there were three Royal Victoria Theatres in the North Island, two in Auckland, facing each other, and one in Wellington. Professional companies soon began to arrive from Australia, some to stay, some for brief tours. Vaudeville flourished, the "gentleman amateur" could do his turns to warm applause, and there were many performances in barracks or associated with the military garrisons. The Australian theatre circuit was highly organized and prosperous by the mid-eighteen-fifties, and New Zealand became its useful and profitable appendage, a status that it has never lost. A national Australian tour of a popular American or British comedy will still conclude in New Zealand. This dependence has been to European observers so complete that as recently as 1951 there was no entry for New Zealand in the *Oxford Companion to the Theatre*, and the full column given to Australia does not mention New Zealand at all.

By the 1880's most of the larger New Zealand cities had built a serviceable Theatre Royal, sometimes a sumptuous opera house in the late-Victorian baroque style, an the Australian-New Zealand circuit had become a recognized and profitable stamping ground for some of the finest British and American actors of the day, by no means always on farewell tours. This marks the beginning of the Theatre of Public Phenomenon, a realm of magical transport, populated by glittering personalities from that fascinating limbo Home, or Abroad, where events occurred and life was lived, the great outer world where meaning resided. The criticism of the period was a gasping celebration; the attitude of audiences grateful and adoring; that of the stars gracious indulgence. The world was Other, Out There, and these were its fascinating representatives.

This period, with a gleam in retrospect of a Golden Age, lasted until 1914, when the regular visits of professional companies briefly ceased. Wartime morale was kept buoyant by the film, which quickly became the great popular entertainment, as it had everywhere else. At the end of the war, the living actor's craft was not extinguished—he could talk, after all, did not flicker, and was in color—but his supremacy had been challenged, limits set to his area: he was no longer in sole charge of public communication. The professional companies soon returned, their vigor unabated, with constant tours from end to end of the country. The most notable of these was the company led by the actor-manager and scholar Allan Wilkie who, with his wife, presented seasons of Shakespeare in every large city in Australia and New Zealand. It is recorded that he once played twenty-five performances of seventeen different Shakespeare plays in nineteen days. He would recruit young New Zealand actors and actresses for his tours, and many learned an exacting craft from him. But he worked in an Indian summer; he and all his professional colleagues were extinguished in 1930 by twin and simultaneous calamities: the worldwide depression and the long-feared extension of speech to the film.

Amateur theatre in New Zealand began, not quite as a response to these disasters—most of the larger societies were founded in the early 1920's—but perhaps somewhat in anticipation of the film's learning to speak. The little theatres and repertories began in the large cities, and the smaller towns followed; by 1939 no city of any size was without one. Repertory did not mean, as it does in England, a weekly, fortnightly, or monthly change of continuous program; amateur groups presented usually not more than three productions a year for a few days at a time. These societies were

242

polite and unadventurous. Their program was devoted to the conscientious and sometimes remarkably accurate reproduction of the look, accent, and deportment of the casts of West End commercial successes, and the doldrums London theatre of the 1930's generously fueled them. The politics and moral sterility of nonintervention, the peace-at-any price attitude of British governments of the day created a theatrical genre of spiritual nonintervention: teacup comedy, transvestite farce, the mildly teasing horrors of the thriller. Cockney maids thus crossed a hundred New Zealand stages as the curtain rose on a timbered cottage in Berks or Bucks; assorted guests, one marked for quick dispatch, would reach a house party outside Oxford or put up at a vaguely sinister inn; the senior member of the society, a capable comic actor, would willingly assume the frozen look and agonizing predicaments ("O, mortifying! O, humiliating!") of Robertson Hare in *Rookery Nook*, *Banana Ridge*, and many another lively farce.

This was the Theatre of Private Artifice. It had no social relevance, nor was it meant to; on the general public, it made no impact whatever. Audiences were drawn from contributing members who formed, not an interested coterie, but a social group roughly approximate to the business and professional elite of the city or town. Artifice, amateur theatricals, or—more crushing— pose and affectation were their public coinage, if indeed their activities struck any coin at all. True, there was the occasional foray into serious modern drama by the longer-established and prosperous groups: the odd O'Casey ("strong meat"), Synge ("quaint"), the lighter, milder Shaw ("clever"), but audiences knew at once that this was not "their" theatre: "When it's all boiled down, you can't beat a good English comedy." Theatre, both in its phenomenal and artificial aspects, was always Other and remote; either sunbursts from Abroad—Dame Sybil Thorndike in 1932 (*Saint Joan, Madam Plays Nap*), Fay Compton in 1937 (*Victoria Regina*) —or if locally performed by amateurs, something made and fashioned elsewhere, something to do for fun, with no questions asked or needed of a form and activity so respectable and so sanctified. This was an appropriate enough response for a provincial society with one certainty only: its origin in the British Isles.

243

PATTERN OF NEW ZEALAND CULTURE

The New Zealand amateur theatre was greatly changed by World War II. Once-glamorous Abroad, source of meaning and font of value, had been almost throttled by events so appalling in magnitude that the imagination could barely hold them; in such a context, the theatre of aping and posturing in a debilitated idiom seemed to the more sensitive amateurs an impertinence and an affront. The larger repertories were faced with groups of rebellious younger members, some hiving off into splinter groups, others persuading their committees to enlarge their scope, to widen the dramatic area. In 1946, Wellington Repertory, for example, much enriched by the war and the largest group in the country, startled its membership by a production of Thornton Wilder's comic-strip fantasy, *The Skin of Our Teeth*, mounted with a skill not effaced by the Old Vic production of 1948, which included Sir Laurence Olivier and Vivien Leigh.

Moreover, a number of new groups formed which would have no part whatever in the Theatre of Private Artifice. Unity Theatre, Wellington, is the oldest of these, and in its history perhaps the most typical. Founded within a year of the entry of the Soviet Union into the war, and largely because of that event, it began on narrowly political lines as a "people's workshop," with the plays appropriate to an aim so restricted, later broadening its policy to include all plays "real and sincere in their presentation of life." This high, wide resolve has now given them twenty-seven years of continuous activity which has seen the production of almost the entire corpus of modern drama: British (Eliot, Wesker, Osborne, Whiting); Irish (Denis Johnston, O'Casey, Synge); American (Miller, Williams, Saroyan, Inge); European (Sartre, Gorki, Ibsen, Brecht, Dürrenmatt). Theatre in their hands and in those of similar groups founded somewhat later, like Grafton (Auckland), Phoenix (Christchurch), and much later, the Globe (Dunedin), began to mean something challenging and awkward, less easily dismissed by those, always vocal, for whom all theatrical activity was pretentious artifice. A coterie audience slowly assembled round these groups, present for one reason only: they wanted to be there. After all, no one goes to O'Casey, Brecht, Osborne, Pinter, Beckett, or Ionesco simply to watch one's friends attempting bogus or alien sophistications: one goes because of the plays themselves, for their power to question, shake, illumine, and appease.

Thus, for those surveying the twenty-odd years of theatrical activity since regular professional visits ceased, the amateurs had been massively engaged and their achievements were not despicable. They had filled the gap, had kept the tattered flag of live theatre flying. Even in their pervasive dim genre of domestic comedy, a number of actors had achieved a modest competence, and there were some talented and vociferous young. Miss Ngaio Marsh, world-renowned for her detective novels, had trained as a Shakespearean actress in Allan Wilkie's company; she proved herself, at the end of the war, a splendid producer of student Shakespeare, working at Canterbury College, Christchurch (now the University of Canterbury). She made a national tour with a student company in 1945 in *Hamlet* and *Othello*, another in 1947 in *Macbeth*, and in 1949 presented a student group in Sydney and Melbourne in *Othello* and *Six Characters in Search of an Author*, the first and, at the time of writing, only Australian tour ever undertaken by a New Zealand company.

A mild theatrical climate had been generated, and it was agreed in sympathetic government circles headed by the late Prime Minister Peter Fraser, who did more for the arts in New Zealand than any predecessor or successor, that the time was ripe for an indigenous professional framework. There was even some talk, more pious and fervent than practicable or feasible, of a National Theatre, even some tentative planning. This all came to nothing, but in 1947, the Regional Council of Adult Education in Auckland formed a drama unit which, as the Community Arts Service Theatre, toured a professional company through the Auckland Province three times a year, within reach of more than half of the total population. A similar group was formed some years later by the Wellington Regional Council for its province, but lasted only a few seasons; its main contribution to community drama, like that of its sister bodies in Canterbury and Otago provinces, came from the roving experienced drama tutor (whose services the Councils provided) working briefly but regularly with amateur groups.

Later, all four regional councils were to sponsor opera and ballet tours.

The C.A.S. Theatre tour was a truly communal effort. A local committee would first engage the company at a nominal guarantee, arrange billeting for actors, provide gigantic suppers, help with the publicity, and sometimes assist with staging and lighting; the Auckland C.A.S. Theatre lasted a remarkable fifteen years. Their program was light to middleweight as it had to be; despite the apparent homogeneity of an audience drawn entirely from one small town or district, it was likely to be more heterogeneous in composition and taste than most city audiences. Neither a coterie nor a social audience, it was a family gathering, a communal outing. When the company presented Tennessee Williams' *The Glass Menagerie* in 1956, they nightly faced an audience of school parties aged fifteen and upwards, young marrieds (with their tots beside them if they had not been able to arrange baby-sitters), the middle-aged, and the elderly. This made the choice of play a risk and a hazard; it was indeed on this rock that the C.A.S. company finally split in 1962.

In October 1948—again, as it happened, through the good offices of Prime Minister Peter Fraser, who personally arranged chartered air transport at the last moment—New Zealand was visited by the Old Vic Theatre Company headed by Sir Laurence Olivier and Vivien Leigh in a program of *Richard III*, *The School for Scandal*, and *The Skin of Our Teeth* for brief seasons in each of the four cities. It was the most gala theatrical season ever staged in New Zealand: it was the Theatre of Public Phenomenon at its grandest. Sir Laurence was not yet quite at the zenith of his powers, but very nearly; it was clear enough that he would soon be the leading actor of the Western world. His wife, after *Gone with the Wind*, was for some years the most celebrated actress alive. Both had been the subjects, not to say victims, of the full power and resources of the modern publicity apparatus; where the reputations of nineteenth-century performers were carried abroad by hearsay or in print, those of twentieth-century actors were established for millions through the potent, glittering shadows of the talking film. "I just can't believe that I'll be seeing them as they really are!" was

246

often gasped in the all-night queues for seats. They came, these infinitely glamorous stars, not merely from Home, but from that much wider Abroad of an alien but fascinating mystery. They were the word made flesh, as it were, a word which one had heard for so long, but so distantly. This was what theatre was, then: glitter, sophistication, fable. For it was not for Shakespeare, Sheridan, or Wilder that the majority of the vast audiences paid such high prices (some to doze quietly through *Richard III*), but to take part in ritual, in phenomenon.

The Old Vic image of theatre as dazzle and glitter was soon to tarnish; within a few months, Sir Laurence's services had been terminated, and the company, briefly of world renown under his leadership, quickly sank in status to London repertory, recognizable only by a debased, mannered style. But it was in the shadow of the Old Vic at its zenith, particularly in the image of the historic New Zealand season, that New Zealand's first fully professional national company was conceived and founded.

After the war, the Government initiated through its Department of Internal Affairs a bursary scheme for gifted acting students from whom no bond to return was asked or expected; with no professional framework for actors, bursars were free to take what chances the English theatre offered them and some have made satisfying careers in it. In 1949, Richard Campion and his wife Edith entered the Old Vic Theatre School, he for the two-year producers' course (extended to three years in his case; his last year was spent mostly "on the road," leading the Young Vic on tours of Sweden, Denmark, and Holland); she for the two-year acting course. Both had worked with distinction in the Wellington amateur theatre; Campion's 1948 production of *King Lear* for Unity Theatre had a most promising bravery and fervor; Mrs. Campion had been successful in roles as various as Amy, Dowager Lady Monchensey, in Eliot's *The Family Reunion*, the Sphinx in Cocteau's *The Infernal Machine*, Nora in O'Casey's *The Plough and the Stars*, and Ella in O'Neill's *All God's Chillun Got Wings*.

They returned to New Zealand at the end of 1951, and in the following year announced their plans for a national professional theatre company, the New Zealand Players, to which they were

247

prepared to devote a large private fortune. A national body of well-wishers, the New Zealand Players Foundation, was formed in every town on the company's itinerary, members paying a small annual subscription to support it. The New Zealand Players opened its first season in Wellington on May 8, 1953, with two plays, *The Young Elizabeth* by Jennette Dowling and Francis Letton—this, remember, was less than a month before the coronation of Elizabeth II—and Pinero's *Dandy Dick*.

For the next seven years, the New Zealand Players spread a theatre grid over the country, from farthest north to deepest south, in three tours a year. The program was catholic rather than popular, including Anouilh's *Ring Round the Moon*, Douglas Stewart's *Ned Kelly*, Ustinov's *The Love of Four Colonels* and *Romanoff and Juliet*, Fry's *The Lady's Not for Burning*, Shaw's *Saint Joan* and *Pygmalion*, Shakespeare's *A Midsummer Night's Dream*, *Twelfth Night*, and *The Merchant of Venice*, the first production outside England of Willis Hall's *The Long and the Short and the Tall*, and the ill-fated *A View from the Bridge* by Arthur Miller.

Tours were long and arduous, three months of mostly one-night stands, and no city season lasting more than ten days. They were exhausting to actors and particularly to stagecrews; Campion's productions, often elaborate, were heavy to move in and pack out. But the Players quickly became a national institution and attendances totaled a million within five years: quite a figure in a population of two million and a half.

Richard Campion set out to dazzle the New Zealand public: for a time he did, with a skill that most Players' audiences had never seen before, and not inferior, in the most sumptuous of his productions, to that of any visiting company. He had as collaborator Raymond Boyce, a graduate designer from the Old Vic Theatre School who joined the company from England for its first season. Together they evolved a style for which, by 1957, the present writer coined the term "Old Vickery," meaning one in which manner conquered matter, for which the way of saying was more considered than the thing said. Outwardly, the company had all the trappings of the Old Vic: settings were as rich, lighting as masterly; even in atmosphere, in the deportment and jargon of its actors, the New Zealand Players irresistibly recalled an English company.

"More matter with less art," pleads Gertrude to Polonius; had she sat through a Players' production, she would be calling for better actors. Actors are few in New Zealand; fewer still are those free to leave safe jobs for the rigors of a Players' tour of three months. At no time was the company able to offer a contract for longer than a single tour, which meant that no permanent body of actors was ever assembled. The more gifted simply used it as a springboard for the high dive overseas. The seven-year history of the Players suggests that while you may find in New Zealand a passable Romeo, an affecting Juliet, even an interesting Hamlet, almost anyone who comes to the audition can end up as Paris, Tybalt, Osric, or Horatio. The company had no home, except Wellington, for rehearsal and administration; thus they put down no roots into the community, assembled no vitally interested audiences. Attempting the allegiance of the whole country, the Players belonged to nobody.

By 1957 the costs of touring, transport, and publicity were so ruinous that the New Zealand Players became a trust under a widely representative and understandably timid board of governors. Campion left the company and was succeeded by a director appointed from England. The State offered, from lottery profits administered by the Department of Internal Affairs, sporadic and grudging grants, drops in the ocean of the Players' now gigantic annual budget. The company limped on with safe, unadventurous productions, except for the brave and brilliant *The Long and the Short and the Tall* in 1959, which was so disastrous at the box office that a planned twelve-week tour was cut in half. Audiences dwindled, the Foundation withered. In 1960, before a full and enthusiastic house for Arthur Miller's *A View from the Bridge*, there were sad speeches from the Board of Governors: the New Zealand Players had collapsed.

Thus ended seven years of continuous professional theatre, involving over two hundred thousand miles of touring, a million and a half paid attendances, forty productions, and a theatrical network

249

laid from end to end of the country. Was it all *folie de grandeur?* Richard Campion has often been accused of it. Yet the plain fact is that in his best productions for the Players, *Ned Kelly, A Midsummer Night's Dream, Saint Joan,* he achieved an authority, a virtuosity, and a precision of style that would be honored anywhere. Recalling, both in his virtues and in his lapses, the brilliant, erratic, and ebullient Sir Tyrone Guthrie, Campion proved himself, in the four years that the company was under his sole artistic direction, unquestionably the finest and most resourceful producer ever to work in this country. And his true measure was taken later, after he had left the Players, in his work for schools and for amateur groups. Distinguished by the same flair, the same passion, his 1959 production of *Oedipus Rex* for Victoria University of Wellington was possibly the finest amateur production ever staged in New Zealand. And his later work in Australia (MacLeish's *J. B.* for the 1962 Adelaide Festival, his productions for J. C. Williamson's theatres in Melbourne and the Elizabethan Theatre Trust in Sydney) confirmed what one knew of a major theatrical talent.

The reasons for the Players' collapse went deeper than a private *folie de grandeur,* as deep as a fundamental misconception of the nature of theatre in the mid-twentieth century, in particular of the temper and character of the New Zealand audience. The public at large in this country will accept professional theatre only as Phenomenon, and this only from glamorous Abroad—even then perhaps only once; the return season of the Old Vic in 1962, led by Vivien Leigh alone, was a financial disaster. The New Zealand Players offered an authentic glitter, but no stars; and it is only to stars that New Zealanders will pay both homage and high prices. The Players' seasons were never Phenomenon, but only Novelty, which soon stales; from novelty, they declined to occasions, to social exercise, "the thing to do." And when the Players, harassed and deviled by mounting costs, appealed to the widest possible box-office returns by presenting cheap thrillers (Agatha Christie's *The Mousetrap* in 1957 and *Spider's Web* in 1958), the company had had its chips. The Players had become the Theatre of Private Artifice, the amateurs' own field, and once amateurs watched, at professional prices, a company performing trivia that they could do as well, if not better, then the professionals might as well pack their bags. What the Players were bitterly and expensively learning was that in the arts, particularly in the art of theatre, New Zealanders' loyalties are local and civic: at widest, parochial.

For the New Zealand audience was not really interested in the theatrical experience at all, nor could they be persuaded to try it on; the word "education" is almost the dirtiest in the national vocabulary. What they wanted, in the country towns, even in the cities, was "a nice, light night out," and the Players' greatest success was, significantly enough, neither Shakespeare nor Shaw, but the agreeably artless English musical *Salad Days*, the only one of their productions ever to justify a return season. The lesson of the Players' debacle was melancholy but unmistakable: New Zealand theatrical taste was for stars, in Shakespeare if they must, or *Salad Days*, with nothing in between.

A further misconception brought the activities of the Auckland C.A.S. Theatre to a close. It was in its twelfth year of continuous operation when, in 1958, Ronald Barker was appointed from England to direct its productions. Mistaking the community audience for a coterie one, he unleashed—the only word—on the unsuspecting country circuit Samuel Beckett's *Waiting for Godot* in a production which, if willful at the edges, was in most areas brilliantly articulate. The entire circuit erupted in rage and disgust; protest meetings were held, furious telegrams were dispatched to the Minister of Education (with whose nominal blessing the production took place), and although the C.A.S. Theatre lasted until early 1962, its back was broken by *Godot*, taken by the unsophisticated audiences as being a yardstick for modern theatre as a whole, of which they wanted no part whatever. If this was its voice, then it would fall on deaf ears. Perhaps by 1962 television would have extinguished the theatre anyway, but all over the North Island *Waiting for Godot* was regarded as the turning point in community drama.

At the time of writing there is no professional theatre in the country whatever with a wider than civic resonance, and even this— the Downstage Theatre in Wellington—is still tentative. The New Zealand Players are not quite dead; the Schools Quartet which

Richard Campion created in 1956 still survives and gives the four young actors the only professional training still available, from February to October, before the toughest and warmest audiences there are; the C.A.S. Theatre is nominally in recess, but seems totally defunct; the Southern Comedy Players, founded in 1957 to provide light entertainment on the South Island circuit, is also in recess while its two directors study in England, but its future is uncertain in the face of the competition, ever more pervasive, of television.

And playwrights? Are there any? There is a horde of them, women outnumbering men by two to one, scribbling away for dear life, it sometimes seems: the Playwrights Association of New Zealand has over ninety members. They fuel the braver amateur groups and the one-act annual *Festspiel* of the British Drama League, active in New Zealand since 1931, always hospitable to and encouraging indigenous drama. Over a thousand actors took part in the 1964 festivals, and six plays were recalled for the final, held on two evenings, adjudicated by a professional producer. In the 150-odd plays presented, perhaps one-tenth were by New Zealand authors, and of these, two-thirds were by women. Where formerly the themes of these plays were minor domestic upsets, mild comedies of errors, playwrights have lately begun to broaden their scope; in the 1964 British Drama League Festival, Alexander Guyan's *Conversations with a Golliwog* more than held its own with a program including T. S. Eliot, Thornton Wilder, Shelagh Delaney, and Paul Green.

But New Zealand playwrights rarely make more than a local eddy, and the waters of public indifference soon smooth it over. The touchstone to success again comes from abroad, and the quickest route for a play originating in Auckland, say, to be produced in Dunedin, is via London or New York, the only sounding boards for a play of national rather than parochial resonance. There are plenty of themes waiting to be explored; New Zealand is a bi-racial community, after all, with 6 per cent of its population of pure or part Polynesian stock, and this theme could be fruitful; such studies as have been made of the Maori people have only been partial successes because of the disinclination of the Maori to take part in *pakeha* cultural activities, though every *pakeha* has some acquaintance with the culture of his predecessors, in however debased a form. Social relationships between men and women are bizarre in New Zealand, and this, too, is being explored: the dislocation of marriages from the war, when nearly one hundred thousand men were absent from the country for years at a time; the question of identity (Who are we? What do we stand for?); the indifference of the community to creative and cultural life—there are plenty of themes, but no vital audience quickening the art by their passionate participation.

In 1946 the enlightened administration of Peter Fraser created the conditions for a permanent National Symphony Orchestra, totally subsidized against loss. Now in its twenty-first continuous year, its annual deficit is close to $200,000. In its first few years, the correspondence columns of the papers seethed with protest. ("Those who like this sort of thing should pay for it themselves, and not leave it to the poor taxpayer.") Time has reduced these storms to heavy breathing. The National Symphony Orchestra of the New Zealand Broadcasting Corporation is now an excellent ensemble which the finest soloists in the world have not disdained; more important still, its existence has created a native school of composers. The New Zealand government saw cleverly enough that a professional ensemble was possible only in a handsomely subsidized permanent framework; it is odd that this has never been conceded as necessary for the theatre also.

The grants to the New Zealand Players were, as noted, limited and intermittent. In 1961 the Minister of Internal Affairs appointed a body to advise him on the disbursements to be made for cultural purposes from the highly profitable Golden Kiwi Lottery. The Arts Advisory Council was generous to opera and ballet, wayward and sometimes incomprehensible in their grants to other causes. Both opera and ballet now have national companies supported both by the State and by handsome private endowment. Like the New Zealand Players, they are as committed to constant touring from one end of the country to the other, but the parochial pull does not operate to their disadvantage, if at all; no amateur, however fervent, could perform in *Don Giovanni* or *Giselle* with-

253

out an exigent training, nor could any one community muster the resources necessary for an opera or ballet season. Both companies were founded at about the same time as the New Zealand Players: ballet, by Poul Gnatt in 1953, opera by Donald Munro in 1954. Mr. Gnatt was a Danish dancer of European reputation who elected to stay in New Zealand after an Australasian tour, and he did seven years' hard work on the community circuit, gaining respect and affection. Donald Munro, a New Zealand baritone who had worked successfully abroad, founded a tiny company in 1954 with a few professional singers; he also pioneered in the country on the community circuit. His success may be judged by the production of *Porgy and Bess* in 1965, with producer, conductor, and three principles from New York, the celebrated Maori bass, Inia te Wiata, from London, and a budget that went over $200,000 before the curtain rose on the first performance, a figure which both London and Broadway would acknowledge as being in their area of risk.

Opera and ballet, as everyone knows, are exotic imports with techniques so demanding that few amateurs ever attempt them; where an amateur group will cheerfully stage a Shakespeare play, the amateur singer or dancer would not dream of a local *Tosca* or *Swan Lake*. On application, however, the Arts Advisory Council made a grant of $10,000 to Richard Campion to pull from the ashes of the New Zealand Players, as it were, the New Zealand Theatre Company. His first production was *Romeo and Juliet*. It was by no means his best; he seemed to have learned little in his four years with amateurs, or perhaps it was that the chance once more to be a national figure made his sense of style falter; in any case, the projected tour was ignominiously curtailed, and though there was one further local production, the New Zealand Theatre Company rapidly disappeared without trace. The Arts Advisory Council announced that there would be no further grants for touring professional theatre.

The Arts Advisory Council was succeeded in 1963 by the Queen Elizabeth II Arts Council, though its members were not appointed until 1964. This autonomous body, freed from an explicit link with the Department of Internal Affairs, was conceived as a commemoration of the second visit of Queen Elizabeth II to New Zealand in 1963.

New Zealand is a maddening country for artists, particularly for those drawn towards the theatre and willing to work here for it rather than go abroad. The arts are precarious undertakings all over the Western world, but at least in Europe and the United States there is the prospect of success, of reputation and reward, of the freedom to work, if only for a few. In New Zealand there are no logical steps to follow, no ladder to climb. The race is to neither the swift nor the persistent; there is simply no race at all. The artist is, to the community at large, an un-person, performing un-work. The temper of the community is thus profoundly hostile and inimical to artistic creation, especially in the performing arts, where it is widely equated with affectation and pose and with less mentionable adherences.

The reasons for this may be sought in the circumstances and climate of the country's founding. The libertarian spirit of the later nineteenth century was strong enough to uproot the early pioneers and settlers, take them half across the world in grueling voyages lasting sometimes six months, for the new life, the fresh start. Things would be better "out there": no class, no aristocracy, no tyranny of property, open lands waiting to be worked. And this is still the impulse that brings a regular flow of immigrants year by year. A correspondent from the United States suggested to the present writer that if New Zealand strikes any chord in the North American imagination, it is of a country distant enough to escape from radioactive fallout. It has always been so, since the first European settlement: but not all fallouts are radioactive.

Since its settlement in the spirit of liberal idealism, New Zealand has become justly famed as the world's most thorough welfare state, where women first had the vote, where a full social security system was first implemented, where citizens are looked after by a benevolent state from cradle to grave. The ideal of such a society will not be creation, but health; its heroes athletes (runners, footballers, Sir Edmund Hillary), its chief art not literature but medicine.

The situation in New Zealand in the 1960's for the artist and intellectual is often so intolerable, the smugness and complacency so monumental, that, paradoxically, the climate may soon be ripe for a masterpiece. This will come perhaps first from a novelist, because his grid of communication—himself to publisher, printer, reader—is somewhat simple and is already established. For a dramatic masterpiece, several preconditions remain to be fulfilled. The history of the theatre in the last ten years has stripped it of all pretensions; it must now be minority, coterie, and fired by a passionate conviction. A devoted few, doing (to adapt Lady Gregory's words about Abbey Theatre policy) what they think is good until in time it becomes popular, will slowly assemble an audience of equal devotion and create that subtle and essential interaction without which no really creative theatre can be viable. And the State, if it is wise, will look at these groups with care and help them when it is necessary. One group, Downstage, Inc, has leased a small restaurant and gives nightly cabaret theatre, with a program that so far has included Edward Albee, Harold Pinter, adaptations of Gogol, original solo performances, Jean Genet, and Eugene O'Neill. Its following is not yet large, but is growing; if the New Zealand Players proved nothing else, it was that such growth is not rapid nor can it be fertilized from above.

There are gleams of hope elsewhere. In the last ten years, the Productions Section of the New Zealand Broadcasting Corporation has slowly assembled a highly competent team of professional radio actors with well-equipped studios in Auckland, Wellington, and Christchurch. They have presented almost the entire body of modern drama, such of it at least that is adaptable for radio, and they are now well equipped for classical drama also, with the best voices in the country at their command. The inclusion of New Zealand plays is not very great, but of some one hundred productions in 1964, over twenty were by local authors. It will be by interaction between the dedicated local professional group and the large studios of broadcasting and television reaching the whole country that a full professional theatre will eventually be fashioned and developed. The next ten years are regarded as crucial for the development of a New Zealand literature. They will be crucial for the theatre also.

MASS COMMUNICATIONS

G. A. WOOD

NEW ZEALAND has a highly centralized system of government, a network of controls to maintain a welfare state and to provide a measure of insulation against overseas trade movements, and government activities extend into every sphere of society. The country's mass communications are locally based but held together, in the case of newspapers, by the Press Association, and of radio and television by the Broadcasting Corporation. Although there is a vigorous and growing indigenous culture, New Zealand still shows its derivative nature and the British origins of its populace. For literature and films it is largely dependent on imports. The inteligentsia still looks toward England, but the majority is both more insular in outlook and influenced by popular films, television programs, and magazines imported from the United States.

The nature of the press has not changed greatly since the introduction of telegraph, railways, and submarine cables in the 1860's and 1870's. Twenty-nine of the thirty-eight daily newspapers still extant were founded in the years before 1880, fifteen of them before 1870. In the past hundred years some major newspapers have died or been absorbed by rivals; no new ones have been launched with permanent success. The one exception is *The Dominion*, the Wellington morning paper which was founded in 1907.

No newspaper has achieved nationwide or even island-wide distribution. Standardized news is retailed in each locality by the local paper selling at about five cents a copy. Nine morning papers cover the whole countryside; the giants, the four papers from the main centers, have divided most of the land between them. Scores of smalltown dailies disappeared when motor transport brought in the big city dailies, and most provincial towns have been reduced to one daily paper published in the afternoon. There are today twenty-five provincial evening papers and one evening paper in each main center.

The main difference among various newspapers lies in their circulations, and hence the number of pages, advertising revenue, and technical facilities. The two papers published in each main center, with circulations ranging from 30,000 to over 200,000, are usually dubbed "metropolitan" papers; provincial dailies range in circulation from less than 2,000 to approaching 30,000. At the time of the 1961 census, one million in a population of under two and a half million lived in the circulation area of the *New Zealand Herald*, the old Auckland Province. In consequence, the *Herald* had a greater circulation than the other three metropolitan morning papers combined, and of a total daily newspaper circulation of under one million, almost one third was provided by the *Herald* and the evening *Auckland Star*.

For all but local reporting, newspapers rely on the Press Association, which was formed by newspaper management in 1879, after the laying of a submarine cable to Australia. The Association is a nonprofit organization financed by striking an annual budget from members. Membership charges are related to the size of the newspaper and smaller papers receive Association services barely at cost price. Today the largest newspapers might be able to maintain an independent news service, but they forego that independence to cooperate in the Association.

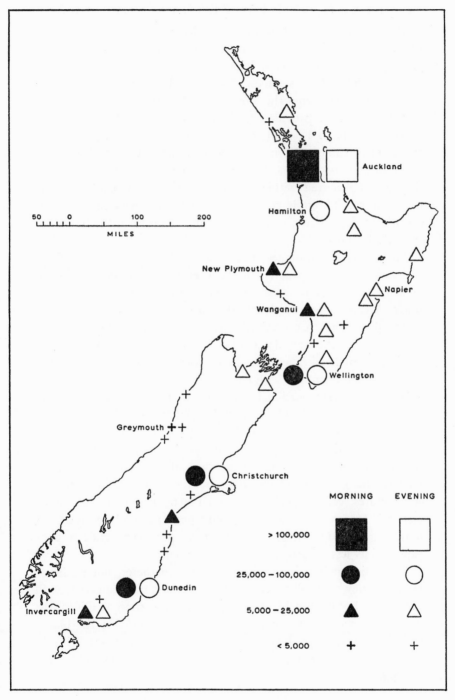

Map 1. Circulation of daily newspapers

Most overseas news is drawn from Reuters, although the Association has the right to buy material from *The Times* (London) and the *New York Times*. In addition, it receives material from two American news services, Associated Press and United Press International, and from the Australian Associated Press, for which, as for Reuters, it provides reciprocal news. The Association has correspondents in London, the United States, Canada, and Australia. They cable news items through Sydney to the Wellington office of the Association, from which, subject to possible editing, they are transmitted within minutes to every newspaper office in the country. Through the Association, newspapers may request specific types of news, and Reuters collects special information for New Zealand needs.

The results are an international coverage beyond the resources of any individual newspaper, and the presentation of closely similar versions of the same news from one end of New Zealand to the other. Members of the Association may not publish any cabled news apart from that received through the Association, although they can, and the best do, publish commentaries sent by airmail. All important local news must be forwarded through the Association to other members without delay.

Only in covering national news outside their own locality have newspapers a free hand in publishing their own independently gathered reports. Except for maintaining political correspondents in Wellington, and covering major sports fixtures, even the largest newspapers tend to rely on the services of the Association. They establish their individual character by their format, local reports and features, editorial comment, and the treatment of Association material, for all must edit the voluminous material received. At most a good paper might use about 60 per cent, while a poor paper prints less or drowns it in poor layout.

Association policy is that it should be a gatherer, not an interpreter, of news. It will transmit straight reports but requires that all statements be attributable to an authoritative source. Given the origins of its overseas material, it is not surprising that the bias is towards coverage of British and Commonwealth news, with in some areas a closer approximation to American views. This may lead to a selection bias against particular regimes. It may be argued, however, that any bias derived from sources of cabled news or the inadequacy of comment is a small price to pay for having a uniformly high and reasonably efficient standard of news coverage.

In a country where, for example, over 60 per cent of the factories employ ten or fewer persons, a large newspaper company is in the small bracket of large-scale employers, with a substantial capital and in some cases returning a substantial profit. Many newspaper publishers also have extensive printing works: publishers of most of the twenty-six daily newspapers with circulations of over seven thousand employ over fifty persons and have an authorized or nominal capital of over $100,000. A metropolitan newspaper employs over two hundred persons and has a capital of over $500,000. A high percentage of newspaper proprietors, even of small papers, belong to such powerful interest groups as the Employers' Association, the Chamber of Commerce, the Master Printers' Association, and the Manufacturers' Association. All belong to the Newspaper Proprietors' Association.

Family control is still marked, for example, in the cases of Wilson and Horton Ltd., which publishes the *New Zealand Herald* and two popular magazines, and of the Wellington and Dunedin evening newspapers. The only important newspaper combination is New Zealand Newspapers Ltd., which publishes the Auckland and Christchurch evening newspapers as well as two magazines. Its directors, like the directors of the Christchurch and Dunedin morning papers, have links with leading city commercial and business interests.

Since 1935, when an intense newspaper war in Christchurch ended in a truce and two papers were closed down, there has been little active competition, newspapers appearing to keep off one another's territory. Since the war they have become more forceful in their news presentation: by 1964 all but one metropolitan and quite a few provincial newspapers had transferred to front-page news; nevertheless, none has reduced to tabloid size, and despite subtle differences in layout and tone, the overall pattern is uniform and restrained. All reflect the interests that control them and support the conservative National party, if with differing degrees of independence. The only exception is a morning paper in the small town of Greymouth on the West Coast. In 1946 the Labour party, which was then in office, attempted to establish a morning paper in Wellington, but without success, and after five years the struggling *Southern Cross* ceased publication.

The most serious challenge to the *status quo* came in early 1964 when *The Dominion* was subject to a series of take-over bids initiated by a $3,200,000 bid by the British Thomson organization. New Zealand newspapers sprang to the defense of one of their number, and the two Auckland companies patriotically offered to take over *The Dominion* themselves. Government reacted vigorously and threatened retroactive legislation, retroactive because Parliament was in its six months' recess. The specter was raised of government licensing of newspapers. The Opposition called for an early session of Parliament to discuss the crisis. Under the circumstances the shareholders rejected the Thomson bid and the others withdrew. Although Lord Thomson had been prepared to guarantee continued New Zealand editorial control of the paper and to reinvest profits in New Zealand, the forces against him were too strong. The New Zealand press avoided the challenge which would have been presented by the expansion of a vigorous metropolitan daily, aiming at increased profits before all else, and able perhaps to dispense with the services of the Press Association. In the next session of Parliament legislation was passed to control overseas takeovers, although this did not prevent the Thomas organization from taking over a major Auckland trade publishing group.

Both political and commercial interests have failed to break the political and commercial monopoly of the daily press. This has not had any great effects on electoral results. Nor can it cause too much harm to the beliefs and cause of the New Zealand Labour party, which is a major political party with a mass following and the resources to fight press discrimination. The first Labour government (1935–1949) introduced broadcasting of parliamentary debates and this has remained an effective means of preventing press distortion or suppression. Newspapers have a strong incentive to avoid provoking an outright clash with a powerful political movement and to maintain a façade of political independence—

except in editorials. In their coverage of elections, the newspapers take care to give equal treatment to the various political parties, although some censor any reference to the campaign of the small Communist party.

The mild and popular views of the Labour party thus receive adequate, if not very sympathetic, press coverage. Evening papers in the main centers may even move towards them to cater for their urban readers. What can and should cause alarm is the effect on the press of its conservative proprietors when the community is deeply divided on emotive issues, especially if the parliamentary leaders of the Labour party do not divide from their conservative opponents. During the industrial upheavals of 1951, when Labour leaders avoided taking sides, or when they crusaded in 1949 for the introduction of peacetime compulsory military training, the free press cooperated with the government to crush minority and left-wing opinion. At the best of times not only small extremist groups, but a significant minority political party like the Social Credit party and even the powerful trade-union movement are unlikely to get a good press.

In addition to the major newspapers there is a host of others, some with a circulation well below one thousand, catering for small towns and the farming areas they serve. Some are dailies and, members of the Press Association, attempt to give a full news coverage, but many are entirely local in interest, appearing once or several times a week. Of the thirty boroughs outside the four main centers which in 1961 had populations of more than five thousand, all but one had in 1964 a paper appearing at least twice a week, and twenty-three had at least one daily. In all, sixty-six provincial cities and towns had at least one local newspaper appearing weekly or more frequently. In addition, there are suburban papers appearing weekly or less frequently which are distributed in the major urban areas, and although the number of newspapers is declining gradu-ally, it appears that such purely local papers will continue to flourish: the ten largest range in circulation from 21,000 to 8,500, and with one exception are centered in or near Auckland, the home territory of the two largest dailies.

They have a vital and continuing role to play in a country

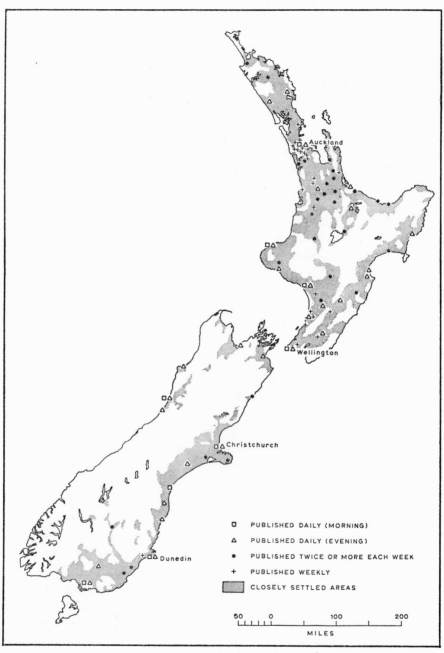

Map 2. Newspapers published in New Zealand

notably lacking in institutional expression of local interest. Local feeling still attaches a meaning to the nine sprawling provinces that were abolished in 1876. The numberless counties and boroughs that since then have administered local affairs are arbitrary creations which in most cases can inspire little loyalty. Boundaries of parliamentary electorates are revised each five years and districts may find themselves shunted from one electorate to another. Various government departments and private organizations tend to divide the country differently for administrative purposes. The press is almost the only organ of local loyalties, traditions, and needs, from the province-wide morning papers to the various types of papers catering for a more restricted area.

There are several national weeklies. The *New Zealand Truth*, with a circulation of 235,000, or 35,000 more than that of the *New Zealand Herald*, is the most widely read paper in the country and its nearest approach to a national newspaper. A tabloid that specializes in court cases and scandal, it is prepared to take up social and political issues and to hammer governments with a vigor unknown in the staid daily press. Other major weeklies are the *New Zealand Women's Weekly* (circulation 190,000), the *Weekly News* (130,000), and the New Zealand *Listener* (79,500), produced by the New Zealand Broadcasting Corporation, which gives weekly radio and television programs but also contains serious comment and reviews.

There are a number of journals and periodicals for sectional groups in the community. Among those, mostly monthlies, that have a circulation of over 20,000 are a *Home Journal*, an agricultural journal, a business journal, a motoring journal, and the journals of the Returned Servicemen's Association, and the Roman Catholic and Anglican churches. Most of the more important journals with circulations under 20,000 are professional or trade publications: for meat-retailers, plumbers, electricians, liquor licensees, orchardists, growers, and so on, or journals for particular sports: golfing, fishing, racing.

A picture of New Zealand interests and tastes can be built from an examination of such periodicals. There are others, however, which have an influence beyond their modest circulation. Literary journals are continually founded, flourish, and die. The longest-living and the best, the quarterly *Landfall*, published with the aid of a grant from the State Literary Fund, has made a particularly important contribution to New Zealand literature and thought. "There have always been for those who seek them dissident journals of small circulation and acid comment, the journals of trade unions and students and independent enthusiasts, and of the Communist Party." [1] A "thread of independent radical comment" has been maintained by the prewar *Tomorrow*, the postwar *Here and Now*, and in the 1960's the quarterly *Comment* and the *New Zealand Monthly Review*. Together with imported products, particularly from England, these provide some of the critical commentary which is less apparent in the newspapers.

Since 1962 radio and television, the major media of mass communications, have been under the control of a three-man corporation appointed by the government.

Broadcasting was first, in 1925, placed in the hands of a private company. In 1932 the company's plant was taken over by a board. The board did not prove a marked success, and in 1934–1935 it was reconstituted and given supervision of private broadcasting, but in 1936 the new Labour Government abolished it and introduced direct ministerial control. From the board the National Broadcasting Service inherited eight low-powered stations, two in each main center, and bought out almost all the private radio stations and introduced advertising on a separate commercial service. Later, in 1943, the National and Commercial services were combined to become divisions under one departmental head.

After the war broadcasting expanded rapidly. Local needs and pressures have led to continuing establishment of new stations. In the late 1940's six part-commercial stations and a short-wave station were established. Since then a large number of wholly commercial stations also have been founded. The number of national stations remained comparatively static, but they were made progressively more powerful and hours of transmission were increased. Today most stations broadcast continuously all day, and New Zealand's most powerful station, 2YA Wellington, continues through the

[1] F. L. Wood, *This New Zealand* (Wellington, 1958), p. 243.

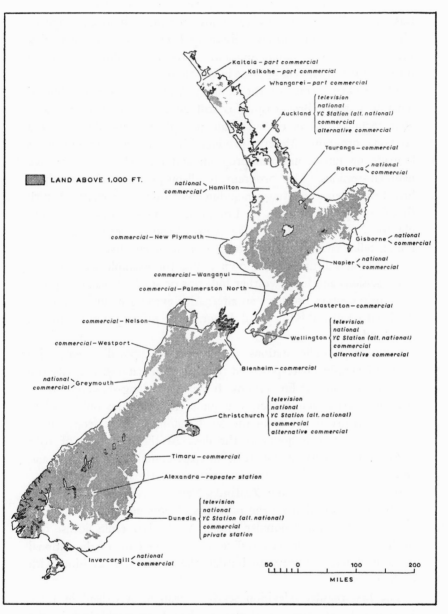

Map 3. Broadcasting stations of New Zealand

night. In March, 1965, there were twenty-three centers with at least one radio station, giving almost complete radio coverage of New Zealand. Some 616,000 listening licenses were granted that year: 24 per 100 of population and an average of almost one radio for every private dwelling place in the country.

The broken terrain of the country made necessary a string of separate stations. Broadcasting is still decentralized, but by 1964–1965 technical advances had made possible the introduction of a "national program." Material produced by the various radio centers is made up into a uniform program and relayed through twelve national stations. The program is all-purpose, providing school broadcasts, news bulletins (including rebroadcasts from the British Broadcasting Corporation in London), farmers', housewives' and childrens' sessions, and coverage of major sporting events as well as music, talks, and official government announcements. Stations may on occasion substitute their own items, for example listeners' request sessions and local weather bulletins or stock exchange reports. The main centers also have an alternative evening national program modeled on the B.B.C. Third Programme, offering serious music, talks, and plays.

Commercial radio stations are devoted to providing entertainment. Generally lower-powered than national stations, they are the local community radio stations. It has been long-standing policy that no district should receive commercial programs only, and in some areas broadcasts from the local station are free from advertisements at certain hours of the day. At the beginning of 1965 there were twenty commercial or part-commercial stations and additional all-music commercial stations in three main centers.

By a strange irony New Zealand's National Symphony Orchestra has been subsidized from the proceeds of commercial radio, which thrives on serials and popular music. As the low radio license fees of three dollars a year only suffice to cover the costs of the national division, it was necessary to burden the commercial division with orchestra costs.

The first regular television service began in Auckland in 1960. Within the next two years stations had been established in the other three centers. With six repeater stations, and aided by a number of local societies operating translator stations, the Corporation by early 1965 gave evening television to the bulk of the population.

At present only one television program is available for a region. Free from advertisements only at certain times, it partakes more of the character of the commercial radio program than of the national. One significant change from radio is that advertisers may not sponsor a program. This gives the Corporation greater opportunity to set its own standards, but inevitably the quality varies considerably. Apart from advertisements, news bulletins, and weather forecasts, a typical evening's viewing might include an early evening session for children, a documentary (travel, nature study), a magazine program (panel discussion, guessing games, singing, and stories), westerns, crime, comic or straight human situations. Increasingly the Corporation may be expected to organize its own programs (early in 1965 it established an overseas program exchange section), but at present for commercial radio (and more particularly television) it draws heavily on American, British, and other material it can obtain overseas.

The production and sales of television sets continue apace, while there has been a drop in the production of radio sets. Television licenses rose from 23,340 in March, 1962, to 81,840 in 1963, and 167,740 in March, 1964. Sheltered behind New Zealand's tight import controls, television sets sell at exorbitant rates. This is a reflection of New Zealand's high standard of living and full employment, and the price of sets is offset by easy time-payment terms. New Zealand has long struggled against balance of payments difficulties, and any economic recession would affect the spread of television-set owners and measures to extend television coverage.

The Corporation has planned a second channel, with the intention of financing one channel from license fees, the other from advertisements. But as was the case with the first television channel, expansion has been delayed for financial reasons. And, as with the initial introduction of television, the question of control is raised. The National party, in office from 1949 to 1957 and again since 1960, has a professed dislike of state control. In 1960 legislation had been passed to place television under ministerial control. The National party came to power later that year and set up the Broadcasting Corporation. The question of a second channel has faced it once more with deciding whether it was advisable to forego the opportunity to intervene in the daily administration of broadcasting, as well as subjecting it to pressures from commercial interests that support it politically.

As the Corporation is dependent on revenue from license fees and the profits of commercial broadcasting, while having to continue community services, it has a strong interest in retaining its monopoly. Applications to operate private stations must reach the government through the Corporation, and it has already shown that it will not recommend licensing. No change is likely in radio service, though the government might bypass the Corporation and legislate to establish separate control of a second television channel.

The 1961 Broadcasting Act gave the Corporation as much independence from government control as could be permitted to an organization with monopoly control of broadcasting, yet it is to comply with general government policy with respect to broadcasting and with any general or specific directions in writing from the Minister of Broadcasting. By late 1964 it had received no written directions. General standards are laid down in the Act. The Corporation is to ensure that nothing in its programs offends good taste or decency, is likely to lead to crime or disorder, or be offensive to public feeling; to maintain a proper balance of subject matter and a high standard of quality; and to present news accurately, impartially, and with due regard to public interest. Occasion for parliamentary discussion and criticism of the activities of the Corporation is provided by the government's placing the salaries of the three members on the annual Estimates, and by the requirement that the Corporation furnish Parliament with an annual report and statement of accounts.

The Corporation is more independent in its finances and staffing arrangements than a state department, but only to a modest degree. Salary scales and conditions of employment must be determined in agreement with the State Services Commission, which controls the public service. The Corporation must conform with general government financial policy both on wages and salaries and on capital expenditure and borrowing. It is required to submit its annual program of capital works to the minister, to have regard to his directions on capital expenditure generally, and to have his consent for capital expenditure for any particular purpose which is in excess of $50,000. Its borrowing powers are subject to the control of the Minister of Finance.

In inheriting the Broadcasting Service, the Corporation inherited both its personnel and its liabilities. The effect of removing ministerial control will only gradually become apparent. The main argument for Corporation control was to remove the political interference to which broadcasting had been subject. There had been examples of censorship by governments of all political persuasions throughout broadcasting history, both of airing views disliked by the government in power and of programs which might embarrass it by offending sections of the community. Increasingly the Broadcasting Service had established an independent and impartial tradition, but ministerial intervention was always possible. In debates on the Corporation Bill members of Parliament cited the banning two years before of all reference to the popular movement to prevent the New Zealand Rugby Union sending a racially selected team to tour South Africa.

There have been occasions since then when the Corporation imposed its own censorship: it decided not to show a B.B.C. interview with M. Bidault, a former French premier who advocated the violent overthrow of the De Gaulle regime, and a talk by a "scientific humanist" was postponed at three and a half hours' notice lest it should offend the Roman Catholic minority at a time when Pope John XXIII lay dying. It may be that the Corporation will become bolder as its traditions become more established and its employees feel freer to take responsibility for introducing politically risky programs.

A danger of corporation control is the introduction of a "twilight zone" in which governmental pressure still operates, although not in the open and not in a fashion in which responsibility can be pinned down. Whether such a zone exists, and whether the Corporation develops ability to resist pressure, depends on the caliber of the minister and of the men composing the Corporation.

The problems were illustrated in the use of radio and television during the 1963 general election campaign. The method of apportioning time for election broadcasts in previous years appears to have been vague and informal. Faced with its first election, the Corporation attempted to absolve itself of all responsibility by setting the total time available and delegating to the prime minister the task of apportioning it. The prime minister allocated times almost exactly as for the past two elections, with the addition of television times, and as in the past, the Social Credit Political League accepted its portion under protest and the Communist party was banned altogether. In the meantime a rather nebulous fourth party emerged, the Liberal party, contesting twenty-three of the eighty seats, the same number as the Communist party. The actual voting showed the Liberals to be equally ineffective as a political force, but mounting public pressure during the campaign caused the prime minister to "request" the Corporation to provide broadcasting time for the Liberals. The Corporation replied by allocating an additional ten minutes for election addresses on television, pointing out to the prime minister that he had only allocated addresses for twenty-three and a half of the twenty-four hours provided on radio, and inviting him to forward a schedule of addresses for the spare thirty minutes on radio and the additional ten minutes on television.

Under the Corporation there has been perhaps a firmer acceptance of the need for controversy on the air, and to permit announcers to develop radio or television personalities, but the most marked change has been the prompt introduction of a full and rapidly expanding news service. Previously there were no news bulletins on commercial radio, and but one New Zealand news bulletin a day on national radio. For overseas news the Service was provided with a token two hundred words daily by the Press Association. Now the Corporation gives news bulletins at intervals throughout the day. It is supplied with overseas news by correspondents resident in London, New York, Malaysia, Thailand, and other centers, and in addition it monitors other radio news services on a reciprocal basis. For New Zealand news it has a growing staff of reporters attached to the various radio stations. Strategically placed radio centers are linked by teleprinter to a central newsroom in Wellington. In addition, commercial radio and television stations also broadcast local news bulletins.

Local production of other forms of mass entertainment and instruction is limited. In the year 1961–1962 books to the value of $350,000 were published in New Zealand. In half that period imports of books, exclusive of school textbooks, amounted to $2,800,000 in value. In consequence it is the Customs Department which has been the chief censor of literature.

Lists of books banned by the department were not published, and the establishment by the government in 1964 of an Indecent Publications Tribunal was a major reform. The Tribunal's task is to determine whether books or sound recordings are indecent and should be banned. It is primarily the duty of the Secretary for Justice and the Comptroller of Customs to submit items to the Tribunal, but with the leave of the Minister of Justice or the Chairman anyone can submit cases. By an Act of 1962 the Tribunal is given liberal guidance in its deliberations: "indecent" includes describing sex, horror, crime, cruelty, or violence in a manner that is injurious to the public good, but the Tribunal is to consider the dominant effect of the work, its literary or artistic merit, the price, and the persons for whom it is intended or who are likely to receive it. As well as considering whether it may corrupt some, it is to assess whether others may benefit. If the work is for the public good, regardless of other considerations, it is not to be classified as indecent. Appeals are allowed to three judges of the Supreme Court. In addition, after three years works may be resubmitted. To prevent members becoming decemvirs of morality, they must retire in rotation and may not serve continuously for more than ten years. The first members of the Tribunal have been liberal and broad-minded in their decisions.

There are other restrictions on books and printed material. Within the limitations of having to wait several months for overseas stocks to be replaced, booksellers have maintained a high standard despite import control in the past. Books were exempted from import control in 1963, but magazines, periodicals, newspapers, comics, maps, and other printed material remain controlled.

Booksellers are assisted by a trade agreement that keeps book prices high. In 1962 the Trade Practices and Prices Commission, which was established by an Act of 1958, ordered discontinuance of the agreement, but the order was reversed by the Appeal Authority.

The film industry is even more dependent on imports, although excellent documentaries are produced locally by the lively, if small, National Film Unit and by private companies. By an Act of 1930 renters of foreign films pay a 25-per-cent tax on net receipts as opposed to a 10-per-cent tax on Commonwealth films. Discrimination toward British or good box-office American films is therefore explicable. The State, in fact, collects twice on films, as an amusement tax is levied on admissions. To assist cinemas to meet the challenge of television this tax was in 1963 removed from the cheapest range of prices. How well cinemas meet that challenge is yet to be seen. Until now New Zealand has had one of the highest per capita cinema attendances in the world. In 1962–1963 there were 204 cinemas, over half of them situated in the four main centers, screening six days a week. (New Zealand's sabbatarian laws prohibit Sunday movies, the publication of Sunday newspapers, and liquor sales.) Ownership is concentrated in the hands of two major organizations: Amalgamated Theatres (49 cinemas in 1964) and Kerridge-Odeon Ltd.

Film exhibitors must be licensed by a tribunal, and a government censor has a free hand in trimming, chopping, or banning films for both cinema and television. In both cases there is right of appeal to a specially constituted authority. (See Table 7.)

New Zealand mass communications are affected on the one hand by the unitary structure of the State and the considerable degree of central control, and on the other by the division of the country's long, narrow terrain into natural districts of varying size and importance. Newspapers, with their restricted area of circulation and local ownership, and the decentralized organization of commercial radio and television foster and encourage local interests and activities. Cultural life is spread through the two islands: musical groups, dramatic companies, and feature shows must tour the country, stopping at least at some of the major urban centers, to obtain sufficient audiences. Despite the smallness of even the main

Table 7. Origins and censorship of films, in films for public exhibition examined by the New Zealand film censor during the year ending March 31, 1964

	35 mm theatre films					
	Feature films			Shorts		
Country	Length in ft.	No. of films	No. of cuts	Length in ft.	No. of films	No. of cuts
Commonwealth	659,220	91	47	200,210	219	0
United States	1,315,810	170	105	219,680	251	0
Other countries	1,303,580	140	42	118,140	104	0

10 theatre films were rejected.

	16 mm films for television					
	Feature films			Shorts		
Country	Length in ft.	No. of films	No. of cuts	Length in ft.	No. of films	No. of cuts
Commonwealth	316,750	145	41	574,820	948	69
United States	1,019,040	562	249	1,566,580	1,926	181
Other countries	0	0	0	47,390	87	21

37 television films were rejected.

centers, urban districts are served with good bookshops and a network of free libraries.

General uniformity of tastes and attitudes is maintained by the common racial origins of the people, assisted *inter alia* by the coordinating work of the Press Association and national radio. The central government, the main if modest patron of the arts and the controller of a centralized education system, is also a unifying influence. By its education policies and through an excellent stream of school publications, it consciously molds New Zealand youth into accepting democratic values. Although broadcasting is no longer under direct state control, the monopoly of the Corporation and its continual responsibility to the government prevent broadcasting from being subjected to purely commercial motives.

There is considerable and increasing freedom of expression. The

Indecent Publications Tribunal has had a marked liberalizing effect on book imports, and film censorship also is exercised in liberal fashion. Newspapers are not subject to external restraints except on publishing pornography; there is no such body as the British Press Council to exercise supervision. Restriction on editorial freedom is imposed from within the industry through the nature of newspaper ownership. The press is now faced with a rival news service organized by the Broadcasting Corporation and, since the introduction of television, with a medium which reaches the public with an immediacy hitherto unknown.

Freedom of expression is used responsibly and with restraint—perhaps too much restraint. There is a danger of a uniform mediocrity. Other than on the job, there is no training to equip journalists and reporters for either major news service to comment critically on their surroundings. The Broadcasting Corporation is conscious of the need to provide commentaries from informed observers, and criticism and dissent can be voiced in a few periodicals. Politically, however, the two major parties tend to combine against radical opinions, and New Zealand lacks the regular and informed assessments of its government and society provided, for example, for Great Britain by a number of Sunday papers and weekly reviews, some of which New Zealand imports.

Mass communications give the public what it wants, as modified by the views of those in control as to what it should have. Perhaps even more than is the case with governments, in its mass communications a society gets what it deserves: they are less an influencing force in, than a mirror of, society. What that mirror reflects depends to a large degree on the few high-minded citizens who are not only the community's arbiters of taste but its very conscience.

BIBLIOGRAPHY

Chapman, E. W., *et al. New Zealand Politics in Action*. Wellington, 1962.

Mackay, I. K. *Broadcasting in New Zealand*. Wellington, 1953.

New Zealand Official Yearbook. Wellington. Annually.

Scholefield, G. H. *Newspapers in New Zealand*. Wellington, 1958.

MAORI CULTURE

R. S. OPPENHEIM

THE culture of the Maori, New Zealand's largest minority group, receives only passing attention from the European (*pakeha*) majority, and indeed its very presence as a separate entity within New Zealand culture is sometimes doubted. This is not to say that some folk arts are not recognized as being distinctively Maori. New Zealand has accepted, usually at their most superficial level, a number of Maori cultural features as typifying the country. Maori culture in this sense is a kind of performance put on at civic functions or as entertainment for tourists; colorful, alien, perhaps a little funny, but nonetheless a national possession.

In spite of this cultural cliché, however, there has been, almost since the earliest days of settlement, a recognition that Maori have a different historical experience, different needs and values, and perhaps different ambitions from the Europeans who now constitute the majority. In the past this recognition served occasionally humane ends, as in the establishment of British sovereignty by treaty rather than by conquest; on the other hand, Europeans frequently used their knowledge of the Maori as a means for exploitation or outright theft.

In the twentieth century the uneasy conscience of white New Zealand has adopted a variety of defenses for the profitable mistakes of the past. Most common is the assertion that Maori have complete equality with whites, or that in a few years, thanks to enlightened social policy, they will have ceased to differ from the majority in any way that matters.

It is significant that color, according to the national ideology, is *not* one of the ways that matter, though the impression that this gives is somewhat marred by the fact that New Zealand discriminates officially against the entry of nonwhite immigrants from all but a few Pacific territories. This is not altogether irrelevant, since the objection to nonwhites generally is expressed in cultural rather than racist terms. New Zealanders feel that what typifies their culture is menaced by the possible immigration in large numbers of Asians or other nonwhite people. It is not surprising, therefore, to find that the general attitude towards Maori progress is conceived in terms that sacrifice all but a tiny part of their cultural distinctiveness.

● In the space of little over a hundred years, Maori have passed from being a majority to being a minority in the land which they first discovered and colonized. With this change in status, changes which continue today have taken place in many aspects of their cultural life. That white New Zealanders are seldom aware of the extent of these changes, or of what is central to Maori social life, might be taken to indicate that significant differences no longer exist between the two groups. How far, then, have the Maori moved toward the point at which cultural submergence will take place? Are there in fact any ways of thinking, acting, and feeling that are characteristic of the social experience of Maori but not of whites? I shall try to chart some of the areas of difference—not so much those of housing or dress, as those which convince Maori that they do not belong to the majority culture. Official statistics give a general picture of the Maori population. At the census of

278

1962, Maori numbered 167,086 out of a total population of 2,414,984, that is, a little over 5 per cent of the total population.

This small minority has some special characteristics. One of these is age; about one half of the Maori population is below twenty years, as compared with under a third of the white population. Another characteristic is fertility; the Maori natural increase rate in 1961 was thirty-eight per thousand compared to twenty-one per thousand for the white population. If this rate is maintained, the Maori proportion of the total population will increase to about 15 per cent in forty years.

Even allowing for this rapid rate of increase, it seems unlikely that the Maori presence would become obvious to a majority of New Zealanders within the century, were it not for certain demographic facts which become more obvious with each census.

Maori, for historical reasons, live mainly in the north and east of the North Island. About 4 per cent live in the South Island. Most are country dwellers, but since 1945 a new trend has arisen: migration to the cities. In 1951, 81 per cent of the Maori were country dwellers, but by 1961 this had fallen to 66 per cent. Although all towns in the North Island show some increases in their Maori population, the focus for the migration is Auckland. Here, between 1956 and 1961, the Maori population increased by 75 per cent to almost 20,000. Wellington, the second largest city in the North Island, had 5,000, while five other main towns in Auckland Province had a Maori population of nearly 14,000.[1]

The increase in Maori population is a regional matter involving both migration and natural increase in a fairly limited area. Although this is an area in which whites have a long history of association with Maori, the association has been neither happy nor, in more recent times, particularly close.

Comparisons on a socioeconomic level are revealing. In 1956 the percentage of Maori engaged as laborers was 41.9 per cent as against 32.87 per cent for non-Maori; in primary production, 26.76 per cent as against 15.82 per cent; as "managers, administrators,

[1] The population totals of the main cities in 1964 were Auckland 482,300; Wellington 261,000; Christchurch 232,700; Dunedin 107,400.

clerical and related workers," 3.13 per cent as against 17.65 per cent. Maori incomes in 1956 were also lower than those of the rest of the population. In that year 56 per cent of non-Maori had incomes below $1400 per year, whereas 81 per cent of the Maori fell into the same group. Five years later the figure had improved to 42 per cent as against 23 per cent of the total population. On the other hand, if the next bracket is included (to $1800) 73.7 per cent of Maori earners fall below as against 48.3 per cent for the total. Gross incomes do not really indicate living standard. The figures, however, support the view that the most striking feature of the Maori situation is the continued existence of enclaves of material poverty.

Generally speaking, Maori households in 1956 lacked many of the amenities that are expected by white New Zealanders, and overcrowding was common. This, as the Hunn Report (1960) pointed out, was far from being overcome, and indeed the proportion of houses built in relation to loan applications to the Department of Maori Affairs had decreased from 37 per cent in 1955 to 20 per cent in 1959. Thirty per cent of houses were estimated to be "grossly overcrowded," and to replace these as well as to accommodate newly married couples, it was estimated that more than six thousand houses were immediately necessary.

At all levels Maori life-expectancies are lower than those of non-Maori, but in the first years of life they are substantially so; the number of deaths per thousand live births at less than one year is 19.4 for whites and 54.37 for Maori. Tuberculosis is still a major cause of death, and the *New Zealand Official Yearbook, 1962* notes that "despite the reductions effected over recent years, Maori rates are still four times those of the European population."

So much, then, for the statistics. One point is clear: Maori do not participate in the services of the welfare state at the same level as whites. Economic, educational, health, and housing disabilities exist for Maori which have not so far been overcome. Economic underprivilege is not cultural difference, though it may sharpen such differences.

The past is one of the cultural determinants which influences the present, but for Maori there are two pasts: the cultural experience

280

that stems from the thousand or so years in which Maori lived undisturbed in New Zealand, and the past that begins in the nineteenth century with the European occupation. The latter has had such a profound effect on Maori that the last century and a quarter has virtually eclipsed all that went before. New religion, law, and technology have all engulfed the orderly conceptual system by which Maori lived before the contact period and have become substitutes for the former way of life. In spite of this some cultural characteristics, whether modified by European usage or not, have survived the impact.

The most important of these is language. There is no satisfactory survey of the extent to which Maori remains a socially important language, and it has no official status in New Zealand; nonetheless, it is still far from extinct. Most, if not all, adult Maori speak Maori to some degree, and many use it as their main conversational language with other Maori. Some, and not merely the elderly, can use Maori in all its elaborate ceremonial idiom. In spite of the policy of the state school system, which until recently suppressed the use of Maori among school children, most Maori children speak or understand some Maori, and many speak the language fluently.

Some pallid attempts have been made by the Education Department to institute limited courses for teaching Maori language, arts, and crafts in the primary schools under its control, but these for the most part lack any real conviction and are largely in the hands of those teachers who feel an obligation to do something. Maori is admitted as a subject for the School Certificate and University Entrance examinations and is taught in a few secondary schools, yet is recognized as a foreign language for degree requirements at the University of Auckland.

If the academic status of Maori gains only grudging acceptance, it is nonetheless a vital social medium. All Maori gatherings include at least the ceremonial use of Maori, for welcoming visitors and so on, and frequently their proceedings are carried on in Maori also. Maori permeates the conversation and doings of any Maori group: it is the language of songs and speeches and of all the occasions which are of real importance to Maori.

Maori possesses a literature, only a part of which has so far been

281

recorded. Of its three forms—narrative prose, poetry, and genealogical history—the recital of genealogy is the most highly developed. It seems to have fulfilled a special function in the maintenance of tradition, in the provision of a cultural time-scale from prehistorical times to the present, and in the conjunction of the activities of gods and men. Maori beliefs about the evolution of the universe were embodied in genealogical accounts that at first seem to be a mere listing of names but in fact become a minor literary genre. Almost all of these accounts make use of a common symbolism, of successive periods of dark or void, occasionally interspersed with periods of light, although other versions liken the birth of the universe to human development or the growth of trees. Almost invariably these cosmogonic genealogies terminate in the names Rangi (sky) and Papa (earth), the marriage of which produced the gods, who in turn produced all life.

In 1849, Wii Maihi Te Rangi-kaheke of Rotorua provided the first written version of his tribe's oral literature. It is a comprehensive, connected, and systematic account of the common Maori beliefs about the origin of the universe and many natural phenomena, of the creation of woman, of the introduction of death, of the development of the islands and continents. Each of these myths is known in somewhat similar versions throughout New Zealand and also thoughout Polynesia. Supplementing the myths are the tribal traditions, which tell of incidents, for the most part human rather than divine, of the past millenium. Knowledge of these traditions is limited to the Maori; they are not mentioned in any other Polynesian oral literatures and can therefore be regarded as a legitimate historical record. The three most general categories of tradition are those concerning origin or discovery, migration or settlement, and local practices.

Maori poetry, like the earliest poetry of the Western world, was always sung or chanted and was distinguished most readily from prose by its use of musical rhythms, speech rhythms, and lilting cadences rather than by its use of alliteration, rhyme schemes, and syllabic meters. Accordingly, it is difficult to distinguish poetry from prose in written versions of Maori oral literature. But when it is sung or chanted, the music itself suggests line division and meter.

In style, poetry differs significantly from prose in its use of repetition, parallelism, euphemism, synonyms and antonyms; these characteristics are found also in Maori oratory, a literary form quite highly praised and much admired. Speeches of welcome are enriched with imagery from the past, and the language of description or discussion is no less vital and inventive. There seems, in fact, to have been a traditional proclivity towards respect for the principles of rhetoric, and Maori languages contain numerous words and expressions that have their equivalents in classical rhetoric.

There is little opportunity for Maori to read their own language, however. The Maori Affairs Department publishes a quarterly magazine, part of which consists of Maori contributions; there are one or two missionary journals; but the newspapers that flourished at intervals during the nineteenth century have disappeared. There is a brief program of Maori news broadcast weekly, but no daily newspaper publishes a column in Maori.

With the authority, power, and techniques of news-gathering firmly in the hands of European private enterprise and the central government, the Maori has to resort to his own method of news-gathering, which is to attend Maori *hui* (gatherings) and so keep in touch with developments which are of particular interest to him.

Out of the past, too, come the traditional arts of carving in wood or stone, plaiting and weaving in geometrical patterns, decorating wood or the walls of rock shelters, and tattooing. Though tattooing has virtually vanished as a cosmetic art and stoneworking has vanished (as it has in Western civilization), woodcarving and weaving in somewhat stylized patterns have gained in popularity among both Maori and *pakeha*, so that they are practiced by artisans of considerable inventiveness and great technical skill.

The Maori carver still holds an honored position in his community, and his skills have always been in constant demand for the decoration of dwellings and canoes. Today his handiwork finds a ready market among tourists. His craft, entered through a selective apprenticeship, is steeped in its own mystique of rituals and prohibitions and conveys both position and prestige.

The common elements of Maori carving are multiple spirals and curvilinear patterns, the human figure (tiki), lizards, birds, fish, and

283

repetitive patterns. The human figure is represented both naturalis-
tically and grotesquely and is most commonly shown with substantial tattooing, with a shortened trunk, in a neonatal or splayed
stance, and with hands of three of four fingers only. As widespread
as human figures are *manaia*, or grotesque carvings of demonic
creatures that are shown full-face or in profile, developed in curvilinear manner, and are given one or two tusklike teeth that pro-
trude from the upper jaw. *Manaia* are frequently distorted or
mutilated and suggest in both appearance and use that they are
Polynesian counterparts of the medieval European gargoyle. It
should be mentioned, however, that there is no known symbolism
in Maori art, and the elements and figures are secular rather than
religious.

Weaving and decoration of a textile made from fine flax fibers
and used in the manufacture of floor mats, baskets, and cloaks have
remained Maori handicrafts of high artistic quality. The textile is
generally decorated with fibers that have been bleached or dyed
black, orange, or red and worked into patterns of large and small
triangles, diamonds, diagonal bars, and stepped patterns. It is therefore a severe contrast to the curvilinear artwork of carving.

Ceremonial cloaks and fine mats, kits, and dancing skirts (*piupiu*)
are still made. All these have changed to some degree in the modern period, but they are highly regarded as cultural expressions. In
ceremonial situations, dances of welcome (*haka* and *poi*) are presented. Clubs for performance of these exist in many parts of the
country. In recent years these groups have tended to search
actively for material surviving from the pre-contact period to add
to their repertoires. The greater part of their music, however, is
based on popular European models. Such clubs are recreational, but
have their part as entertainment groups in specifically Maori social
situations as well as those in which "Maori culture" is paraded as
being distinctive of New Zealand. A curious cross-cultural fertiliza-
tion exists in the *haka* performed by the New Zealand Rugby team
in its overseas tours.

Central to the Maori's identity in the past, though less so today,
was his membership of a kin-based group. The most inclusive
group, often called a "tribe," was the *iwi*, a named group associated

with a particular territory whose members traced themselves to one or more remote ancestors.

Below the *iwi*, in order of inclusiveness, came the *hapuu*, also a named group but more narrowly localized and made up of a group of lineages and various kinfolk who chose to associate themselves with it. Lowest in order of segmentation came the *whaanau*, an extended family group of three or four generations' depth, several of which together composed the *hapuu*.

Membership in the *whaanau* and *hapuu* carried with it the obligation to give mutual aid and allocated rank to the senior members of the various lineage segments. Political power, however, was achieved rather than ascribed, though descent was a prerequisite for the *mana* necessary to wield political power. At best this was limited; the most important *rangatira* (man of high rank) could hardly exert power over more than his closest kin and had to act rather by persuasion than coercion.

Something of this structure is still acknowledged by modern Maori. The *iwi* and the *hapuu* are insignificant politically, but they are a focus of sentiment, and membership of one or other may still be quoted with pride when the occasion is appropriate. *Iwi* and *hapuu* membership are significant in the ceremonial situation. The means to establishing identity in the group, by reciting genealogies (*whakapapa*), is a valued branch of knowledge usually guarded with some jealousy.

"Chieftainship" remains, though it is hardly more than the acknowledgment of descent from a noted ancestor combined with the personality and intelligence to make something of it; aristocracy, as Maori understand it, is highly diffused. The descent system is such that most Maori are confident of the possibility of finding chiefly ancestors if they choose. As in the past, Maori do not acknowledge a pre-emptive right to lead except in the ceremonial context, where it is the combination of ability, age, and experience as well as descent that establish the individual's reputation. Senior men in a community are usually treated with respect and affection, but their opinions, while they are deferred to, are not regarded as being in the nature of commands.

The interlocking nature of descent, descent group, prestige, and political and religious power, thus, has largely disappeared from Maori society. What remains is a respect for the principles that underlay this organization, tempered by an egalitarianism that is fundamentally anarchic, since it places more value on the peer group and on mutual aid than on an authority structure in which some make decisions and others follow. The result is to provide a structure that is extremely flexible, but which nonetheless places a high value on cooperation with, and loyalty to, one's immediate segment. In return the individual is provided with a series of roles in which his abilities, and finally his age, can find adequate expression.

The basic unit of modern Maori structure is the extended family group resembling the *whaanau* of earlier times, but less narrowly circumscribed by residence. The essential feature of the "family" is that its members acknowledge the responsibility to give mutual aid. Families unite to perform the main ceremonials: weddings, twenty-first birthdays, funerals, and tombstone unveilings.

In the activities of the family are expressed all those deeply held cultural values that Maori mean when they use the term *Maoritanga* (Maoriness). The cultural forms, however, consist of a reworking of traditional custom to fit new social circumstances, a mark, surely, of their vitality.

Death affords a focus for the whole set of cultural values. The ceremonial centers around the complex of buildings and open ground called the *marae*, which is to be found in every rural area in which Maori live. The *marae* consists of the meetinghouse (*whare hui*), the open ground before it, the *marae* proper, and an adjoining dining hall and kitchen.

The meetinghouse is named and is regarded as having a certain degree of *tapu* (sacredness); eating within it is usually forbidden and sometimes smoking as well. Sometimes it is carved elaborately, but more often it is an unpretentious one-roomed wooden building.

When death occurs the corpse is taken to the meetinghouse to lie in state for a customary period of three days. During this time relatives and friends from all parts of the district gather to pay their last respects. The deceased person is lamented in the traditional fashion with wailing and speeches of eulogy that often also include allusions to tribal history and to the values of *Maoritanga*.

The visitors to the *marae* are accommodated in the meetinghouse where the corpse lies. As each new party arrives it is ceremonially welcomed, first by being "called" from the door of the house by several of the oldest women and then, as its members enter the house, by one of the spokesmen for the family of the deceased. When the ceremonial lamenting is finished the visitors are absorbed into the main gathering of people.

The evening and the greater part of the night is taken up with speech-making. This is confined to men, but there is no restriction as to the subject that may be raised, and consequently many matters of signficance or general interest are discussed. People sleep or listen as they feel inclined. In the meantime the kinsfolk of the deceased, other than his or her immediate family, are kept busy with the organizing of the food and accommodation for the visitors. On the third day, after a Christian service, the body is buried in a cemetery chosen, often after long debate, by the relatives. Throughout, the weight is taken from the immediate relatives, who are the focus of the ceremonial. The combined efforts of the kinsfolk meet, in cash, labor, and kind, the expenses and arduous tasks of the gathering.

This manifestation of the mutual aid principle is so well established that it survives the effect of migration to the city. The dead are usually taken back to the home *marae* for the ceremonial and burial. The reasons are clear enough. Whereas in the home area there is, at a guess, a *marae* to every two or three hundred people, in Auckland there are only two to serve some twenty thousand. These, furthermore, are associated with particular tribes. Sensitivity to the reactions of white neighbors, inability to draw together and suitably feed and accommodate visitors, all inhibit the possibility of a suitable farewelling of the dead, but even if this did not apply there would still be the overriding sentiment in favor of the home *marae*. The city-dwelling Maori is inextricably entangled with his kinsfolk and with his home district. When he cuts himself free of them he ceases in an important way to be culturally identifiable by other Maori.

City and country, then, are interdependent societies for Maori, in ways that they are not, and never have been, for whites. Many city-dwelling whites have, of course, spent their early years in a rural environment, but their experience differs fundamentally. The land, for Maori, has different uses from those to which it is put by whites. The Maori system of land ownership, for example, has important consequences for group membership, and is a further extension of the kinship and political systems. In Kootare, the community in Northland studied by Metge,[2] only nine farmers out of sixty-four lived by full-time farming, and only one had exclusive title to the land which he worked.

The Maori system of collective ownership, determined by descent from an ancestral owner, is antagonistic to the individualization of titles, which is thought of as essential for efficient farming. It is generally held, and there is some truth in the contention, that collective ownership has paralyzed the development of those lands that still remain to Maori, but there are other factors which are equally important: the shortage of capital, of technical knowledge, of imagination in the kinds of solution offered to Maori, as well as the nature of the land itself.

The rural Maori society does not in any case depend on the economic use of land in the ordinary sense. Land is a focus of sentiment. The right to use it has existed in tribal groups time out of mind; the fact that a migrant owns a share in land, however small, in his home district ties him to that place, gives him rights on the *marae* as a *tangata whenua* ("man of land"), and establishes for him a sense of continuity with his cultural past. For Maori it is the social role of the land, rather than what it will produce, that is important.

Land, kinship, ceremonial, family and tribal identity, make a Maori what he is. For the migrant the course is between compromise and complete alienation. Few Maori at the moment choose the latter.

The migrant Maori society, according to Metge, differs from the rural in that the city environment is more permissive and allows for a wider range of actions in a given social situation. Whereas, for example, people in Metge's rural community would refuse to call in

2 Joan Metge, *A New Maori Migration* (London, 1964), p. 33.

288

the police when some offense against their property occurred because this might involve kinsfolk, they would more readily do this in the city. Nonetheless, as Metge observes, the greater number of contacts of these people were with Maori, and their strong consciousness of being Maori tended to counteract the divergence of development that might arise between urban and rural families.

Urban Maori make a conscious compromise between the rural culture and the restrictions that they inevitably encounter in the city. The compromise is effected in various ways. It is not feasible, for example, to hold *tangihanga*, the funeral ceremonial, in a crowded suburb; for this a *marae* is necessary, and not simply any *marae*, but one on which the people concerned have full status. When a death occurs, then, the body will be taken back to the home *marae* for burial. Conflict arises, however, between the demands of the employer and the social demand of the kin group. For the closest kin no compromise is possible, but it is generally being recognized by the more traditionally minded that the demands of work have to be met. It is usual now for the body to be held for several hours in the city so that those who cannot get away still have an opportunity to pay their respects.

The demand of the other ceremonial is less stringent; nonetheless there is generally some attempt to use the home *marae*, and there will certainly be visits for country kin to the city if ceremonial is held there.

In some groups, whose history as migrants is fairly long, the unity with the home society expresses itself in the formation of committees which act as a liaison between the town and country groups, with the former making cash contributions to the maintenance of the *marae* and the cost of major ceremonial occasions.

These compromises make it possible for city-dwelling Maori to retain their cultural identity, while at the same time adapting the culture to the changes in social circumstance. Some of the vitality which Maori institutions show must be attributed to the fact that Maori themselves wish to retain their identity because it offers satisfactions not available in white society as they see it.

Racial difference also plays a part. Since a Maori cannot be other than a Maori, there is no loss in maintaining a discrete social and cultural life. Many, perhaps most, Maori tend to identify the bio-logical fact of being Maori with cultural and social life, and thus to expect people who look like Maori to have at least some allegiance to Maori values. For them the frontier between the cultures is not abolished by removal to the city. Maori value structure remains a consistent whole, not differentiated to any marked degree by the change of environment.

The most commonplace reaction of whites to Maori is one of easy paternalism. The frequently expressed view that Maori are the equal of whites has in fact little more meaning than that they are not actively discriminated against. In government Maori have sepa-rate representation; in law they are subject to the same machinery as whites; in the use of public facilities there is no legal ground for discrimination, though there is no legal remedy if it occurs.

This general indifference to Maori and insensitivity to their culture has received some shocks in recent years. The attitude that "New Zealand leads the world" in race relations has had some criticism. Two major incidents have focused attention on discrimi-nation and have given point to the doubts that New Zealanders are beginning to feel about the racial harmony that is said to exist in their country. The first of these was the refusal of service in an Auckland hotel to a prominent Maori and the second the protest occasioned by the decision of the New Zealand Rugby Union in 1960 to exclude Maori players from the team chosen to tour South Africa.

Although the first incident was smoothed over, the second was more important. A protest movement which gained considerable impetus arose, marches were held, and a petition circulated. The prime minister was asked to intervene with the Rugby Union, but took the position that it was no concern of the government. Tempers ran high. A Maori member of Parliament publicly stated his support for the protest. The security service attempted to investigate the political background of members of the movement. Those who carried petitions met with a wide range of reactions, from enthusiasm to violence.

For the most part, however, New Zealanders took the view, as letters to the newspapers showed, that the Rugby Union had acted wisely on behalf of the Maori, and a few Maori were found to speak up in favor of the Union's decision. (The team left at the scheduled time in spite of the protest and conducted a successful tour of South Africa.)

The taste left behind by this incident was unpleasant, however, and it revealed to white New Zealanders for the first time that there was a degree of dissent not only from the view that theirs was the best of all possible worlds, but also that attitudes of paternalism were still acceptable. Maori had taken little part, at the popular level, in the protest, but those whites who associated with them at the time could not fail to be impressed by their public embarrassment and private bitterness that it had taken a matter of this kind to draw attention to something that they felt went much deeper in New Zealand society.

The predominating attitude, after all, was one of kindly patronage. The best excuse for keeping Maori out of the team was that they would be protected from insult in South Africa; the best reason for including them was to protect them from discrimination in New Zealand. Either way, the responsibility that whites felt toward Maori was apparently that of sophisticated to unsophisticated, senior to junior.

The Rugby tour issue helped to sensitize New Zealanders to the immediate facts of life in a plural society. Although sporting relationships with South Africa inevitably contain elements of political significance, the Rugby Union consistently denied this. More recently it has realized that it has a responsibility to clarify its policy. In its most recent public statements the emphasis has been on attempts to gain entry for Maori to South Africa as part of the team and therefore exclude them from the inconveniences of *apartheid*. Two Maori members of the Rugby Union—an experimental shipment, as it were—went to South Africa in 1964 and returned, predictably, praising the conditions that they had seen in that country.

The Rugby tour protest was significant of deeper issues of uncertainty in the conscience of New Zealanders. The antithetical positions of South Africa and New Zealand is apparently not immediately obvious to New Zealanders, and although press correspondence is now more openly critical of South Africa or of discriminatory acts within New Zealand, the majority view seems to be concerned with practicality rather than principle. New Zealanders, it is stated by no lesser person than the Maori advisor to the Rugby Union, do not understand South Africa's problems. This faithful parroting of the South African government's views, followed by an approving chorus of letters to the editor, indicates that New Zealanders' perceptions of race relations either within or without their own country are deplorably naive.

The shock of the 1960 protest was followed, fortuitously, by a drastic reappraisal of government policy towards Maori. The Labour government had commissioned J. K. Hunn, a senior civil servant, to report on the work of the Maori Affairs Department, and with the change of government in 1961 this report was published. The Hunn Report, as it came to be known, was more than a scrutiny of Maori affairs, however. It was, in fact, an analysis of policy at many levels.

The results were refreshingly controversial. Hunn revealed that Maori housing and land policies were so restricted by budgetary considerations as to make them nearly ineffective, and that Maori educational development was well behind that of white New Zealanders. More importantly, Mr. Hunn developed in the report a master theory of race relations, which he termed "integration." The term was unfortunate. The author was little aware of the extent of cultural differentiation, and what he conceived as integration turned out to be a reworking of the former policy of assimilation, a concept which Mr. Hunn had himself criticized. Mr. Hunn regarded integration as a step on the road to the disappearance of what he regarded as the undesirable elements of Maori culture. Some of these he said were "relics," which might be retained if the people so chose, but that the aim was to bring the Maori into a "modern" culture by which it seems he meant a modern technological mastery.[3] If this were to happen at the cost of those things that made the Maori distinctive, then, so far as the theory went, this was merely part of the process of history.

[3] It will be clear that "integration" is used differently here from the way in which it is used in the United States.

The naiveté of Mr. Hunn came in for considerable criticism, from both Maori and whites. The report, however, gained the support of the government and has since become the touchstone of policy on Maori affairs. Mr. Hunn was appointed to the director-ship of the Department, presumably so that he might personally supervise the reforms he envisaged. B. G. Biggs, in reviewing the report, remarked, "Since assuming the portfolio the new Minister of Maori Affairs, Mr. Hanan, has acted with energy. In November, 1960 he was reported as saying that he knew nothing about Maori; at Omarumutu in 1961 he was able to assure his audience that he was completely familiar with the Maori situation, and that he knew what to do about it."

That Mr. Hunn should have made some assumptions that were out of tune with Maori feeling was hardly his fault; there was, and is, a paucity of sociological research in New Zealand. This, in turn, is hardly the fault of the sociologists, but rather a failure of New Zealand intellectuals to perceive an important area of social criticism.

The concerns of social criticism in New Zealand have in fact centered upon the white society and its problems. The themes of isolation and social experiment have seldom been far from the work of New Zealanders; indeed there has been not infrequently an obsessive scrutiny of the differences existing between white New Zealand society and that of the outside world. Thus, in 1961 a volume of essays was published that reflected the views of seven contributors in various fields to the influence of isolation on this country. There is, as far as I am aware, no volume by writers of equivalent status on the relationship of the white New Zealander to the Maori.

So it is that when one tries to locate the dimensions and details of what constitutes "they" and "we" in New Zealand, either for whites or Maori, it is difficult to find any large body of critical opinion. What little sociological research has been done has been mainly in the areas of race relations and community studies. General discussion of Maori affairs or of the immediate necessities of Maori-white relations in the 1960's has been confined to working papers at one or two conferences either of church groups or under the auspices of the Department of University Extension, Auckland. For the most part, New Zealand's intellectuals view this area as a matter of welfare theory rather than for any serious analysis of the form of New Zealand society.

Two recent contributions are those of James Ritchie and Bill Pearson. The first, assessing the capacity of Maori society to adjust to contact with whites, says:

Within its own world of conflict Maori society is well experienced in handling this kind of task [i.e., to deal with prejudice]; it is alert to schism and interested in strife and argument. Pakeha society is not; it leaves its stones unturned; covers itself with conformity; curbs consciousness with taboos. It leaves its public washing of dirty linen to the newspapers, public enquiries and the law courts.[4]

And Pearson, discussing integration, says:

The way of life we have been trying to "integrate" on to Maoris is a spiritually impoverished version of a deeply anxious, individualistic and often sadistic (and dirty-minded) Euro-American culture. If instead of forcing them into our uniform, we would allow Maoris to be themselves, we could at once rid ourselves of our intermittent worry about 'what we are doing for the Maoris', and at the same time could enter more confidently into bi-racial New Zealand activities, to our enrichment.[5]

In the opinions expressed by both these writers there is an implicit condemnation of the value system of New Zealand white society and a recognition of some other—and perhaps more rewarding—value held by Maori. If this is so, then it, more than the external marks, is what constitutes the difference in culture between Maori and white.

Whether the values which Ritchie and Pearson admire can endure in the face of "a modern culture" as Mr. Hunn terms it, is a moot point. What is clear is that there is a deep insecurity in the minds of these New Zealanders about the values which their own society holds.

The purpose of this essay was to locate the differences between Maori and white culture in New Zealand and to trace the response of the society to them. Maori, it has been shown, retain to a large

[4] James Ritchie, *The Making of a Maori* (Wellington, 1964), p. 17.
[5] Bill Pearson, "The Maori People," *Landfall*, XVI, ii, 7.

extent their language, some of their arts and other means of expression, and a number of social institutions. They retain a set of values which reflects their social and cultural experience, and they have shown the capacity and tenacity to adapt their culture to new demographic patterns. Above all, they are concerned to remain Maori even if this means that they must lose out to the dominant culture in some respects.

The prevailing characteristic of the white majority's attitudes, however, is ignorance. Lack of contact, lack of interest, and principally lack of imagination, leave white New Zealanders at a loss to understand either that Maori aspirations might differ from their own, or that Maori might value what to the white majority is valueless. The very speed of the increase in the Maori population must throw the two groups together increasingly, particularly in some restricted areas. It will not be possible for the white society to forget the Maori in the future nor, it would seem, to integrate it out of existence.

Social change may in time stretch the differentiation of Maori and white culturally beyond all meaningful limits, but it will not mean the total disappearance of Maori as an element in New Zealand society. Not the least important element in cultural differentiation is the consciousness of difference held by the minority group. For Maori this cannot be evaded while there are still white and brown New Zealanders.

While, however, Maori remain as a group distinguished by language, ceremonial usage, tradition, and kinship organization, they are likely also to be the inheritors of a particular set of values. These may ultimately disappear and the distinction become one of race only, but in the meantime there is a specifically Maori cultural experience setting apart the two groups. It is with the fact of this difference that New Zealanders must come to terms.

BIBLIOGRAPHY

Best, E. *The Maori*. Wellington, 1924.
Biggs, B. G. *Maori Marriage*. Wellington, 1960.

Buck, Peter H. (Te Rangi Hiroa). *The Coming of the Maori*. Wellington, 1949.
Campbell, J. L. *Poenamo*. Christchurch, 1881; 1952.
Firth, Raymond. *Primitive Economics of the New Zealand Maori*. Wellington, 1929.
Grey, Sir George. *Polynesian Mythology*. Christchurch, 1855; 1956.
Harre, John. *Maori and Pakeha*. Wellington, 1967.
Maning, F. E. *Old New Zealand*. Christchurch, 1863; 1956.
Ritchie, James. *The Making of a Maori*. Wellington, 1964.
Turner, Denis. *Tangi*. Wellington, 1963.
Vayda, A. P. *Maori Warfare*. Wellington, 1960.

NOTES ON THE CONTRIBUTORS

R. D. Batt is professor of biochemistry and dean of the faculty of Biological Sciences in Massey University at Palmerston North.

D. A. Hansen, associate professor of sociology in the University of California at Santa Barbara, has taught at the University of Otago and at Purdue University. While in New Zealand he made a special study of the effects of the introduction of television.

Bruce Mason, perhaps the best-known dramatist in New Zealand, has given a solo recital, "The End of the Golden Weather," over three hundred times in his own country and in Europe, has had his play *The Pohutukawa Tree* produced in the Soviet Union and on British television, and is author of a collection of theatre criticism, *Occasions* (1965).

A. L. McLeod has contributed articles on aspects of New Zealand culture to two encyclopedias and edited *Walt Whitman in Australia and New Zealand*, *The Commonwealth Pen*, and *The Pattern of Australian Culture*. He is professor of English and speech and dean of the School of Liberal Arts and Science at Rider University, Trenton, New Jersey.

297

PATTERN OF NEW ZEALAND CULTURE

KENNETH MELVIN, now professor of international education in Boston University, was formerly senior lecturer in education at the University of Otago. He holds degrees and diplomas in education, philosophy, music, and social studies and is the author of seven books, including *A History of Education in New Zealand*.

AUSTIN MITCHELL, formerly lecturer in government in the University of Canterbury at Christchurch, now Official Fellow of Nuffield College, Oxford, has devoted special attention to Australian and New Zealand politics.

J. J. MOL, who was born in the Netherlands, has studied at Princeton University, Union Theological Seminary, and Columbia University, where he worked under Reinhold Niebuhr. In 1961 he became lecturer in sociology in the University of Canterbury and in 1963 was appointed research fellow in sociology at the Institute of Advanced Studies of the Australian National University at Canberra.

R. S. OPPENHEIM is lecturer in Maori studies in the University of Auckland. He is a frequent contributor to professional journals, has made an intensive study of Polynesian cultures, and translated a number of Maori *waita* for the *Penguin Book of New Zealand Verse*.

J. C. REID, who is a professor of English in the University of Auckland, is the author of *Creative Writing in New Zealand, Francis Thompson: Man and Poet, Thomas Hood*, and *The Hidden World of Charles Dickens*, and editor of eight volumes.

JOHN A. RITCHIE, professor of music in the University of Canterbury, is well known throughout New Zealand as composer, conductor, music educator, and musicologist. In 1967–1968 he was a visiting professor of music in the University of Exeter.

P. A. TOMORY was for many years director of the Auckland City Art Gallery, was senior lecturer in art in the University of Auckland from 1965 to 1967, and is now associate professor of art history and archaeology at Columbia University.

G. A. WOOD, senior lecturer in the department of history at the University of Otago, has made a special study of the role of the mass media in New Zealand society and has published several articles on related topics.

298

INDEX

INDEX

INDEX